Kicking Off the Week

Kicking Off the Week

A History of Monday Night Football
on ABC Television, 1970–2005

WESLEY HYATT

McFarland & Company, Inc., Publishers
Jefferson, North Carolina, and London

LIBRARY OF CONGRESS CATALOGUING-IN-PUBLICATION DATA

Hyatt, Wesley.
Kicking off the week : a history of Monday night football
on ABC television, 1970–2005 / Wesley Hyatt.
p.   cm.
Includes bibliographic references and index.

ISBN-13: 978-0-7864-2969-1
(illustrated case binding : 50# alkaline paper) ∞

1. Monday night football (Television program)—History.   I. Title.

GV742.3.H93 2007   796.332—dc22   2007000880

British Library cataloguing data are available

On the cover: John Madden from the 2002 season; and (on screen, from left)
Don Meredith, Howard Cosell and Frank Gifford from 1980 (ABC/Photofest)

Manufactured in the United States of America

*McFarland & Company, Inc., Publishers
Box 611, Jefferson, North Carolina 28640
www.mcfarlandpub.com*

To my friend Jimmy Lancaster,
who cheers me on before, during
and after every football season

Acknowledgments

Anyone who attempts seriously to cover a series that ran more than a third of a century needs as much help as he can get. Fortunately, I received it from several people beyond the multitude of books, magazines and newspapers that also proved essential for my work (see the bibliography for all those sources). First off, Freddie Kiger, my old high school teacher and family friend, gave me some essential contact information he had that proved particularly enlightening about the *Monday Night Football* story. I also tip my hat to vintage television collector Russell Wells, with whom I traded my own special finds to get his hard-to-find copies of early *Monday Night Football* games to watch. He provided me with six rare copies of games from the first five years to view (with commercials included, no less). Thank you, Freddie and Russell.

The people I interviewed for this book were Rupert Hitzig (telephone interview September 11, 2005); Alex Karras (telephone interview July 3, 2006); Marvin Schlenker (telephone interview May 1, 2006); Edwin "Bud" Shrake (telephone interview May 3, 2006); Martin Starger (telephone interview May 19, 2006); and Fred Williamson (email interview August 15, 2005, telephone interview follow-up August 16, 2005). I thank them all for the time and effort they spent with me in illuminating various parts of the *Monday Night Football* story.

Finally, I thank my dad and mom, Ronald and Gayle Hyatt, and my friends Jimmy Lancaster and Renee Duncan for providing particular moral support for me on this project as always. I love and respect them dearly for everything they did for me.

Table of Contents

Introduction

"Our baby is gone. I'm tearing up as we speak. It's like the child just left the house at an early age... Unbelievable."

That was the initial reaction Robert Kekaula, sports director of ABC's Hawaii affiliate KITV, related to reporter Leila Wai of *The Honolulu Advertiser* when he heard in 2005 that ABC was ending *Monday Night Football* the next year. Like many people, he was stunned at the news.

Keep in mind that KITV had aired the games on a delayed basis after the local 6:00 news, where during the sports segment they would tell viewers to "close your eyes" while they showed the results of that night's games. The contests already had been played, yet even in the westernmost U.S. affiliate, most viewers waited for tape-delayed versions of them, something the station did not do regularly.

Such was the power of *Monday Night Football*. It was a tradition every fall on the first evening of the work week for 35 seasons on the air — in every part of the United States.

Yet now, with a simple announcement with few regrets from network officials, a TV institution would become history, at least on ABC. Professional football on Monday nights would continue on ABC's sports cable operation ESPN in the fall of 2006, and on NBC Sunday nights that autumn as well, to make up for those without cable or satellite service who had been watching them on ABC.

But neither would be the same as the original show.

When it debuted, *Monday Night Football* revolutionized the coverage of TV sports, putting not two but three announcers in its booth to deliver its games and using more cameras than had been employed regularly by the other networks. It gave the audience just about every possible angle to watch a football game or see plays again at another view in slow motion. If activity on the field lagged, commentary between the regular announcers often made up for the ennui on display, making it more than just a football game. In the process, *Monday Night Football* made household names of those sports personalities, including Howard Cosell, Frank Gifford, Don Meredith, Al Michaels, Dan Dierdorf and many others.

Given that, why would ABC get rid of the series, anyway? Indeed, ponder these astounding feats. By the time of its cancellation, *Monday Night Football* had:

- Finished at number 10 in the ratings for the 2004–2005 season, making it just one of a handful of nighttime series ever to be cancelled while in the top 10.
- Finished in the top 10 seasonal ratings 15 times, the second highest total of any nighttime series (*60 Minutes* leads all with 22 times).
- Been the only ABC series to finish in the top 10 for more than two seasons in the 21st century.
- Been the only ABC series in the top 10 during two different seasons in the 20th century.
- Been ABC's top-rated series for seven seasons.
- Been ABC's longest running nighttime TV series ever, excluding movies. Its nearest competitor, *20/20*, started in 1978 and was seven seasons behind the tally for *Monday Night Football* when the latter's cancellation notice came out.

All told, based on its lengthy run and high ratings over the years, *Monday Night Football* was the second most popular TV series in America of all time, behind only *60 Minutes* (which started in 1968).

And now it was ending, even though it was still a hit, due to production costs that were not covered by advertising. Under its onerous contract with the NFL, ABC was losing $150 million yearly. With the notoriously penny-pinching Walt Disney Corporation owning the network and unable to adjust the contract, the bottom line became the bottom line in determining whether it should stay.

Figures alone do not convey the impact of *Monday Night Football*. It influenced other networks to upgrade their graphics and overall presentation of TV sports. It allowed ABC a strong platform to promote its programs, which no doubt helped the perennial third-place network move into first by the mid–1970s.

It also gave ABC a winning program on Monday nights, one of the most contested time slots on television. Consider that since it started, *Monday Night Football* competed against four of the five CBS Emmy-winning Outstanding Comedies, excluding *The Mary Tyler Moore Show*, and three of the five CBS Emmy-winning Outstanding Dramas, excluding *The Waltons* and *Picket Fences*. It had movie blockbusters such as *The Godfather* run against it on NBC too. Later came challenges from other broadcast and cable networks, yet throughout it all, *Monday Night Football* remained either first or second in its time slot for much of its run, a testament to its popularity.

Perhaps most striking was how it influenced a generation (and then some) of pro football players. "I can remember when I was a little boy saying, 'Boy, wouldn't it be great to play on *Monday Night Football?*'" Dallas Cowboys quarterback Troy Aikman reminisced in the show's 25th anniversary special, *Monday Night Football Mania*, on September 2, 1996. His teammate, Cowboys running back Emmett Smith, noted on the same special, "Friends come over and watch the big game on *Monday Night Football*." Smith did his part on the show when he set the record for most touchdowns in a season by a running back in the December 25, 1995, contest against the Arizona Cardinals.

"It's the national exposure, the excitement of being the only game on TV at that time," added Miami Dolphins quarterback Dan Marino in the special. He also claimed to be such a devoted fan that he could remember watching the first *Monday Night Football* game all the way back in 1970.

There were drawbacks with *Monday Night Football*, of course. The announcers found themselves scrutinized constantly for mistakes, biases, and overall performance and often came up short. Several of the on-air personnel put out books sniping at each other in print (more about them later). Others just became punchlines to bad jokes, especially around the turn of the century. Say the names of Dennis Miller, Eric Dickerson and Lisa Guerrero to *Monday Night Football* fans, and watch them either roll their eyes or relate how wrong they were to do the show. Given that *Monday Night Football* was America's premiere sports show, viewers felt they deserved the best from it, and while technically the show never let them down, the commentary could be downright awful. Some would argue that was part of the series' appeal. Others would say it cheapened the show that should have set the standard for TV sports programming.

For ABC, *Monday Night Football* was a double-edged programming tool. It was swell for the network to have it in the fall, but since the football season ended in December (and later in January), that meant ABC had two hours it automatically had to replace in midseason. Usually the network played it safe by running theatrical movies, but with increased cable and home video exposure of those films by the 1990s causing lower ratings, ABC found itself having to run series in the slot instead. The problem was, by that time, CBS usually had its series already in place for the season, and so the likes of *M*A*S*H*, *Cagney & Lacey*, *Designing Women*, *Northern Exposure*, *Murphy Brown* and others were ahead of the game with viewers, and there was little to entice them to change the channel. Likewise, ABC's abandonment of movies gave NBC the field all to itself in the 1990s and NBC recovered some of the audience that had gone to ABC. Naturally, no successful series emerged on ABC Mondays in the "football period" (9–11 P.M. Eastern and Pacific, 8–10 P.M. Central) between seasons.

There was another programming hang-up. Throughout its run, *Monday Night Football* either came on after an hour of programs in the East and Midwest (8–9

P.M. Eastern, 7–8 P.M. Central) or before one in the West. Finding a hit series that could run prior to and following the football games was difficult for network executives. A mere three series ran at least two years in that time slot — *The Rookies*, *That's Incredible!* and *MacGyver* — and only *The Rookies* managed to crack the top 20, and just for the 1974–75 season. More often, the slot found itself the home for quick losers like *The San Pedro Beach Bums*, *Timecop* and *Dangerous Minds*. "We were never really successful," said Martin Starger, vice president for programming at ABC from 1969 to 1975, about filling that period.

Even given those difficulties, however, ABC by and large was proud of *Monday Night Football*. It was the culmination of the network's boast about being the leader in TV sports, and it gave ABC the distinction of being more than just the perennial runner-up among the Big Three broadcast networks, behind CBS and NBC. For a network known for having flashy hits that failed to run the distance (besides *Monday Night Football* and *20/20*, the only other nighttime ABC series to run at least a decade are *The Lawrence Welk Show*, *The Adventures of Ozzie and Harriet*, *Happy Days*, *N.Y.P.D. Blue* and *Primetime Live*), the series lent it stability and credibility. It was a show no other network could emulate due to the special circumstances under which it was created, a rarity indeed in TV's copycat creative world.

In short, *Monday Night Football* was an original. And now it's gone, hard as that may be to believe. NBC probably will do fine with football Sunday nights. And ESPN certainly won't regret having the biggest sports draw on Monday nights added to its lineup either. But the loss of what we knew as *Monday Night Football* really hurts. For both football fans and TV viewers. Its story on the following pages will explain why.

1

The NFL Before
Monday Night Football

We have become so accustomed to rabid, huge swarms of fans, glitzy plays and just overall energy at NFL games, thanks in part to *Monday Night Football*, that it is hard to comprehend a period when such enthusiasm did not exist. But actually, most people were rather indifferent to pro football for the first part of the 20th century, and if TV had not come onto the scene, it may well have folded due to apathy.

The sport of football in America derived from rugby. It began as an amateur affair played between college teams with its rules being refined from 1869 through 1883 before anyone competed professionally. The first pro football player was William "Pudge" Heffelfinger in 1892. He earned $500 in his first game to lead the Allegheny Athletic Association to a 4–0 victory versus the Pittsburgh Athletic Club. This achievement did not result in establishing regular professional football, however.

Instead, the sport faced setbacks over the next years. The biggest in the early 1900s were the many publicized deaths of players on the field, prompting no less than President Teddy Roosevelt to encourage reform through better and safer helmets and equipment. Not long after that got into place, the United States found itself involved in World War I, which depleted potential players and spectators in 1917 and 1918. Finally, in the wake of the prosperity and stability of the post-war years, pro football on a regular basis looked to be a viable proposition.

The National Football League (NFL) first sprung to life in 1920 by organizers in a Hupmobile automobile showroom in Canton, Ohio. (As with most items associated with the NFL's origins, Hupmobile later went out of business.) Originally titled the American Professional Football Association (it became the NFL in 1922), its teams played in moderate-sized cities in Ohio, Wisconsin, Illinois and Indiana via sponsorships from local businesses and civic groups. Franchises included the Akron Pros, the Canton Bulldogs, the Massillon Tigers, the Hammond Pros, the Muncie Flyers, the Racine Cardinals, the Rock Island Independents, and the Decatur Staleys.

This humble beginning led to an inauspicious slate of activity during the league's first 15 years. Most games contained activity not much better than what you could get with amateurs, many teams fielded fewer than 20 players per game, and names and locations of franchises switched often. Salaries were so paltry that most players held off-season jobs to be solvent financially.

The NFL grew to 22 teams by 1926, but the stock market crash three years later hurt it badly, and by 1931 only 10 NFL teams existed. The only modern day survivor from the chaotic first 15 years are the Green Bay Packers, sponsored originally by a meat processing plant, hence the team name. Later, as team sponsorships died out with the NFL, the Green Bay Packers converted its ownership into a corporation held by fans, thus allowing the town of Green Bay, Wisconsin, a chance to compete against much bigger cities such as New York and Los Angeles as the league expanded into those metropolises.

It was not until 1936 that all NFL teams finally stayed in one location more than one year. Significantly, that was around the time the league finally received decent radio coverage, even though college football had been receiving network radio airings for nearly a decade. This was because NCAA football had a much classier and important image at the time than did pro football. As Ted Patterson noted of the contrast in *The Golden Voices of Football*, "Just about every school of importance was airing its games on radio. Not so in the professional leagues. It wasn't until the late 1930s that the NFL began making a name for itself, and not a very big name at that."

Getting on the Air

One of the first pro teams to go out over the airwaves was the Brooklyn Dodgers (not the baseball team) in 1933 on New York radio. Stan Lomax covered the game. Two years later, broadcaster Harry Wismer started covering action for the Detroit Lions.

Joining the fray in 1936 were the Pittsburgh Pirates (renamed the Pittsburgh Steelers in 1940), although their games were not live. Sportscaster Joe Tucker had to recreate the game as radio coverage at the field was banned at the time. Tucker eventually earned the right to be with the team and covered the Steelers on radio through 1967.

Next to arrive were the Cleveland Rams in 1937. Significantly, Tom Manning, the top sportscaster in Cleveland at the time, did not announce their games, sticking instead with doing the more esteemed Ohio State Buckeyes schedule. Bob Kelley presided over the matchups instead, and he stayed with the Rams when they relocated to Los Angeles after winning the 1945 league championship.

While radio coverage expanded for the league in the 1930s and 1940s, as indicated it remained mainly local in nature, and the real prestige in national radio lay with college football. The game also lagged in appeal compared to baseball (in the 1940s, NFL games would draw at best 40,000 attendees vs. 50,000 for the World Series), and like most other industries it felt the impact of World War II military service. For example, a lack of players due to the war caused the Philadelphia Eagles and the Pittsburgh Steelers to merge as the "Steagles" in 1943.

The War Ends; Bert Bell Rings In

After the war ended, the NFL looked poised to grow. Its new commissioner installed in 1946, former Eagles owner Bert Bell, planned to exploit the new medium of television in a way the league never did with radio. It was a decision that was farsighted; it helped pro football establish itself as America's number 1 favorite sport to watch on TV.

However, there were a few drawbacks to how Bell ran the NFL. It took him a while to keep the league solvent—as late as 1952 NFL franchises still managed to go bankrupt despite increasing profits and video exposure. Also, he ran his large operation like a mom and pop shop—he preferred to do his business out of his home in Narberth, Pennsylvania, near Philadelphia, even as the NFL expanded franchises and secured larger TV contracts. This hardly gave a professional, classy image to a sport that required that approach among the general public for most of the 1950s.

Mind you, this did not mean Bell was over his head as NFL commissioner. He did make some major accomplishments as the organization's leader, including TV exposure of course, but also in a few other areas. Most notably, under his leadership the NFL managed to quash the rival All-America Football Conference (AAFC), which had three of its teams join the NFL after it folded, including the Cleveland Browns.

But against this triumph, one has to weigh the fact that Bell unintentionally created an even bigger threat to the NFL after that. Its name was the American Football League, and its origins are a direct result of Bell miscalculating others' desire to tap into the growing market for professional football.

The AFL Challenge

In 1958, Texas millionaire Lamar Hunt met with Bell about establishing an NFL team in Dallas. Bell turned him down. Hunt then offered to buy a NFL franchise in 1959, particularly the Chicago Cardinals, and relocate it to Dallas. Again, Bell used his influence to nix that notion.

Rather than quit after the second rejection, Hunt pressed forward and learned several other money men — Bud Adams of Houston, Bob Howsam of Denver and Max Winter of Minneapolis — also wanted NFL franchises in their cities but could not get majority ownership from the league either. Meeting with them, Hunt came up with the notion of starting a new league that included franchises in America's two biggest metropolises, New York City and Los Angeles, to give the new league legitimacy, even though he had not talked to anyone representing them.

Hunt corrected that by approaching former radio and TV sportscaster Harry Wismer about owning a New York franchise. Wismer liked the idea, but as with other backers of the planned league who met in the summer of 1959, they agreed they would need a TV contract to survive in the long term. They also picked Joe Foss as their commissioner of eight planned teams.

Then Bert Bell himself unknowingly gave the competing group a big boost. Called to testify before Congress on July 1959 to see whether or not the NFL should be exempt from the Sherman Antitrust Act, Bell asked Hunt if he could mention the latter's plans to convince legislators the NFL did not have a monopoly on professional football players. That testimony generated publicity and interest in the league in New York City, Los Angeles and other cities with clubs under consideration for the new league. Soon Hunt and crew announced that they planned to have in operation by 1960 their new American Football League, abbreviated naturally as AFL. (Only experts realized there had been three other aborted efforts using the name previously over the years to compete with the NFL. The first American Football League lasted just one year, 1926, the second one from 1936 to 1937 and the third from 1940 to 1941.)

Amid this growing threat, Bell died dramatically from a heart attack at a Philadelphia Eagles game on October 13, 1959. To replace him, the NFL owners selected the following year a diminutive, unassuming, little-known 33-year-old. He seemed unlikely to lead effectively, but quickly and decisively, Alvin Ray "Pete" Rozelle soon made himself as much a household name as he did with his sport thanks to his canny actions.

Meet Pete

Pete Rozelle's initial NFL experience was in 1946 as a gofer for Maxwell Stiles, public relations director for the Los Angeles Rams, just newly relocated from Cleveland. He left to be athletic news director at the University of San Francisco, then was public relations director for the Rams in 1952–55 before starting his own p.r. firm.

Rozelle returned to NFL in 1957 when Bert Bell drafted him as general manager for the Rams, whose owners by now hated each other. Rozelle smoothed out the situation. Still, he attended the NFL's annual meeting in 1960 without plans to replace Bell, but after 10 days deadlocked over who should do the job, Dan Reeves suggested his general manager Rozelle get the job, and he did.

As a relatively unknown candidate picked as a compromise, Rozelle looked to have his work cut out for him just keeping the NFL going in 1960. Adding to his problems was the growing presence of the AFL too. In one notable court case that year, a judge ruled that Louisiana State University running back Billy Cannon had to go into the AFL rather than NFL after signing contracts both with the AFL's Houston Oilers and NFL's Los Angeles Rams, because Cannon signed with the Oilers first. Emboldened by this decision, the AFL soon launched an antitrust suit against the NFL to gain more money and leverage.

The AFL also threw the NFL off guard with its proposed TV package. In the 1940s and 1950s, the TV networks established deals with individual NFL teams to cover them. The AFL proposed a package whereby all its franchises would be available for national coverage for one fee. The only network without an NFL contract at the time was the American Broadcasting Company (ABC), and it had $8 million available in sports advertising from Gillette to help it in 1960. With that support, ABC negotiated a deal to give the AFL $8.5 million for five years on a graduated scale, depending on ratings generated by it. Of course, Gillette sponsored ABC's AFL broadcasts. The deal impacted Rozelle by prompting the other networks to complain about having to pay for contracts for different NFL teams rather than having them collected into one purchase package like the AFL. Rozelle considered that a fair notion, and when he won approval from Congress to do so via the passage of the Sports Antitrust Broadcast Act on September 30, 1961, he began doing so in 1963, to great future benefit for the league.

Rozelle was able to get one thorny TV-related issue out of the way early in his career, though. He engineered relocating the Cardinals franchise from Chicago to St. Louis in 1960 because the Cardinals had shared the Chicago market with the Bears franchise there. Up until 1973, court rulings upheld that TV coverage for pro football games could be "blacked out" in a 75-mile radius from where a home game took place, as an effort to promote and protect gate attendance. That situation meant that with Chicago having two NFL franchises, it doubled the chance that viewers in the Second City would not get a NFL game to watch that week, thus hurting ratings. By moving the Cardinals to St. Louis, Rozelle not only solved the blackout dilemma but also moved his organization into another major TV market. (The blackouts rule received modification by Congress in September 1973 when it passed laws requiring that any game sold out at least 72 hours in advance could be televised in its local market. Legislators did so knowing that President Richard Nixon, an avid fan of the Washington Redskins and pro football in general, resented not being able to watch the local games from the White House.)

That Chicago quandary was an easy fix, but several other issues faced Rozelle for the long term, and many of them involved TV exposure. Among them was getting NFL games onto a regular nighttime schedule. That plan would take nearly 10 years, and ironically it would involve the network that secured the AFL's first TV contract — ABC. But if Rozelle was considered incorrectly a lightweight at first glance when drafted as NFL commissioner in 1960, he at least had more respect initially than ABC did within its industry at the time, and ABC had been around some 15 years by 1960. As we will learn shortly, ABC was doing so poorly in its first couple of decades of existence that it needed NFL football more than NFL football needed it.

2

ABC Pre–*Monday Night Football*

If you've ever eaten a Life Saver while at a major movie theater, you have in a condensed form represented the early years of ownership of ABC.

ABC grew out of a ruling by the Federal Communications Commission (FCC) that the National Broadcasting Company (NBC), in operation with two radio networks (NBC Blue and NBC Red) since January 1, 1927, had a monopoly in its setup. Forced to sell a network as a result, NBC began plans to sell off the smaller Blue operation in 1942.

The winning bidder was Edward J. Noble, chairman of Life Savers, Inc., for $8 million. The change took effect on October 12, 1943. For his payment, Noble received a network then consisting of 168 affiliates and 715 employees. Its name was just Blue until the next year, when Noble purchased the name "American Broadcasting Company" for it. The network became ABC officially on June 15, 1945, with 197 radio affiliates then in operation.

Yet as anybody familiar with broadcasting knew then, the big news among the networks was the expected explosion of commercial television as World War II ended. NBC already had plans for it, as did its primary radio competitor, the Columbia Broadcasting System (CBS), established in 1928. Another company called DuMont had been experimenting with TV in preparation to operate its own network too. With all these plans, ABC leaders realized they would have to do TV to remain competitive. With ABC having less capital and advertising revenues than its competitors, this would not be easy.

Getting Into Video

The savviest move ABC made initially on TV was to apply for broadcasting licenses on Channel 7 in five of the top six markets at the time — New York City, Chicago, Los Angeles, Detroit and San Francisco. The network wanted these licenses for its owned and operated stations, of which the FCC limited each network to just five at the time. While NBC, CBS and DuMont scrambled to get rights for Channels 2–6 in markets haphazardly, ABC's decision gave the network a coherent base to launch its operations, as viewers in those five major cities soon would realize that ABC was on Channel 7 for all of them.

On the downside, ABC lacked quality programming for its emerging TV operations. While ABC gave late 1940s audiences such non-entities as Skip Farrell and Jacques Fray, NBC and CBS offered Ed Sullivan, Milton Berle and Arthur Godfrey. Naturally, ABC attracted few viewers. The only hit ABC had in 1949 was the western *The Lone Ranger*.

Hurting matters more was beyond its owned stations, few of its TV affiliates took direct feeds from the network. Most of the 60-odd other ones connected to it aired programs on a delayed basis using kinescopes (films of live TV shows shot off a monitor, usually not of the best picture quality). With this structure and poor entertainment to offer, it was no wonder that ABC struggled in its early TV years. By 1950 ABC barely made a profit amid losses on its TV production of almost $2 million.

Amid this gloomy atmosphere, the network had a savior the next year when a 45-year-old ex-lawyer bought it and over the next 34 years oversaw its bumpy transformation from a struggling entity to the top banana in broadcasting. His name was Leonard Goldenson.

Golden(son) Years

Joining Paramount Pictures in 1933 as counsel for the film company in its theater division, Goldenson moved up to become its vice president in 1941. After the Supreme Court ruled in 1948 that it was illegal for movie studios to own theaters showing their films as well, Goldenson became president of United Paramount Theatres in 1949. The group owned 1,298 theaters wholly or in part.

Goldenson realized that TV's growing popularity now ate into his company's profits, so he pursued buying ABC, using his company's capital to purchase it. The FCC had the final call on whether a TV network could merge with a movie theater group without the result being a monopoly, however, and it did not do so favorably until February 9, 1953. It is this date that ABC has since considered its real "birth" as a network.

As part of the deal, Goldenson had to keep Robert Kintner as ABC's president, a job Kintner had held ever since ABC went into network TV. However, Kintner disliked the new men Goldenson installed as ABC executives, and after several clashes, Goldenson fired Kintner in 1956. Kintner then became president of NBC through 1965. Goldenson replaced him with Oliver "Ollie" Treyz, who upped ABC's ad sales. But Treyz's unreliable promises to agencies eventually proved to be his undoing, and despite all his efforts, ABC remained in third place with fewer affiliates than CBS and NBC when he was fired in 1962. (Unable to get its act together, DuMont went out of business in 1955.)

To be fair, there was little to entice a station owner to join ABC in the early years anyway. On weekdays, for example, the network never programmed more than two hours of shows before 7 P.M. until January 1956, whereas CBS and NBC provided a near-continuous slate of programs daily from morning to evening. At the other end of the day, it was not uncommon for ABC to "go dark" and offer no programs after 10:30 P.M. while CBS and NBC sent out their own shows to stations. (In fact, ABC decreased its 10:30 to 11 programming from nightly in 1950 to just once a week in 1955, 1957 and 1958.)

Perhaps no better illustration of how the network fared on TV prior to *Monday Night Football* can come from reviewing ABC's Monday schedule over the years. Get ready–a lot of shows you won't recognize make up the bulk of this tale.

The Monday Night Mess

From its start as a TV network in 1948 through the fall of 1959, ABC had only seven series that lasted more than one season on Monday nights. Two were documentaries (*The Big Picture* and *Bold Journey*), one was a news show (*Junior Press Conference*). The three stayed on ABC despite drawing tiny audiences because they were cheap to produce.

As for the others, *Hollywood Screen Test* has been credited as the first network TV series for ABC, having run on its Philadelphia and Washington affiliates starting April 15, 1948, before ABC inaugurated its New York TV affiliate's operation four months later. Apparently sentimentality for the talent competition was enough to help carry it on Mondays from 7:30 to 8 P.M. from 1950 to 1953, where even despite running against news on CBS and NBC it failed to attract many viewers, especially in relation to the similar *Arthur Godfrey's Talent Scouts* that aired on CBS from 8:30 to 9 P.M. the same night.

The Voice of Firestone was ABC's way to sop up advertising from the titular tire company. NBC forced the series off its Monday night lineup in 1954 for low ratings; ABC generated the same results when the series moved over to the network at the same 8:30–9 P.M. time slot. ABC officials moved *The Voice of Firestone* back to start a half hour later in 1957 to try to bolster its ratings. They then watched in horror as the series flopped against a show that had been airing on ABC Monday nights before *The Voice of Firestone* for two years, *Make Room for Daddy* (a/k/a *The Danny Thomas Show*). Never a hit on ABC, *Make Room for Daddy* became the top-rated comedy on TV when it inherited the 9–9:30 P.M. time slot formerly held by *I Love Lucy* on CBS.

Indeed, CBS and NBC owned Mondays totally in the 1950s. Viewers not watching *The George Burns and Gracie Allen Show* or *Studio One* on CBS checked out "Peter Pan" on *Producers' Showcase* or *Twenty-One* or *Robert Montgomery Presents* on NBC instead. Tired of low ratings for *The Voice of Firestone* by the 1958–59 season, ABC cancelled it after the company refused to move it to a less competitive Sunday afternoon slot.

Finally, *Lawrence Welk's Top Tunes and New Talent* was a spin-off of the network's surprise 1955 hit *The Lawrence Welk Show*. Never as popular as its parent, *Lawrence Welk's Top Tunes and New Talent* ran two years on Mondays from 1956 to 1958 (and one more on Wednesdays in 1958–59)—actually pretty good given ABC's variety series track record. Apart from *The Lawrence Welk Show*, the only variety shows that ran more than three years on ABC prior to 1970 were the *Paul Whiteman's TV Teen Club* from 1949 to 1954, *Ozark Jubilee* from 1955 to 1960 and *The Hollywood Palace* from 1964 to 1970.

Then, emboldened by its triumphant 1958–59 schedule, when it placed four series in the seasonal top 10 (but had enough stinkers otherwise to finish still in third place), ABC totally revamped its Monday night schedule in the fall of 1959 for the first time since it began broadcasting, with four big Hollywood adventure film productions— *Cheyenne, Bourbon Street Beat, Adventures in Paradise* and *Man with a Camera*. The last three did not dominate their slots, but the western *Cheyenne* became the first ABC Monday series to break the seasonal top 20 (finishing at 17), thus forcing the cancellation of its 7:30–8:30 competition of *Masquerade Party* and *The Texan* on CBS and *Richard Diamond, Private Detective* and *Love & Marriage* on NBC. With that victory, ABC appeared poised to steal the lead for the evening in the 1960s. Unfortunately, *Cheyenne* slid in popularity thereafter and went off Mondays by the end of 1962.

Still, the network did OK with the addition of *The Rifleman* on Mondays in 1960 after *Cheyenne*, with *The Rifleman* ranking in the top 30 in 1960–61 and 1961–62 before declining and being canceled in 1963. But ABC's real triumph was its 10–11 P.M. medical drama added in the fall of 1961, *Ben Casey*. A solid performer reaching number 18 in its first season, *Ben Casey* zoomed to number 7 in 1962–63, the first top 10 Monday night series for ABC ever. *Ben Casey* was in fact about the only thing ABC had going for it that season—the network's next highest-rated series was *Wagon Train* all the way down at number 25.

Flush with the success of *Ben Casey*, or maybe woozy from it, ABC moved the series to Wednesdays opposite CBS's top sitcoms *The Beverly Hillbillies* and *The Dick Van Dyke Show* in 1963–64 and replaced it with the drama *Breaking Point* on Mondays, with a lead-in for the latter being a newly expanded 90-minute version of *Wagon Train*. The results were disastrous. Viewers overwhelmingly preferred CBS's comedy lineup of *The Lucy Show* and *The Andy Griffith Show*, and even a return of *Ben Casey* to its Monday time slot in the fall of 1964 could not stop its rating downfall that began when it aired on Wednesdays. Nevertheless, *Ben Casey* would be the only ABC show to last more than two seasons on Mondays in the mid–1960s until its cancellation in 1966.

Sliding Down: ABC Mondays Mid- to Late–1960s

The faltering progress on Mondays oddly came at the time when the network fared the best it had done ever in the ratings. Helping the network's rise greatly was Edgar J. Scherick, formerly from its sports division (more on him in the next chapter). Moved to vice president in charge of programming at ABC in 1963, he oversaw the network's effort to come out of the 1962–63 horror by rejiggering the lineup to where ABC actually finished in first place several weeks during the first few months of the 1964–65 season.

Part of this had to do with a decent schedule of new shows from Scherick (the sitcoms *Bewitched* and *The Addams Family* and the soap opera *Peyton Place* all finished in the top 25), and part came from Tom Moore, ABC's president since 1962. Moore made a successful concerted pitch to establish ABC affiliates throughout the country so that the network could compete on an equal footing with CBS and NBC in most markets. Meanwhile, CBS (the number 1 network since 1956) suffered a larger-than-usual number of new shows bombing, including three network president James Aubrey added due to being friends with Keefe Brasselle, an actor whose production company created the shows.

But Aubrey was out in 1965, and CBS returned to first while ABC slumped back to third at the end of the 1964–65 season. Monday nights were part of the reason why. ABC bet on the sitcoms *Wendy and Me* (starring George Burns) and *The Bing Crosby Show*, but they could not overturn CBS's established comedies. Testing a different strategy, ABC employed two dubious westerns for its 1965–66 schedule, *The Legend of Jesse James* and *A Man Called Shenandoah*. CBS barely flinched; both oaters went off within a year.

Finally, in the fall of 1966, ABC unveiled the half-hour dramas *The Rat Patrol* and *The Felony Squad*, an edition of *Peyton Place*, and the hour-long western *The Big Valley* for its Monday night offerings. They didn't stop the CBS sitcom juggernaut at all, but they did better than their predecessors, so ABC kept them in place for two years.

When Scherick left in 1967, ABC replaced him with Len Goldberg, who as head of ABC daytime programming in 1966 installed such hits as *Dark Shadows* and *The Newlywed Game*. However, Goldberg and ABC president Tom Moore quarreled often over leadership, with Moore resigned to the idea that ABC always would be the number three network. Even worse, ABC faced other considerable challenges besides its programming.

One was the conversion to color. By 1965 most NBC and CBS shows aired in color, so ABC naturally had to do the same. Leonard Goldenson estimated the cost of converting ABC's programs to color would be about $113 million, so he considered merging with other companies to help out with expenses. On December 7, 1965, an announcement came that ABC would join with the International Telephone and Telegraph Corporation (ITT).

But two weeks before the merger was to be finalized on February 1, 1967, the Department of Justice halted it, concerned that ITT might censor ABC's news due to the former's multinational operations. Justice officials threatened to challenge ABC all the way to the Supreme Court over the matter; meanwhile, ITT did a confidential study learning that mid-level ABC executives had little belief in their bosses, and ITT's stock would cost it nearly double the original price of $388 million for the acquisition. With all these circumstances, both parties called off their deal officially on January 1, 1968.

Exactly six months later, ABC officials learned Howard Hughes intended to take over the network with a $150 million deal. Goldenson feared the buyout until he learned Hughes would have to appear personally before the FCC to say how he would divest himself of a Las Vegas TV station he owned before he could take over ABC. As the last thing the reclusive billionaire wanted to do was to show up in public, he had to drop his plan. But the legal wrangling led ABC to lose $20 million in 1968, its worst year ever financially.

With ABC focused on these deals more than programming, its lineups suffered in quality and ratings. In 1967–68, only the sitcom *The Flying Nun* and the spy drama *It Takes a Thief* ran more than two years among newcomers, and in 1968–69 only one show met the same qualifications — *The Mod Squad*, which ran until 1973. Meanwhile, the highest rated series ABC had for both seasons was *Bewitched* at number 11; it was one of just two programs ABC had in the top 20 for both 1967–68 and 1968–69. During this time, to make a better pitch for ABC's future, Goldenson installed Elton Rule as the new network president in 1968 (as a nice gesture of dignity, he promoted Tom Moore before letting him go).

Also, in the 1968–69 season on Mondays, ABC faced new competition from NBC, which had been fighting ABC for second place on Mondays in the 1960s. *Rowan and Martin's Laugh-In* joined the CBS Monday stalwarts *Gunsmoke*, *Here's Lucy* (a new series starring Lucille Ball), *Mayberry R.F.D.* (the spin-off of *The Andy Griffith Show* after its star had left the show in 1968) and *Family Affair* in the top 10 in 1968–69. *The Carol Burnett Show*, which followed *Family Affair* on CBS from 10 to 11 P.M., made the top 25. With these powerhouses against them, the 1968–69 ABC Monday slate of *The Avengers*, *Peyton Place*, *The Outcasts* and *The Big Valley* crumbled and forced the network to redo the whole night for 1969–70, the first time it did so since its horrendous 1962–63 season.

The Pits: ABC Mondays 1969–70

For 1969–70 Mondays, ABC launched the night with two 45-minute series, the variety show *The Music Scene* and the drama *The New People*, with the break between shows coming in the middle of *Gunsmoke* on CBS and *Rowan and Mar-*

tin's Laugh-In on NBC in an abortive attempt to stop viewers from checking out either one of those shows.

"When you're fighting like that, you'll try anything," said Martin Starger, who became vice president of programming for ABC in 1969. He said the network knew it could not get anyone to tune in at 8 P.M. Mondays given the competition, so they thought if they started a half-hour show that ended after *Gunsmoke* and *Rowan and Martin's Laugh-In* were already in progress, it would convince viewers to stay with ABC. It did not work.

Then from 9 to 10 P.M., ABC displayed *The Survivors*, an expensive soap opera starring Lana Turner in the type of melodrama she excelled in during the early to mid 1960s. Unfortunately for her, that genre was out of favor by 1969, and the show had scathing reviews to boot. It joined the other ABC Monday shows in going off the air after four months. ABC had more faith in its other Monday night series, the comedy anthology *Love American Style* from 10 to 11 P.M., so it moved it to Fridays despite so-so ratings in January 1970.

The rest of the 1969–70 season on Mondays, ABC programmed the fading *It Takes a Thief* from 7:30 to 8:30 P.M., then a movie followed by a half-hour documentary called *Now* from 10:30 to 11 P.M. Ratings remained pathetic, and the CBS and NBC competition grew even stronger. *Rowan and Martin's Laugh-In, Gunsmoke, Mayberry R.F.D.* and *Here's Lucy* were all in the top six for 1969–70, *The Doris Day Show* (which took the 9:30–10 P.M. slot *Family Affair* had in 1968–69) was at number 10, and *The Carol Burnett Show* was at 13. As with 1967–68 and 1968–69, ABC finished in third place overall with only two top 20 series in 1969–70 (the highest was *Marcus Welby, M.D.* at number 8).

With such a bleak outlook, ABC could and would use just about anything to program its Monday night lineup. Then came a notion from NFL Commissioner Pete Rozelle to do a regular slate of football games for that night. It was not an easy choice for the network to make despite its difficulties on Mondays, particularly in light of the network's up-and-down history with sports in general, and the dicey record of sports in the nighttime too. For one thing, there had not been a regularly scheduled nighttime sports show on TV in six years, and among the ones that had aired prior to that, few were ratings smashes.

Though ABC would boast about being the leader in network sports by its promotions in the 1970s, the fact was the network had its fair share of problems with the field over the years, and there were certain circumstances that made pro football on Monday night not necessarily a choice that would be a smash. An examination of that history is in order to understand the tentatively optimistic air that ABC had when it announced it finally would begin airing *Monday Night Football*.

3

NFL and ABC Merge

How novel was the idea of doing sports regularly on nighttime network TV in 1970? Well, consider while daytime weekends overflowed with such activity, it had been six years since any network sports series had aired past 7 P.M. That show was *The Fight of the Week*, which ended on ABC September 11, 1964.

The Fight of the Week grew out of *The Gillette Cavalcade of Sports*, which focused on boxing. It was a top 25 series for NBC from 1950 to 1954. In 1960 NBC canned the Friday night series for low ratings. Yet its title sponsor liked how the program propelled the company to be the leading razor in America. So Lou Maxon, president of the ad agency handling the Gillette account, won over ABC programming and sports head Tom Moore by saying that Gillette would guarantee $8 million annually in advertising for ABC to spend on any shows as long as it kept the series on the air. The retitled *The Fight of the Week* stayed in the ratings cellar for four years, but Gillette's revenues helped ABC bid successfully for the rights to the American Football League and NCAA football.

The only other nighttime sports series to crack the top 30 before *Monday Night Football* was *The Pabst Blue Ribbon Bouts*, a CBS series retitled *Wednesday Night Fights* when it moved to ABC in 1955. *The Pabst Blue Ribbon Bouts* was a top 30 hit on CBS in 1950–55. The series went off ABC in 1960 because Gillette demanded *The Gillette Cavalcade of Sports* be the network's only boxing series as part of its transfer from NBC.

The Gillette Cavalcade of Sports and *The Pabst Blue Ribbon Bouts/Wednesday Night Fights* were the only regularly scheduled nighttime network sports series to appear in the 1960s except for the maligned *Jackpot Bowling Starring Milton Berle*, where the title comedian uncomfortably hosted a game of tenpins on NBC Monday nights in 1960–61. In fact, apart from the two boxing series, only a handful of nighttime sports series had aired on the networks since the mid–1950s, and most were summer shows — *The Big Moment* (historic sports highlights) on NBC in 1957, *Cowtown Rodeo* on ABC in 1957 and 1958, *Baseball Corner* on ABC in 1958 and *Harness Racing* on ABC in 1958.

Previously, there had been considerably more network nighttime sports series in the late 1940s through mid–1950s, but they existed primarily on ABC and DuMont as cheap programming to use to fill time and make money. Pro wrestling was a featured attraction on DuMont, while ABC boasted heavy exposure of the roller derby for a time.

But it was mainly men who watched sports, and most big nighttime advertisers wanted to appeal to women, the main purchasers of household products. As audiences for most nighttime sports were not large, they became less favored by the networks, to the point where they were nonexistent by the mid–1960s. With the announcement of *Monday Night Football*, ABC executives took the risk that nighttime TV was ready to embrace regular sports programming again, and they were counting on the how pro football had grown in popularity over 30 years on television to lead the way.

Pro Football on TV: The Early Years

TV's first NFL game occurred on October 22, 1939, on NBC's experimental New York City station W2XBS. It was a two-and-a-half-hour contest with no commercials, played between the Philadelphia Eagles and Brooklyn Dodgers at Ebbets Field with Allen "Skip" Walz doing play-by-play. Reviewers noted how there was snow on the screen and deep shadows later in the game that darkened part of the field. Hardly an auspicious beginning between the game and the medium.

Nevertheless, NBC broadcasted other pro football games during 1939 and 1940 (locally only), but the sport did not get significant exposure on the tube until after World War II. The first regular network effort was on NBC in 1947 from October 4 through November 23. Bob Stanton, a network staff announcer, gave play-by-play for contests featuring the New York Giants, joined by commentator Arthur Daly, a sportswriter with *The New York Times*. It aired in New York City, Philadelphia, Washington, D.C., and Schenectady, New York — basically the whole lineup on NBC's fledgling East Coast network. The series apparently did not impress its sponsor, Pabst Blue Ribbon Beer, or NBC that much, as it lasted just that one season. In fact, NBC did not carry another pro football series until 13 years later.

The following year, more than 30 ABC affiliates in the Midwest joined to air the home games of the Chicago Bears and the Chicago Cardinals (except, ironically, for the Chicago station due to the local blackout rule). It was popular enough that it attracted the attention of a time buyer at the Dancer Fitzgerald Sample ad agency named Edgar Scherick. A magna cum laude Phi Beta Kappa graduate of Harvard, Scherick told network officials his client, Falstaff beer, wanted to sponsor half of the shows. According to Scherick, ABC President Robert Kintner did not realize many of its stations had been carrying an NFL game, but naturally the network accepted the business, and Scherick would prove to be pivotal for ABC in the future too.

By 1951 ABC's NFL series aired on 15 stations including as far south as Miami, and its popularity led another struggling network called DuMont to air its own slate of Sunday afternoon pro games. DuMont carried several different games each week, with the main one being the New York Giants games called by Harry Wismer (the same Wismer who later was owner of the New York Titans in the AFL from 1960 to 1963). It became the network's most popular and widely seen series, even airing on some NBC and CBS affiliates, and probably was the only DuMont program to run on more than 100 stations.

Given that strong popularity, DuMont tried to exploit it for all it was worth and added pro football to its Saturday nighttime lineup in the fall of 1953. Ray Scott served as the initial sportscaster of *The Game of the Week* on DuMont, giving the NFL its first national nighttime coverage. The series also aired Saturday nights in the fall of 1954. It did well for the network, even though its ratings did not challenge its popular competition, *The Jackie Gleason Show* on CBS and *Your Show of Shows* on NBC.

However, DuMont faced financial difficulties that required it to cut back its programming to virtually nothing by the spring of 1955, and it could only muster rights for Sunday afternoon games in the fall of 1955 before going off by the end of the year. ABC had kept its own Chicago games at the same time, so it looked like with the crumbling of the DuMont network ABC would assume full rights for the NFL in the 1956 season.

But ABC underwent a nasty experience with amateur football in the 1954–55 season for which reverberations affected its NFL coverage. After the incident, in fact, ABC had such distaste for weekend sports series that it barely carried any the rest of the 1950s.

NCAA for ABC? No Way

In 1954 Robert O'Brien, an ex–Notre Dame football player who was ABC's financial vice president and secretary, secured a deal to do 13 NCAA football games for ABC for $2.5 million. As part of the agreement, he promised NCAA officials that the network would cover 26 weeks of Saturday afternoon winter and spring college sports too.

However, ABC President Robert Kintner resented the deal because he himself did not initiate it and, worse, it came from O'Brien, one of the new executives thrust upon him under ABC's new ownership by Leonard Goldenson. To spite O'Brien, Kintner delayed finalizing advertising for the program, forcing several last-minute bargain basement sales. The result cost ABC $1.8 million and loss of respect from the NCAA, which dropped ABC from carrying spring sports and offered football rights to NBC the next year.

With that bungling, ABC had little revenue to pursue future sports programming, and with DuMont out of business, the NFL wanted to keep wide distribution of its product on TV. It found a willing buyer in CBS, who envied NBC having NCAA football rights for most of the 1950s and wanted a comparable product to offer its affiliates. Starting in 1956, CBS would own at least part of the rights to the NFL for the next 38 years.

Assisting in producing CBS's 1956 NFL coverage was Edgar Scherick — yes, the same Scherick who placed advertising on ABC's NFL games earlier in the 1950s. He had helped ABC get rights to air major league baseball games Saturday afternoons in 1953 for a series that became a hit despite having to be blacked out in half the homes served by TV at the time because baseball officials wanted to protect home attendance. When CBS got the rights for *Game of the Week* in 1955, Scherick left ABC too (no doubt the NCAA football debacle influenced his move as well). Scherick left CBS in 1957 to establish Sports Programs, Inc., an entity that acquired rights to sports shows, sold commercials for them and supplied talent for them on and off camera.

The next year came an event that really put pro football into the national consciousness. On Sunday, December 28, 1958, the Baltimore Colts met the New York Giants in the NFL championship game on NBC. The spirited contest became the first NFL championship game to go into sudden-death overtime, and Colts quarterback Johnny Unitas helped lead his team to the exciting win, passing for 349 yards, a record for a championship game.

As no other games were on that afternoon (it started at 1:45 P.M.), and it was played right in the middle of the Christmas and New Year's holidays between college bowl games, the contest resulted in a large audience that loved the show it saw. The game made Unitas a household name and the NFL more of interest to TV viewers — and at least one network president. ABC's Tom Moore realized he needed more sports for his network to survive, as the immediacy of sports would naturally require ABC affiliates to clear the schedules and program such series live. Even by the late 1950s, many ABC affiliates relied on getting network shows taped or filmed and sent to them rather than using cables for simultaneous feeds across the network. That setup would have to change if ABC seriously wanted to compete with CBS and NBC.

However, Moore found that overseeing both entertainment and sports series would be too much for him to do successfully. So going back to an old friend, Moore drafted Scherick to supply the latter's company services to ABC — for a nice price for Scherick.

Building a Foundation of Sports on ABC

One of Scherick's early efforts for ABC was *Saturday Night Football* in 1959, a tape-delayed broadcast of a pro game earlier that day that aired starting at 11 P.M. The late night offering attracted few, but its commentator, Howard Cosell, would be back doing the same job on a different night a little more than a decade later.

Saturday Night Football was just a warm-up to what Moore and Scherick planned to do in televising sports. Moore had ambitions of getting back to ABC the rights for NCAA football (on NBC since 1952), pro baseball (on CBS since 1955) and a few other events. The previously mentioned Gillette advertising money helped the men get some of these activities, along with a little ingenuity.

On March 14, 1960, bids for TV rights of the next two years of NCAA football occurred. Scherick knew he could get them only if NBC Sports President Tom Gallery put in a low bid, which he assumed would be likely if both CBS did not participate and Gallery did not recognize anyone from ABC ready to put in a counteroffer. Scherick wisely gambled CBS would not participate due to its already having won the rights to most NFL games. Now he just had to have a representative for ABC do his work surreptitiously at the meeting of NCAA officials in the Manhattan Hotel.

In an ingenious stroke, Scherick sent to the meeting nondescript Stan Frankel, ABC's assistant controller, and instructed him to act low key until after Gallery looked around, saw that no other network representatives were there and placed NBC's low bid on the table for consideration. It worked like exactly as planned. Frankel shocked Gallery by topping him with ABC's bid for the NCAA, which offered $1,051,114 more than NBC's proposal (NBC's low bid was 10 percent over the previous $5 million it paid for college football). With NCAA and the new AFL football league coming together in the fall of 1960, ABC was on the move to establish its sports presence on TV after years of neglect.

Now all Scherick had to do was to get his production team into place. He planned to install Jack Lubell to produce and direct both the Saturday college and Sunday AFL games. However, Lubell wound up doing only the AFL due to a man Scherick interviewed in April 1960 at the recommendation of his buddy Pat Hernon, the weathercaster at NBC's New York City affiliate WNBC. Hernon hosted a pilot (a proposed show) earlier in 1960 featuring male-oriented informational spots called *For Men Only*. NBC rejected it, and so did Scherick, but the latter did think the show's producer held more promise than its premise, so he invited the producer to his office.

From their meeting onward, TV sports would never be the same again.

Introducing Roone Arledge

He was distinctive from his birth on July 8, 1931, in Forest Hills, New York, just by his odd first name alone. Roone Arledge claimed he took his name from his father, whose father in turn chose "Roon" for his son from a minister's last name he found in an old family bible. It was Roone's dad who added an "e" to the end, for reasons unknown.

Growing up in a well-to-do family (Roone Sr. was a lawyer), Arledge possessed two main ingredients needed to succeed in the world of network television — ambition and luck. He did well attending Columbia University in the early 1950s as a business major, and while serving as headwaiter at the Wayside Inn in Chatham, Massachusetts, one summer between his schooling, he befriended a family that wanted food after the kitchen had closed. That family's father was DuMont programming chief James Cadigan. He remembered Roone when the young man interviewed for a job at the network after he graduated with a bachelor's in business administration in 1952. Roone became a DuMont assistant to the assistant program director (yes, they had such complicated titles in network TV even then) until he was drafted into the Army to serve stateside. When his year-long tour of duty ended in 1955, he had no job — DuMont was now defunct.

Luckily, Roone's wife Joan was a number two secretary to NBC's founder General David Sarnoff, and with that connection he secured a job interview there. Roone became stage manager for various live NBC shows before getting a regular job as co-producer of a five-hour (7 A.M. to noon) weekend block of entertainment on WNBC called *Sunday Schedule*. When it ended, he went to produce a Monday-through-Saturday 9 to 10 A.M. show for the station called *Hi, Mom!* starring ventriloquist Shari Lewis and her sock puppet Lamb Chop that ran from 1957 through 1959 and earned Roone his first Emmy.

A year later, Roone met with Scherick, who tested the producer's knowledge of sports by having Arledge identify three sports stars pictured in Scherick's office. Roone passed with flying colors, so Scherick offered Roone a job at his company on the spot. Despite the lack of prestige associated with ABC, Arledge felt like doing something new, so he accepted the offer, even though Scherick's operation was not officially ABC Sports yet.

Originally, Roone's job was to be in charge of keeping track of production talent not tied down by other commitments to ABC and line them up for potential work in Scherick's sports empire, such as for regional NCAA football telecasts. He made a huge blunder his first week on the job by unwittingly telling a reporter with the entertainment periodical *Show Business* that he would be the NCAA games producer before getting the official approval on doing so from Scherick, who reprimanded him in response. This situation also made Roone wary about dealing with the press the rest of his life and gave him a reputation of being difficult to meet, even among his employees.

But luck and ambition struck again, as Roone did wind up having that producing job by the start of the season. What happened was that Arledge mentioned to Scherick how unimpressed he was with the way NBC and CBS used just four cameras (usually two at the 20-yard line and two on the 50-yard line) for football coverage and how ABC could do it better. Wanting to know more, Scherick asked Arledge to come in with a full proposal in the summer of 1960 to present to ABC executives, specifically on how to improve NCAA football coverage. Roone eagerly accepted the task and laid out a ton of ideas.

What Roone proposed was stated upfront in his own opening words: "Heretofore, television has done a remarkable job of bringing the game to the viewer — now we are going to take the viewer to the game!" He proposed adding directional mikes for better sounds, and more cameras to cover the action at all angles — some in the end zones, some on jeeps going down the sideline, some handheld to get close-ups of players. There would be more use of graphics, such as split screens to cover different parts of the action. ABC would show crowd shots too, to give a sense of how spectators felt at the time. It was all to convey to viewers the feeling of being at the game, to the point of visiting the area around the stadium and using video recorders to show highlights of the game so far during halftime. These were radical notions, but Roone's superiors lapped them up.

In fact, Roone so impressed the executives that Scherick named him producer of the NCAA football games following his proposal, forcing Jack Lubell, who previously did the job at CBS, out of the post. Roone offered to let Lubell direct the games, but understandably Lubell did not want to do only that task and concentrated instead on supervising the AFL games. Roone went with Bill Bennington as director instead.

The rest of Roone's staff for NCAA football included production assistant Chuck Howard (hired in August shortly before the first game was played), associate director Marvin Schlenker, producer Jim Spence, engineer Bob Trachinger and technical chief Julie Barnathan. All stayed devoted to Roone for years. The game announcers were Curt Gowdy (play-by-play) and Paul Christman (analysis or "color" man).

Schlenker said 46 years later that Arledge was determined to stake out a distinctive approach in sports coverage on NCAA football from the start. "I think the first game we used six cameras, which was unheard of in those days," he recalled.

Roone's innovations in his football coverage attracted notice in the industry, and he kept striving for them. The biggest occurred on a Thanksgiving face-off in 1961 when Texas played Texas A&M. During halftime, ABC pioneered the first on-air use of slow motion replay of a score of that happened in the first half of a game. (Schlenker credited engineer Bob Trachinger for crystallizing the process into a reality.) Thereafter, ABC used such replays in halftime shows or during timeouts fairly regularly. To Roone's everlasting distress, however, CBS beat him in being the first network to use instant replay immediately after a football play occurred — in the Army-Navy game of December 7, 1963.

Then came more luck for Roone. In March 1961 ABC purchased Sports Programs, Inc., for $500,000 from Ed Scherick in order to make it ABC's official sports department. Scherick became its vice president in charge of sales before leaving it in two years to join the network's entertainment department. He left the leadership to his administrative assistant Chet Simmons, who had been second in command to Scherick at Sports Programs. However, ABC President Tom Moore favored Arledge for the post due to his innovations. Facing this situation, Simmons went to NBC to become vice president in charge of sports there in 1963. That same year, Roone replaced Jack Lubell as producer of the AFL games on ABC along with doing the same chores for NCAA football.

Arledge also took charge of a then little-noticed anthology program aired during the spring and summer months on Saturday afternoons which launched April 29, 1961, to compensate for ABC not having baseball to offer its affiliates like CBS and NBC did, and according to Marvin Schlenker, to keep together on an active basis the solid production crew the network now had in its sports department with NCAA football. The show was called *ABC's Wide World of Sports*. It became a mainstay on the network for nearly 40 years.

Thus, in three short years, Arledge went from being an outsider at ABC sports to its head man in his early thirties. His launch into being a major sports figure coincided with the climb of NFL Commissioner Pete Rozelle. Not surprisingly, soon the two men crossed each other's paths in ways that initially disappointed but ultimately satisfied them both.

Rozelle Propels the NFL

Apart from the initial trouble he had when it formed, Rozelle found the American Football League not to be a major concern for the NFL for a few years. The AFL's exposure on ABC did not become a huge challenge to the NFL games on CBS and NBC in the early 1960s. Attendance alone was lousy. ABC had to frame shots on both punters and receivers during kicks in order to avoid following the football's trajectory at the start of the play, as that would reveal the fact that the stands were often empty. And ABC started the games at 3:30 P.M. in the hopes that the NFL games that began at 2 P.M. would be at halftime and bored NFL viewers would check out the activity, but it never translated itself that way.

Indeed, Rozelle probably was thankful for the AFL's creation, as its notion of having all league teams share in the profits from a TV deal gave him the model to use in the NFL. It also probably saved some NFL franchises. For example, CBS had been restless in the late 1950s, having to make deals with individual teams to get game rights, as the amounts each team cost varied widely (in 1959, for example, Green Bay got $30,000 versus $200,000 or so for the New York Giants) and resulted in CBS paying the rights for nine teams to carry in regional action. In contrast, NBC made contracts with Baltimore and Pittsburgh to air their games nationally (the remaining 12th club at the time, Cleveland, sold its games to its own lineup of stations). With NBC's apparent advantage in ease and costs, CBS threatened to drop coverage of the weaker teams in its NFL slate. Rozelle, realizing CBS had legal ties to the nine clubs through 1963 that could have left the smaller ones with no network TV, consolidated all TV rights into one national contract on January 10, 1962, that gave CBS rights to all regular season games in 1962 and 1963 for $4.65 million.

Though the cost skyrocketed (prior to that the networks paid no more than $2 million a year for NFL rights), it was next to nothing compared to bidding for two years of NFL TV rights among all networks in 1964. Though ABC had the AFL as a decent performer, it knew that it could win the NFL with a solid bid and forget all about the other league. After all, it had made the top bid with NCAA football back in 1960. Unfortunately for ABC, it made NCAA football so attractive that the other networks outbid them, so the sport aired on CBS in 1962 and 1963, then on NBC in 1964 and 1965. Losing the NCAA was a mixed blessing for Roone — ABC now had more money to put toward a NFL rights bid, but if he did not get it, he faced a future with only AFL games to show in the fall of 1964, and possibly no football at all on ABC in 1965.

Roone was frank about his feelings for the NFL in his autobiography: "I wanted a piece of it so badly I could taste it." Too bad for him, other network executives shared his enthusiasm. While ABC's offer of $13.2 million per year outdid what NBC proposed by $2.5 million, CBS topped them both with a $14.1 million yearly offer.

The astronomical rise in fee rights to some $28 million for NFL games in 1964 and 1965 astounded casual observers, but CBS instantly recouped its costs by securing two $14 million ad contracts, from Ford Motors and Philip Morris. The network also had room for additional spot announcements that would represent profits. As for the NFL, the winning amount divided per franchise left each club with $1 million a year from TV rights alone, 10 times what they had made for similar rights under Commissioner Bert Bell in the 1950s. Clearly the league and its commissioner, Pete Rozelle, had moved into the big time on TV.

But even losing its shot, ABC was not quite finished with the NFL.

The NFL in Nighttime, Part One

When ABC President Tom Moore cancelled *The Fight of the Week* on Friday nights in 1964, he recognized the profitability CBS had with its new NFL deal, and at the same time the disappointments ABC faced with its Friday night lineup for the fall of 1964. Almost all the Friday night shows on ABC during the 1963–64 were losers in their time slots, and with none being strong candidates to return the next season, inspiration hit him — why not slot NFL games on Friday nights? It would give the league wider potential exposure, as more people watch TV at night than during the day, and it would solve a major scheduling problem for ABC. Moore pitched it to Rozelle, and he thought it a possibility worth considering.

The trouble was that before a real deal was in place, Walter Byers, executive director of NCAA sports, got wind of Moore's notion and raised a fit. He knew that such a show would affect attendance of high school football games slated Friday nights across the country, and those games directly impacted the scouting of players for college matches. Rallying his troops, Byers had school athletic directors protesting this plan, and even Congress got into the act by passing a resolution banning pro games on Friday and Saturday nights.

With this development, options for nighttime NFL games became limited quickly. Sundays were out due to fears of burning out interest from games played earlier in the day, and Tuesdays through Thursdays didn't leave teams enough time to recover and practice for next week's games. That left Monday nights for NFL to try games. But Mondays were a huge risk for ABC previously, and the network felt more confident about returning *Ben Casey* to its 10–11 P.M. slot that night for future success over the still iffy prospects of the NFL, particularly for facing CBS's top shows. Moore forgot about the idea — but Rozelle did not.

When 1964 ended, ABC prepared to air pro basketball and then pro baseball in the next year, yet the lack of having the same level of football on the network gnawed at Roone Arledge. The bidding deadline for the NFL TV rights for 1966 and 1967 occurred on January 24, 1965, and Arledge rounded up his financing as much as he could to put together a package he felt was unbeatable. But once again, CBS was not to be outdone.

The first bid from NBC was for $20.6 million yearly. ABC proposed $26.1 million. CBS edged the latter out again with $27.2 million. The amount stunned industry watchers even more than the 1964–65 deal, but number crunchers at CBS reviewed projected ad revenues and believed the network would come out ahead despite paying out nearly double its last two-year deal with the NFL.

If Arledge was disappointed with the NFL decision, he was positively flabbergasted by the AFL's response to it. The league's contract with ABC came up for renewal in 1965, and having seen how much the networks were willing to settle for the competition, AFL leaders adjusted their sights accordingly. They contacted NBC and suggested a deal of $42 million for five years, more than five times ABC's 1960–64 AFL deal. The AFL offered ABC a chance to beat the proposal, but Tom Moore said his network would lose $5 million a year to do just at the minimum and dropped out of negotiations. Thus, ABC had no football to show on the network in the fall of 1965.

As it turned out, NBC did lose about $1 million a year those five years with the AFL. But the influx of cash made the league much more competitive with the NFL in getting players. For one, the New York Jets (previously known as the Titans franchise until 1963), signed popular college quarterback Joe Namath for an unprecedented $400,000 annually, drawing huge crowds for the team and increased visibility for the league. Sensing a threat, Rozelle approached Tex Schramm, general manager of the AFL's Dallas Cowboys, for a meeting in March 1966 to propose a merger using the angle that the two leagues were raiding each other. Schramm met with Lamar Hunt of the AFL the next month for an initial proposal. The public learned of the merger plan officially on June 8, 1966, with a four-year interim period set before all the teams would compete under the NFL aegis in different conferences. With the AFL competition out of the way, Rozelle could now focus TV-wise on getting the NFL nighttime exposure under its next contract for the 1968 and 1969 seasons.

The NFL in Nighttime, Part Two

At first glance, Rozelle's options looked limited. NBC's AFL contract precluded it from bidding, while Arledge, desperate to have any football on ABC, agreed to conditions set by the NCAA's Walter Byers to air college games without any NFL matches on ABC at the same time if the NCAA gave him a guaranteed deal for Saturday games from 1966 to 1969. CBS was in the driver's seat by default and appeared able to dictate the terms.

But Rozelle had a negotiating tactic up his sleeve. He threatened to have the NFL establish a deal with stations to air them nationally rather than use the network. Worried about losing the property, especially to its own affiliates in the fall, CBS ponied up $37.6 million for two years along with the provision of letting one game a year run on Monday nights effective with the immediate season. The first aired October 31, 1966, and scared up a nice 31 share of the Halloween audience that night (meaning that 31 percent of all TV sets turned on while it aired were tuned to the football game). The October 30, 1967, game dipped a little to a 26 share, but the next year on October 28, 1968, it increased to an impressive 36 share. And that was with the 1967 and 1968 games starting at 9:30 P.M. Eastern.

With these figures in hand, Rozelle approached CBS in the spring of 1969 with the option of doing Monday night football on a regular basis under its next NFL contract. The network had all its Monday shows in the top 25 (as mentioned in Chapter 2, they were, from start to end, *Gunsmoke, Here's Lucy, Mayberry R.F.D., Family Affair* and *The Carol Burnett Show*) and felt no need to change its winning hand, so it told Rozelle thanks but no thanks.

NBC was up next, and it looked more promising to the NFL. The bulk of its Monday night lineup since 1968 consisted of movies that could be delayed until the fall season ended each year, particularly since they were not doing a bang-up job against CBS's powerhouse lineup. But there were a few negatives in the face of that strong positive.

One was the concern of how *Rowan and Martin's Laugh-In*, then the number 1 show on TV, would fare on the West Coast if it had to air after football in the late evening (since it ran from 8 to 9 P.M. Eastern and 7 to 8 P.M. Central, those time zones would not be affected if NFL football started at 9 P.M.). Rescheduling it to another night was a possibility, but given that the series gave NBC its best Monday night numbers in a decade, the network was not keen on that option.

Worse yet was that when NBC ran an AFL game on Monday, September 9, 1968, as an experiment, reportedly *The Tonight Show* host Johnny Carson was upset at how its late conclusion ate into the starting time and the audience for his show, at the time airing live from New York City. Carson had already walked out on NBC in 1967 to get a better contract, and with his show being the top generator of ad money for the network, officials did not want to see him do that again. Indeed, no executive wanted to tell him his show would start Mondays after the NFL games ended around midnight rather than in its normal 11:30 P.M. slot. With that in mind, NBC nixed Rozelle's nighttime notion.

That left ABC or syndication to local networks. Rozelle first approached Roone Arledge, who naturally was receptive, but he faced immediate opposition. For one, Tom Moore, a passionate believer in Arledge and ABC Sports, left as network president in 1968, and his successor, Elton Rule, did not care to have football on his nighttime schedule. Other naysayers were ABC sales executives who questioned how the show would appeal to women viewers and operators of smaller ABC affiliates who worried the deal meant the network would dump NCAA football games that had become established with them and the local schools that often appeared on the regional college contests. Faced with these initial obstacles, Arledge let the idea go.

Then came word in late August to Roone that Rozelle was talking about syndicating Monday night football the next year as an option. Roone told the news to his superiors, who fretted about the potential defections of ABC affiliates to such a proposal, given the network's weak standing on the night. That threat affected their position on the proposal, as did an endorsement for the show itself from the network's newly installed vice president of programming, Martin Starger. "I supported it, being this was a big decision for the network," Starger said. "It was an excellent programming decision."

Starger felt publicity about the novelty of the series would draw attention to it, plus its length would alleviate the recurring problem ABC had with filling its 25-hour nighttime schedule at the time (7–11 P.M. Sundays and 7:30–11 P.M. other nights). It was routine every year for ABC to come up at least a half hour short of national programming in those periods because it did not have as much money as NBC and CBS, or as Starger put it, "There were never enough good programs to go around."

The one big nagging fear he had concerning "Roone's baby," as Starger termed the nighttime football proposal, was the insistence by Rozelle and Arledge that the games start at 9 P.M. Eastern. Starger understood them wanting to get the biggest national audience as possible, so that required a 9 P.M. start so that West Coast viewers could see it live at 6 P.M. after most had presumably come home from rush hour traffic after work. The problem was that Starger, being the programming expert he was, recognized how difficult it would be to schedule a series or two that would appeal as a lead-in to viewers in the Eastern and Central time zones before the game and as a lead-out after the game to viewers in the Pacific time zone. It was a legitimate concern that would bedevil ABC programmers throughout most of the run of *Monday Night Football*. Still, Starger approved the offer overall. "It seemed like a no-lose proposition," he said.

With the blessing of Starger and his other bosses, Roone had lunch with Rozelle to iron out a deal, but to Arledge's dismay, Rozelle insisted on giving NBC and CBS right of first refusal in response to ABC's proposal, given the NFL's longer association with both networks. Luckily for Roone, neither network made a counterproposal.

So, ABC now had a three-year, $25.5-million contract with the NFL to do Monday games. That gave the network the beginning of what would become an institution.

The ABC Family and Friends React

Upon the announcement of the plan, ABC affiliates overwhelmingly endorsed the proposal. Starger said most of the East Coast and Midwest affiliates could handle the encroachment of games that could last until the late night hours and figured their news teams could handle staying up later than usual to do their reports after the game.

A dicier situation was the matter of ABC's new late night talk show hosted by Dick Cavett that started on December 29, 1969. ABC faced the same difficulty NBC did with Johnny Carson in forcing Cavett to start his burgeoning show live after the local newscasts that followed *Monday Night Football* in the Eastern and Central time zones.

"I was a big supporter of *The Dick Cavett Show*," Starger said. Nevertheless, he realized that football would have to take precedence over the talk show on the network for financial reasons alone. He admitted that *Monday Night Football* "kind of dislodged it" from its normal airing time and that the show's staff was not happy about being pushed back because it would give its competition the advantage of starting earlier.

But Cavett was not as established as Carson, so of course he could not and did not walk out on this setup. Nonetheless, football clearly hurt him in the ratings on Monday nights, particularly when the games ended in blowouts.

The biggest dissenter to the Monday night games plan in public was NCAA Sports Executive Director Walter Byers. He was infuriated with the deal, feeling it diminished the network's attention to coverage of college football. To placate Byers, Roone promised not to promote NFL games on NCAA ones, yet he would promote NCAA ones on the Monday games. Additionally, he promised not to switch Chris Schenkel, ABC's main college football play-by-play announcer, to NFL coverage. Byers relaxed somewhat but still viewed the new show warily.

Some skepticism about the new program remained privately within ABC as well. Marvin Schlenker, who had worked with Arledge on NCAA football in the 1960s before leaving the sports department entirely in 1969 to work for ABC News, was one of the doubters.

"I thought, well, OK, let's try it, but really I didn't have much faith in it. But I was wrong. Just a little wrong," he chuckled while recalling the announcement.

Readying for the Launch

Although virtually pressured by circumstances to do the show, ABC officials did have encouraging figures to think the Monday games could be a success. For one, pollster Lou Harris found a shift in American public opinion about favorite sports during the 1960s toward the game. In 1964, for example, 45 percent of Americans liked baseball best, followed next by football at 23 percent. But by 1969, the two sports were in a statistical dead heat in popularity, with 31 percent favoring football and 28 percent baseball.

This upgrade of affection for football came through the ratings for the pro game's premiere event, the Super Bowl. It started in January 1967 as the end-of-season contest between the winners of the merging-in-progress AFL and NFL systems, and each year its ratings grew bigger, to the point where the 1970 Super Bowl on CBS scored a rating of 39.4, just a few thousand shy of the daytime sports record rating of 39.5 for the fourth game of the 1963 World Series. (A year later, NBC's telecast of Super Bowl V on January 17, 1971, would set a new record by getting a 39.9 rating; thereafter, the show would air in the nighttime.)

Best of all, sponsors judged *Monday Night Football* a solid hit, particularly of course ones oriented toward men. Four months prior to its premiere, *Monday Night Football* had sold out all its ad spots for the 1970 season. The marketing experts who bought the advertising time seemed to agree with what Rozelle told Melvin Durslag in *TV Guide* in explaining the need for the new NFL show. "Our lifeline is TV and, revenue-wise, we have gone about as far as we can on Sunday," Rozelle said. "Monday night means not only extra money, but opens exciting new possibilities for reaching people who haven't been in the habit of watching on Sunday."

To get those people to watch was the main challenge Roone faced. As with other dilemmas in covering sports, of course, he naturally looked forward to meeting it.

4

The Kickoff (1970–71)

As visionary as Arledge was in setting up *Monday Night Football* as its founder and executive producer, one should be careful not to overlook the impact of the man Arledge named as its director and co-producer (with Dennis Lewin), Fulvio Chester "Chet" Forte.

Forte (pronounced "FOUR-tee") had been a college basketball star in the mid–1950s despite standing just 5'9". In his last season (1956–57), he was a first-string All-American guard at Columbia University as well as AP Player of the Year thanks in part to ranking third in scoring nationally, averaging 28.9 points per game at the time.

The Cincinnati Royals drafted him to play pro, but he did not pass the training camp. Undaunted, Forte became a production assistant to CBS Sports President Bill McPhail in 1958. He stayed there for five years until Arledge recruited him to come to ABC. Forte gained respect for his pacing and coverage of events there, while those in the know also realized Forte had a serious gambling addiction. That was not enough to discourage Arledge from using him on *Monday Night Football*, however.

Working with Arledge on a vision to present football on TV as never seen before, Forte put up to 11 cameras in stadiums to cover games. These included four on the stadium roofs (three of them usually covering the running backs and wide receivers), one each on both end zones, two handheld miniature cameras on the sidelines, one on a wheeled platform on the sidelines, one inside the production headquarters to superimpose statistics and, if available, an 11th one from the Goodyear blimp circling overhead. The total was more than double what NBC and CBS used for their NFL games.

"The three cameras isolating on players feed into separate video machines," ABC cameraman Don Farnham told Wayne Dunham in the *Chicago Tribune TV Week*. "Thus, we are able to have an instant replay from a different angle than that shown by the live-action cameras on almost every play."

Besides more cameras with more options, there also was a greater variety in framing the action too. Big lenses showed a kicker at the end of the field full screen, for example, and there were more sideline shots and head shots of participants than ever before. With these implementations, Forte and Arledge made sure that *Monday Night Football* was going to be visually distinctive from other network football shows.

It also would be unique in the way viewers heard the game, and not just by better mikes catching field action. The *Monday Night Football* announcers would have something to say about the game too — plenty, since there were more of them than usual there.

Triple Play

When it came to announcing sports on TV prior to 1970, it had usually consisted just of a play-by-play man to detail action and an analyst or "color man" to give commentary. *Monday Night Football* heralded the first time that three men would do the job for the sport — but, contrary to what most reports said, this was a first only on the pro level.

In 1965, NBC went with the trio of Lindsey Nelson, Terry Brennan and Bud Wilkinson as the lead team covering that week's slate of NCAA football games. Nelson was a veteran play-by-play man who did his duty for college gridiron matches on TV from 1953 to 1959, when the games alternated among NBC, ABC and CBS. After ABC lost the rights for the games in 1962 to CBS after having them in 1960 and 1961, when Curt Gowdy and Paul Christman announced them, Nelson came back as the announcer, with Brennan joining him. Brennan had been the head football coach at Notre Dame from 1954 to 1958 prior to going into the broadcasting booth.

The duo moved to NBC when the network got the NCAA rights in 1964, then became a threesome the next year when the network drafted Wilkinson, formerly Oklahoma's head football coach in the 1950s. Carl Lindemann, then vice president and later president of NBC Sports, claimed the lineup floundered because Brennan and Wilkinson were at each other's throats in giving their opinions on air and this forced Nelson to be a traffic cop of sorts between them along with his regular duties. If there was that much dissension occurring, however, then why did NBC keep them together throughout the whole season from September through December? Without having seen any of the games, and with Wilkinson and Nelson both dead and Brennan unable to be reached for comment, it's hard for this writer to know if Lindemann's assessment was true.

The fact that NBC lost the NCAA rights to ABC for the following season while the trio was active could have colored Lindemann's perspective, as well as the contrast between the obscurity of Brennan-Nelson-Wilkinson and the popularity of *Monday Night Football* and its setup. In any event, ABC used its own announcer duos when NCAA football came to the network in 1966 and dropped Nelson and Brennan from the coverage. Nelson returned to do college football for CBS in the 1980s before retiring.

Arledge planned his own three-man booth at the outset for *Monday Night Football* to shake up the status quo. It was because Arledge desired to have a new man as the focus for it, one who had not called a regularly scheduled network football series in more than a decade. He was not a play-by-play announcer or ex-player color man, so he would need both to assist him while the show would be fashioned around him. He was, however, a "name" in TV sports, and arguably the biggest and best it ever had.

The Mouth That Roared

During practice sessions for the game show *Family Feud* before it debuted in 1976, participants had to give the most popular answers among 100 people surveyed to this question: "Name someone who Americans hate the most." Disgraced former President Richard Nixon finished first in the voting; Satan came in third. Players named them both, but no one knew who received second place until the game ended. The answer prompted a knowing "Of course!" response from those who saw it — Howard Cosell.

Throughout most of his professional career, Howard Cosell was a loathed man in sportscasting. He knew it himself and even reveled in it to a degree. "Arrogant, pompous, obnoxious, vain, cruel, persecuting, distasteful, verbose, a showoff. I have been called all of these," he noted in his 1973 autobiography *Cosell*. "Of course, I am."

Secretly, though, Cosell did want to be liked, but he was his own worst enemy. Even his defenders had a hard time proclaiming his brilliant insights about what was wrong with sports and what corrections were needed when Cosell told them he was right about it in his insistent, imperious nasal tone. It was not the way others covered sports on TV, which is why Arledge thought Cosell to be a crucial ingredient for *Monday Night Football*.

Born Howard William Cohen in Winston-Salem, N.C., on March 25, 1918, he would change his surname and his birth year as an adult (he claimed to be born in 1920 in *Cosell*). Those alterations made media pundits question Cosell's boast that he was the one sportscaster who could "tell it like it is." His love of sports emerged as a teenager when, attending Alexander Hamilton High School in Brooklyn, he wrote a column called "Speaking of Sports" for the school paper.

Pressured by his mother and father, Cosell attended New York University and became a lawyer. His love remained with sports, though, and in his mid-thirties he managed to secure a sports column called "Cosell's Clubhouse" in a now-forgotten men's magazine called *Real*. Around the same time in 1953 he hosted for free on ABC radio in New York City a panel show for Little League players, letting them ask questions of baseball stars.

The latter activity led to a contract with ABC to do weekend sports shows. To enliven his presentations, Cosell went to spring training in 1955 to tape interviews with players on location at a time when most radio interviews were done live in a studio. This is where Cosell believed he created his first enemies, specifically with print journalists who felt he infringed upon their sacrosanct arena. He said Dick Young of *The New York Daily News* was so infuriated that he uttered profanities in the background to spoil the tapings of interviews. Cosell overcame that obstacle, and his reporting grew strong enough that ABC put him on TV with a nightly 15-minute (7 to 7:15 P.M.) roundup of news in the athletics world called *Sports Focus* from June 3, 1957, through September 12, 1958, followed by the Saturday night NFL game in 1959.

Thereafter, ABC President Tom Moore put an embargo on Cosell for network TV appearances for five years, feeling that his receding hairline and nasal accent made him unappealing to viewers outside New York City (he did allow Cosell to do sports on ABC's Manhattan affiliate WABC, however). Cosell valiantly ventured onward and stood out on ABC radio sports, especially in announcing boxing, which he first covered for the network in 1956. His diligence in interviews on radio and local TV convinced Roone to pressure Moore into installing Cosell as a pregame interviewer when ABC won the rights to cover major league baseball coverage in 1965.

That job did not bring Cosell prominence, as the program was low-rated and ABC lost the rights for baseball to NBC for nearly a decade afterward. What did push him to the forefront was serving as the top announcer for boxing on *ABC's Wide World of Sports*, which showcased pugilists frequently starting in the mid–1960s. During that time, a boxer named Cassius Clay announced he had become a Muslim and henceforth would be known as Muhammad Ali. And since he was a Muslim, Ali refused the draft for the Vietnam War in 1967 on religious grounds.

Cosell supported Ali in both developments. For that he received much hate mail charging him with being a "nigger loving Jew bastard," as Cosell often put it. But it brought him respect from others, such as ABC President Tom Moore, who made a 180-degree turn about Cosell's appropriateness for TV and embraced him before leaving ABC in 1968.

Ali had his own take with Cosell, threatening to pull off the man's toupee on air during their interviews. Cosell was sensitive about that happening, but it did eventually come out that he owned 12 different hair rugs at his disposal for public appearances. Other personal traits about Cosell were that he puffed stogies freely off the air even though he had to have known about the dangers of smoking, and he drank vodka prodigiously before and after each *Monday Night Football* game.

The most irritating habits Cosell conveyed were his love of ornate commentary that detractors found pretentious and his cocksure attitude that he was always right even while sometimes being wrong. The latter applied to his time with *Monday Night Football*. For example, in his 1985 book *I Never Played the Game*, Cosell claimed *Monday Night Football* outrated such competition as *I Love Lucy* and *I Spy*. Impressive, except both shows had been off the air by the time *Monday Night Football* debuted. *I Spy* ended on NBC in 1968 after three years on the air, while *I Love Lucy* had been out of production for CBS since 1957. (In his defense, Cosell was not the only one who confused *I Love Lucy* with Lucille Ball's later series *Here's Lucy*—so did at least two other reference books and the 2002 TV-movie *Monday Night Mayhem*.)

Yet even given the above failings, apologizing and modesty were apparently not part of Cosell's vocabulary. "Let's put it on the table. I'm great," he once told Dinah Shore on her 1970s talk show. Talking to Frank Deford in *Sports Illustrated* in 1983, Cosell proclaimed the following: "I never had any idea that I—that any person in sports—could become so important in U.S. society." To all that, Johnny Carson once prompted laughs from his audience on *The Tonight Show* by calling Cosell "a legend in his own mind."

There was one overriding factor in Cosell's defense of his greatness, however. Simply put, he could speak off the cuff better than almost any sportscaster at the time. He proved this on *Monday Night Football* when he narrated the halftime highlights of the previous day's games and needed only one take to do so every occasion — and he did this just as he saw the film clips in slow motion for the first time. His most dramatic moment during each of these segments came when a runner or receiver headed down the field to the goal line and he would intone deliberately "he, could, go, all, the, way!"

So Arledge now had his main analyst for *Monday Night Football*. Next came his play-by-play man. The winner was not the first one on Roone's list. In fact, he was not a leading candidate at all until others convinced Roone to use him.

"Whoa, Nellie!"

Roone now thought of Curt Gowdy to join Cosell for the play-by-play spot, but Gowdy still had still two years remaining on his NBC AFL contract and could not do it. Next up was Vin Scully, who did not want to travel (his hosting of a game show on NBC daytime in 1969 called *It Takes Two* may also have influenced his decision). Then ABC President Elton Rule suggested he used an ABC Sports personality who was not a major name at the time — Keith Jackson.

Born and raised on a farm near Carrollton, Georgia, on October 18, 1928, Keith Jackson joined the Marines for more than four years before studying political science at Washington State University in Seattle. Rather than pursue that field, however, Jackson went to work at KOMO-TV, ABC's Seattle affiliate, doing various jobs for its sports department, including play-by-play on Washington State football games starting in 1952 followed by AFL games in the early 1960s. He also made history announcing the first live radio broadcast of a sports event from Russia to the United States in 1958, covering via satellite a University of Washington team competing in the Soviet Union.

Jackson could have remained comfortably as a sports reporter in Seattle were it not for a bit of serendipity. In 1962 the father-in-law of ABC President Tom Moore told his relative to check out Jackson while Moore was in Seattle to see the Gold Cup Hydroplaning Championships event being taped for *ABC's Wide World of Sports*. Moore liked the way Jackson covered the event and recommended that Arledge consider putting him under contract for ABC Sports. Arledge liked Jackson's work too, so by 1964 Jackson was an ABC sportscaster.

Not long thereafter, Keith Jackson made his movie debut in the 1966 comedy *The Fortune Cookie* starring Jack Lemmon and Walter Matthau and directed by Billy Wilder. Announcing a game between the Minnesota Vikings and the home team Cleveland Browns, Jackson is the first voice and face seen at the movie's start. What startles a viewer is that Jackson is playing an unnamed sportscaster for CBS, not ABC. Lemmon's character is a CBS cameraman on the sidelines whose injury propels the plot. Jackson disappears after that incident.

That same year, Jackson became a supporting play-by-play man on ABC's NCAA football telecasts. He was not given the primary games — that honor went to Chris Schenkel. Yet because he was considered a secondary announcer, there was barely a peep from NCAA officials about his selection to work on *Monday Night Football*.

Still, he remained a distinctive presence on NCAA games, yelling out "Whoa, nellie!" in appreciation of a particularly showy play (he did not originate the saying, but he certainly popularized it) and dramatically describing the action with phrases like "Fum-BALL!" when the ball was dropped. Home viewers by and large loved his approach.

Jackson realized the new post would no doubt give him added visibility over the limited audiences there had been for the Saturday college games and other ABC sports. What he did not count on was the mix of personalities and egos that made doing the show a challenge for an unassuming man like himself, a blend that left him surprisingly without a job after just one year with *Monday Night Football*.

Let's Not Forget Dandy Don

To complete his team, Arledge wanted Frank Gifford. An ex–NFL player, Gifford started announcing on TV in 1957 during the off-season. He became a full-time sportscaster in 1965. Roone met Gifford at a party and mentioned that he already had Cosell to work with him. That did not impress Frank, but in any event he could not do the show then due to his contract with CBS. He suggested Arledge pursue Don Meredith instead.

Gifford recommended Meredith because of a post-game interview the two did when the Dallas Cowboys lost to the Green Bay Packers on December 31, 1967. Meredith had been quarterback for the Cowboys since 1960 and led them to an NFL championship win over the Packers in 1966. He expected to do the same a year later, but they lost 21–17. With the game ending some 40 minutes earlier than planned, then–CBS sportscaster Frank Gifford met with Meredith in the locker room, and the player emotionally recounted how hard the team wanted to win, ultimately blaming himself for the loss. It was gripping TV in which Gifford and Meredith bonded, and when Meredith's team lost in the playoffs a year later, he resigned from the Cowboys and hung out with his new buddy Gifford.

Gifford believed with his open, casual air, Meredith would be an excellent sportscaster now that he was no longer a Cowboy. Yet few others in broadcasting felt that way at the time, so Meredith had resigned himself to pursuing employment in the insurance field.

Then when he learned of Arledge's interest in him for *Monday Night Football*, Meredith left Arledge five phone messages over a week in 1970 to discuss doing the show. He told Roone in the last one that he and CBS were in negotiations about him being a color man for the network's games that fall, which forced Roone to confer with him at dinner. When they met face to face, Don told him he was a horse's ass for the way he made him chase him down. Roone said that was the kind of candor he wanted on the show. That caught Don's fancy, so he signed on as the third sportscaster for *Monday Night Football*.

Yet Meredith was still "green" as an analyst, and it showed up during the 1970 preseason. To give everyone preparation for the new show, Arledge held a "dress rehearsal" (aired only in house at ABC) when the Kansas City Chiefs visited the Detroit Lions in August. Technically it was flawless, and Jackson and Cosell accommodated themselves fairly well. But Meredith flopped badly and he knew it. He nearly gave up doing the show entirely in its wake until Cosell urged him to keep trying.

Meredith did so, and he soon cultivated a laid-back, down-home approach of being himself that viewers found quite appealing. He often called himself on air "Jeff and Hazel's boy from Mount Vernon, Texas" (he was in fact born there as Joseph Don Meredith on April 10, 1938; Mount Vernon lies 100 miles from Dallas) and occasionally burst into a country song. This included singing "turn out the lights, the party's over" whenever it became apparent that a game's outcome had been virtually decided before time expired.

"Don's always been a ham," according to Meredith's old Texas pal, sportswriter Edwin "Bud" Shrake. Shrake recalled how Meredith entertained people even as a youngster during a shrub judging contest for the local 4-H club. Still, it would be in sports rather than show business where Meredith made his first professional mark.

Meredith set records for scoring while playing football in high school, then went on to attend Southern Methodist University, where he started at quarterback for three years and became named an All-American player there in 1958 and 1959. The Chicago Bears drafted him in the third round of the 1960 NFL draft but traded him to the Dallas Cowboys for future higher draft picks. He was the backup quarterback to Eddie LeBaron with the Cowboys until Coach Tom Landry installed him as a starter in 1965. Even though he was the NFL Player of the Year in 1966, made the Pro Bowl twice, tied several franchise records and delivered three straight division titles to Dallas, he earned boos from fans there when he failed to lead the team to a NFL championship, a fact that gnawed at him even after leaving the team.

When it came to doing *Monday Night Football*, despite commonly held beliefs then and now, Meredith did indeed prepare for each game and did not simply speak off the cuff, as some thought watching his easygoing delivery and observations. He watched films of the competing teams and looked over scouting reports on them too. However, he made sure he didn't study so much he'd lose his spontaneity on air.

Meredith found deflating some comments by Cosell to be an easy and popular task. Cosell laughed them off initially on *Monday Night Football*, but later he wondered if Meredith really disliked him and, if so, why he ever helped him succeed on the show.

The First Shows, the Reviews and Howard's "Virulent Virus"

After an unofficial "preview" on August 28, 1970, the real debut of *Monday Night Football* occurred on September 21, 1970, between the Cleveland Browns and the New York Jets. There were memorable moments as the Browns won it 24–21, and not just on the playing field.

"Leroy Kelly has not been a compelling figure out there tonight!" Cosell shouted about the star Cleveland running back's performance in the debut (Kelly had only gained 45 yards at that point in the game). That was something most other more genteel sportscasters did not do. Cosell also pointed out New York Jets quarterback Joe Namath's game-losing interception as the key play of the game too, thus managing to have ticked off both Browns and Jets fans within a single game.

Meredith kept the mood lighter. When he learned one Cleveland player bore the moniker Fair Hooker, he could not help himself and risked raising the wrath of network censors when he quipped, "Now there's a name. Fair Hooker. I ain't never met one yet!" As for his part, Keith Jackson did a solid job of exposition. Privately, he felt he was treated as an anonymous voice on the show, and Meredith's game commentary did not impress him.

Jackson might have been the only person on the broadcasting team who felt disappointed by the show. That same optimistic sentiment among the staff did not come through among media critics who watched it, however. Almost all the major reviews praised Chet Forte's direction and the work of the technical crew, particularly the cameramen. The talent provoked more varied reactions.

Frank Deford in *Sports Illustrated* gave the opener a mixed call, albeit slightly favorable. "The opening game found the ABC team unduly timid and too often working at cross purposes," he noted. He felt that "Meredith was tight" and that Cosell did merely "play-by-play footnotes" rather than offer solid analysis. He also believed Cosell was wasted doing the halftime highlights narration and would have preferred an essay or interview by the sportscaster instead. Still, he summarized, "As first steps go, it wasn't too bad."

More positive was Pete Axthelm in *Newsweek*, saying that the announcers "while sometimes erratic and indisputably controversial, were seldom dull." He noted that Cosell "grates on some, but his perception of the game far outstrips that of anyone else."

An anonymous reviewer for *Variety* made little reference to the sportscasters while applauding the overall presentation, noting that "on the basis of the opener, nighttime football looks like a winning proposition."

Later critiques were just as mixed. After seeing the first four games, John Leonard in *Life* said that "Cosell has been uncharacteristically bland." Leonard called himself a Cosell fan, but "right now Don Meredith is stealing the show."

At the end of the season, Cleveland Amory of *TV Guide* finally gave his take. "However you feel about too much football, ABC's camerawork during its new Monday night games has been superb, even amid some bad weather conditions," he opined. He praised Jackson as "smooth talking but not too smooth, fast but not too fast, and knowledgeable." Meredith did not impress him ("In the Cowboys-Cardinals game, he was unbelievably bad"), but Cosell did. "He is overfull of himself and underfull of humor, but we like him. In fact, we think he stands almost alone in daring to say what everybody (a) is thinking and (b) would like to say."

Amory was a rather lone voice in favor of Cosell in the first season, among critics and viewers. "It was unbelievable, the pressure to throw Howard off the show," Arledge told Robert Daley in *The New York Times Magazine* in 1974. "I used to come in Tuesday and my office was filled with boxes of mail. I got tired of letters that all started, 'We the undersigned,' with 300 signatures after it." One who wanted Cosell gone was Henry Ford II, president of Ford Motor Company and a major sponsor of *Monday Night Football*. It took much cajoling from Roone to turn Ford around by the end of the season.

Hating Howard reached a peak in the first season on November 23, 1970, when the New York Giants visited the Philadelphia Eagles. To hear Cosell tell it, he suffered chills while at the stadium without power for two and a half hours before the energy came on and he was able to do his highlight reel, then felt woozy at a pre-show party and cold again having to tape an opening interview on the field. After that, he claimed to have run wind sprints with ex–Olympian John Carlos to combat his chills, but that did little good when he returned to the broadcast booth and it was open to the cold air. That did not help him any, and midway through the second quarter he threw up on Jackson and was unable to finish his sentences or even say "Philadelphia" properly. According to Howard, this all happened because he had toxic vertigo resulting from an inner ear infection.

"Yeah. He poured three martinis in his ear," sneered longtime Cosell nemesis Dick Young in the *New York Daily News* in response.

Young and many reporters said flatly that Cosell got drunk and that Roone had to take him off the air out of necessity, not by Howard's call. Arledge confirmed Young's assessment in his autobiography, saying he knew Cosell had martinis available to him not only at the pre-game party but also had alcohol with him in the booth. Arledge covered for Cosell (who took a taxi all the way home from Philadelphia to New York City that night) by saying he had a reaction to flu medication, but he had to let his announcer know that everyone thought he was drunk. Nonsense, Howard said, noting that he had never been drunk in his life, and that a "virulent virus" was the cause of the problem instead. He returned to the broadcast booth the next week without mention of the incident.

The situation would be the first of several times where Arledge found himself getting poor treatment from a man he loved and defended against a chorus of critics. Cosell saw the whole brouhaha differently, as a personal triumph versus those who he thought wanted to get him off *Monday Night Football* permanently. "The writers never laid a glove on me," he wrote in *Cosell*. "And they never will."

A Personal View

Given all these contradictory views, what was it really like to watch *Monday Night Football* in its first year? Well, here's my take, after having seen the second show played on September 28, 1970, when the Kansas City Chiefs visited the Baltimore Colts:

The show opened with a recorded bit of Forte saying "Take tape — three, two, one" before it went into animated graphics for the introduction, the sort of digital action now usually seen on Jumbotrons. Then the camera cut to the stadium, where the spectators were sedate, a true shock to anyone accustomed to the rowdy ones later seen at the start of every *Monday Night Football* game.

Cosell stood on the field to interview each team's starting quarterback. Of Kansas City's Len Dawson, he observed the team's losing record after having won the Super Bowl earlier in the year and queried, "Has the spark left your club?" To the Colts' Johnny Unitas, he asked, "Some of the would-be experts have said you throw the short one with all of the old brilliance, but the ability to throw the long one is no longer there. True or not true?" Such blunt questions stunned many viewers in 1970, but to their credit both men took them in stride, especially Unitas, who responded, "Well, you'd have to ask the experts." Unitas smiled, and Cosell laughed.

After swinging it to Jackson to discuss the defensive talents on each team, Cosell then intoned, "Now to our other colleague, loose and easy, with a magnificence of a Texas drawl and a background in professional football that in its time will be legendary, Dandy Don Meredith." Meredith stressed how the quarterbacks would need to patient against the defenses they faced that night and concluded, "And you know, the Good Lord takes care of those who wait, so we'll just find out tonight."

After the singing of the national anthem, Jackson narrated urgently and compellingly the game's activity for roughly seven minutes before Cosell and Meredith jumped in to give observations. Cosell dropped such words as "theorem" while folksier Meredith reminisced about playing against KC's Billy Ray Smith. Both spent time commenting on the particulars of the game for the benefit of fans who did not watch football regularly ("Don, I think you want to point out that that bump between the two was perfectly legal"; "That's right").

Technically, the show was not quite as smooth as later broadcasts, but still with high caliber features, such as often employing a split screen in slow motion to show what both the quarterback and the receiver did during the play. Jackson read many promos for upcoming college football games and shows like *The Mod Squad* to give the requisite network support.

The problem was the game was a loser, with KC rolling up a 31–7 lead by halftime amid an abysmal performance by Unitas, who was five for 15 in pass completions before being replaced by Earl Morrall prior to the end of the second quarter. Cosell was subdued at halftime about the situation, calling the Chiefs' domination "little short of amazing" while saying that the touchdown the Colts scored before the end of the half gave fans something to cheer about. In fact, it was Meredith who was more direct later in the game, stating flatly that "Baltimore has not played very sharp tonight" en route to the team being on the losing end of a 44–24 blowout.

Part of Cosell's reticence had to have come from seeing injured Chiefs running back Mike Garrett on the sidelines early in the second quarter and mistakenly telling the audience, "He's a tough, slippery kid. He'll be back very quickly." In fact, Garrett never returned to the lineup, and after Arledge chastised Cosell for such a brash prediction, Cosell went quiet for five minutes, then spoke only four more times the rest of the period. He spoke only 10 more times after the halftime, still grousing about the situation apparently, and in fact he did more talking during the excellent halftime highlights.

Supposedly, Cosell threatened to quit after this show, as did Jackson, upset with a lack of airtime. But they stayed — as did a lot of the audience from the first show.

The Multiple Impacts of Monday Night Football

The *Monday Night Football* opener got a huge 35 percent of the available audience (a 30 share was considered a success at the time, given there were only three commercial networks then). It dented CBS somewhat, but that network's Monday night lineup still finished ahead of it for the season. NBC was a different story. Not only was that network's movies hurt by *Monday Night Football*, but three Bob Hope specials running against the show could not stop it either. Even though Ol' Ski Nose racked up some of his best ratings ever for his specials in the late 1960s and early 1970s, his fall 1970 Monday outings did little to drive down the considerable audience for *Monday Night Football*.

There were other ways to measure the power of *Monday Night Football*. Movie theaters, particularly ones playing X-rated films, claimed poor business on Monday nights. Restaurants reported their activity was off by 25 percent to Robert H. Boyle in *Sports Illustrated*. The real shock, though, was the show's appeal to females too — 40 percent of its audience consisted of women.

Perhaps the most notable gauge of the show's appeal came in Milwaukee. Grade school teacher Dick Benson thought the series' popularity had been overstated by the press, so he polled his class. To his surprise, 29 of his 31 pupils reported having seen the October 5 game between the Detroit Lions and Chicago Bears, both undefeated up to that point.

There was an unplanned aspect to having games on Monday for NFL players: Because of the shortened time for practice with the loss of one day, the Monday games made it more difficult for them to recuperate and get ready for Sunday games the next weekend. Indeed, four of the five first *Monday Night Football* winners lost the following Sunday they played. In his weekly tips oddsmaker Jimmy the Greek automatically deducted three points in his projections for any team facing that circumstance.

End of the First Season

When its season ended in December, *Monday Night Football* averaged an 18.5 rating and a 31 share of the audience. That was respectable enough to put it among the top 40 shows for 1970–71, but it was not as big a ratings hit as three other newcomers, *The Flip Wilson Show* on NBC (which finished the season at number 2), *The Mary Tyler Moore Show* on CBS (number 22 for 1970–71) and *The Partridge Family* on ABC (number 25; this series actually improved its average toward the season's end). *Monday Night Football* did finish ahead of the ABC sitcom *The Odd Couple*, the only other series besides *Monday Night Football* and *The Partridge Family* to debut on ABC in the fall of 1970 and be renewed for another season.

In fact, most of the other new 1970 fall ABC series could not manage more than a 23 share and went off by the middle or end of the season. Among them were the *Monday Night Football* lead-ins (or lead-outs, for those on the West Coast) *The Young Lawyers* and *The Silent Force*. The first show starred Lee J. Cobb shepherding a group of eager attorneys from 7:30 to 8:30 P.M. Eastern, the second was a half-hour spy adventure featuring Ed Nelson.

Martin Starger, then vice president of programming at ABC, said he installed the two series because he thought they would appeal to a mostly male audience and be compatible with *Monday Night Football*. Their failure left him with a nagging question he had for Monday nights until he left in 1975: "'What programming could lead in and lead out?' And the answer is probably nothing." ABC replaced them in January with *Let's Make a Deal*, *The Newlywed Game* and *The Reel Game* (more on them later).

The network dropped and did not replace two and a half hours of other failed series that same month in preparation for the Prime Time Access Rule to take effect the following fall. That rule from the Federal Communications Commission forced the networks to give back a half hour of air time each night to their affiliates in a quest for more diverse programming. Letting go of its losers helped improve ABC's average rating temporarily by not counting them in the mix, and during the week of January 18–24, 1971, ABC won that week's nighttime ratings, the first time the network had done so in more than six years. As was the custom, however, CBS and NBC rallied ahead of ABC by the end of the season. Nevertheless, ABC favored the Prime Time Access Rule because losing the 7:30–8 P.M. nightly slot meant ABC could save $20 million to use for other programming.

Though its first season of ratings were not spectacular and still had ABC in third place Monday nights, the network nonetheless was thrilled with *Monday Night Football*, given how its predecessors in the time slot in the fall of 1969, *The Survivors* and *Love American Style*, generated a measly 12 rating in the same time period. A survey in the February 10, 1971, issue of *Variety* showed the series' demographic appeal among the young was strong too —*Monday Night Football* ranked number 13 among

12- to 17-year-olds for all nighttime network programs. Also, the ratings were notorious for not counting TV sets people viewed in bars and college fraternity houses and dorms, areas where *Monday Night Football* no doubt performed well too.

However, despite what some sources claim, the series did not lead to the cancellation of its direct competition in its first half hour, *Mayberry R.F.D.* CBS dropped the series because it was trying to "de-ruralize" its schedule of series deemed to have little appeal to young, urban viewers and thus not as attractive to advertisers, and even a number 15 series like *Mayberry R.F.D.* in 1970–71 fell under this category. (Others CBS rid itself of in this manner at the end of 1970–71 were *The Beverly Hillbillies*, *Green Acres*, *Hee Haw*, and *The Jim Nabors Hour*.) To replace it was not difficult. With the loss of the 7:30–8 P.M. slot, CBS simply moved *Gunsmoke* up a half-hour to start at 8 P.M., and *Here's Lucy* likewise followed it at 9 P.M., meaning *Monday Night Football* would have the imposing challenge of taking on longtime favorite Lucille Ball, whose series finished third in 1970–71, in the fall of 1971. *The Doris Day Show* remained at 9:30–10 P.M.

Also in spite of previous reports, *Monday Night Football* did not drive off *The Carol Burnett Show* to another night. Though her ratings dropped some from the previous season to number 25 in 1970–71, her show still beat *Monday Night Football*. She moved because CBS wanted a strong series to lead off its Wednesday schedule, where *The Storefront Lawyers* bombed miserably in 1970–71. Burnett did well enough there to knock off ABC's *Bewitched* and *The Courtship of Eddie's Father* sitcoms in 1971–72, then CBS switched her before the end of 1972 to Saturdays from 10 to 11 P.M., where she prospered until shortly prior to her decision to end her series in 1978 after 11 years on CBS.

Even given these caveats, when ABC officials met with station owners in February 1971, there was nothing but praise about *Monday Night Football* and its future on the network. There was still talk among some affiliates about getting rid of Cosell, with a third of them complaining about him at the meeting, but Arledge and others held firm in keeping him.

Jim Duffy, president of the ABC television network (as opposed to Elton Rule, president and CEO of ABC and thus Duffy's boss), told *Variety* the network originally had wanted to fill out the remainder of the 1970–71 season with professional hockey or basketball games instead of movies, but the schedules for both sports already had been established so far in advance that the games were sold out in arenas that could not easily reschedule them without losing money.

When affiliates got wind of this idea, they strongly objected to it, feeling neither sport was as solid a draw as football, and they threatened not to carry them if ABC tried to do in later seasons. (Local pre-emptions of ABC shows were a real possibility and continual problem for the network at the time—*Variety* reported that ABC's newscast aired on just 145 stations versus 202 for CBS's and 210 for NBC's in 1971, for one thing.) Thus, movies filled out the period when *Monday*

Night Football ended its run every season through 1974, even though they never generated quite as high a ratings average as *Monday Night Football* and generally finished behind the competition on CBS and NBC.

One more note involving *Monday Night Football* came out at the end of the season and probably slipped by all but the most astute TV observers. Under a new deal he had, Johnny Carson would no longer host *The Tonight Show* on Mondays starting in May 1971. Now, obviously, no one said officially it was due to competition from *Monday Night Football*. In fact, one could cite the precedent Carson's predecessor, Jack Paar, took in the early 1960s when hosting *The Tonight Show* and took Fridays off. But with Carson deciding Mondays would be his time off, one can't help but get the suspicion maybe he thought it a waste of time to try to compete on a day now where a sizable chunk of his audience would be watching football rather than himself.

Around the same time, at the Emmy awards held on May 9, 1971, *Monday Night Football* was up for two statuettes. It lost Outstanding Sports Programming to *ABC's Wide World of Sports*, but Don Meredith tied with Jim McKay of the latter show as an individual winner. Cosell was not even nominated, and was very much upset with the omission. At least he still kept his job, as opposed to what happened to Keith Jackson.

Exit Jackson, Enter Gifford

As decently as *Monday Night Football* had performed in its first season, Arledge remained unsatisfied. He wanted a bigger name in the booth. Knowing that Gifford's contract with CBS was up, he went for his old pal to join the team in March 1971.

Before doing so, Roone informed Cosell of his plan to replace Keith Jackson with Gifford. Cosell favored keeping Jackson, believing him to be a better announcer than Gifford, but he said he could live with the change. However, he warned him to tell Keith before it became public and make it up to him with other plum announcing jobs. Roone did not heed his word, nor that of others in ABC Sports who felt Arledge's affection for Gifford blinded him to the solid job Jackson had been doing on *Monday Night Football*.

By April 20, 1971, word about the deal leaked out in the press. They sought a word from Jackson, who was in Milwaukee preparing to cover a pro basketball game for ABC. Some 40 reporters called Jackson at his hotel and left messages before he heard about the change from Roone. He told Kay Gardella, TV critic for *The New York Daily News*, that he did not appreciate learning about his ouster from the media and not his boss.

Arledge did meet with Jackson in person in New York City after the stories broke and tried to defend himself by saying he called him the same day the media did. The only problem with that explanation was that Jackson kept all the messages from his hotel stay and pointed out that none of them came from Arledge. Jackson was as disgusted by Arledge's behavior, and that of Meredith, of whom he flatly said was "bullshit."

"Keith Jackson, I handed miserably," Arledge candidly admitted in his autobiography. Jackson went back to doing NCAA football, and Arledge tried to make it up to him by promoting Jackson to lead announcer there, demoting Chris Schenkel, who had held that post for ABC since 1966. In that position, Jackson became a legend as ABC's top college football announcer and won National Sportscaster of the Year honors five times, a Peabody Award and Emmys in 1995 and 1997 as Outstanding Sports Personality — Host/Play-by-Play.

Planning to retire in 1998, Jackson changed his mind when ABC let him cover NCAA football games only on the West Coast near his home in the Pacific Northwest, thus cutting down his travel. He officially announced he would stop calling all college games in 2006, ending 40 years of national football coverage on TV. Yet despite that, Arledge and Jackson never had a personal relationship thanks to his botched dismissal in 1971.

Arledge did not dwell on the Keith Jackson fiasco at the time, focusing instead on promoting his new announcer, for whom he had high expectations. "Frank will not only set the game but will also say what the color man used to say, thus freeing Cosell and Meredith to make their commentary on a more sophisticated level," Arledge told Edwin Shrake in *Sports Illustrated*. To underline his confidence in his fresh addition, Arledge gave spots to Gifford on *ABC's Wide World of Sports* and the 1972 Olympics as well.

Gifford also had one more job at his new network, albeit at a local level. He became the sportscaster for *Eyewitness News* from 6 to 6:30 P.M. nightly at WABC in New York City. He replaced Howard Cosell there. This move fermented Cosell's discontentment with Gifford, whom he previously had denounced as a mere "pretty boy" announcer.

Regardless of the roughness in change of personnel, sponsors felt *Monday Night Football* would not be affected adversely. In the May 5, 1971, issue of *Variety*, ABC announced that its fall 1971 slate of *Monday Night Football* games already was sold out. That was an impressive feat, especially given that one sponsor, Marlboro Cigarettes, would not come back due to a ban on smoking ads on TV taking effect after January 1, 1971.

NFL Action in Action

In light of the advertisers' enthusiasm for nighttime football, and in the hope of bigger ratings, NFL Films, the league's official branch recording movie highlights (and lowlights) of each game, took a chance by putting its premiere series *NFL Action* on ABC nighttime starting May 12, 1971. The series began in syndication in 1967, then went onto CBS Sundays 4:30–5 P.M. during the summers of 1969 and 1970. Ironically, Frank Gifford hosted the show when it started, followed by Pat Summerall in 1969 and then John Facenda in 1970. Facenda, the news anchor for the Philadelphia CBS-TV affiliate WCAU from 1948 to 1973, lent his rich, robust tone as narrator for the highlights as well, as he would for all NFL Films until his death at age 72 in 1984.

With Facenda on hand, *NFL Action* premiered on ABC Wednesdays from 10:30 to 11 P.M. Why did ABC not schedule it on Mondays like the football games? Well, since midseason, ABC actually generated decent ratings for its nighttime versions of its hit daytime game shows *Let's Make a Deal* and *The Newlywed Game* on Mondays at 7:30–8 P.M. and 8–8:30 P.M. respectively, and their relatively low production costs made them ideal to stay on the schedule through the summer before they were cancelled. The show that followed them, however, *The Reel Game*, was a real disaster of a game that generated low ratings from 8:30 to 9 P.M. opposite *Rowan and Martin's Laugh-In* and *Here's Lucy* and appeared to be the perfect spot for the half-hour *NFL Action*.

The difficulty for ABC and the NFL was that the Bristol-Myers pharmaceutical company, a major advertiser, had its heart set on sponsoring *It Was a Very Good Year*, a nostalgic informational show hosted by Mel Torme, on Mondays from 8:30 to 9 P.M. starting May 10, 1971, to replace *The Reel Game*. Given the organization's buying power, ABC did not want to let them down, and the operators of NFL Films convinced themselves it might be worth trying the show on another night, just to show how expansive the desire was among viewers to see NFL-related series in the nighttime.

Oddly, ABC decided to clear the time for the series Wednesdays from 10:30 to 11 P.M. Conventional programming wisdom among the networks at the time — and still today — is that one did not put a half-hour show leading into the 11 P.M. newscasts, as movies and hour-long dramas were better draws, and that a half-hour show would have a tough time competing with programs already in progress. So it was the case with *NFL Action* here as well. Starting midway opposite the top 10 hit *Hawaii Five-O* on CBS, *NFL Action* suffered greatly in trying to induce the largely male audience of that series to switch over and view it. Also, the relatively late time slot for *NFL Action* meant that male teens would not be able to see it in many households, unlike what they could do for at least part of *Monday Night Football*.

Given all these factors, *NFL Action* flopped as a prime time series on ABC during the summer of 1971. After finishing up on September 8, just before the official start of the second season of *Monday Night Football*, the series returned yet once again on CBS Sundays 4:30–5 P.M. from January 23 through March 12, 1972, before going back into syndication, still with Facenda as its host and announcer. A somewhat chastened ABC and NFL decided there would be no more offseason series involving the two parties afterward, leaving both to concentrate on just *Monday Night Football*.

Showdown with Archie Bunker?

Another development during the summer of 1971 was the possibility that CBS would let its hottest new series, *All in the Family*, run opposite *Monday Night Football* on Mondays from 10:30 to 11 P.M. *All in the Family* had launched from the CBS schedule slowly on Tuesday nights in January 1971. Its ratings built up slowly to become the most talked-about show on TV, particularly after winning the Emmy for Outstanding Comedy Series.

CBS planned to have *All in the Family* as its final show on Monday nights in the fall of 1971. But CBS programming whiz Fred Silverman felt it would be buried there, so he switched some series around to put *All in the Family* as the leadoff series on Saturday nights for CBS, where it became the number 1 show the next four seasons it stayed there.

Instead, CBS moved two other sitcoms it had on Saturdays, *My Three Sons* and *Arnie*, to 10–11 P.M. Mondays. *My Three Sons* was going into its 12th season after having remained strong enough to finish at number 19 in 1970–71. *Arnie*, which followed *My Three Sons* Saturdays in 1970–71, was not as popular as the latter, but it did merit an Emmy nomination as Outstanding Comedy Series that season. Even though network programming strategies long accepted that networks should end their nighttime schedule with hour-long series and not half-hour sitcoms, CBS had enough faith in both shows (not to mention five half hours less to schedule in 1971–72, thanks to the Prime Time Access Rule) that the network gave them a shot there.

Would *All in the Family* have become the cultural phenomenon it had on Saturday nights had it run opposite *Monday Night Football* at 10:30–11 P.M., perhaps even beating that series? We can only wonder in retrospect. One thing was certain—*My Three Sons* and *Arnie* flopped on Monday and went off, proving that *Monday Night Football* now had enough power to beat CBS.

Yes, *Monday Night Football* was getting more popular each year. Too bad this success did not convert into making things more congenial in the atmosphere behind the scenes.

5

Gifford Arrives, and *Monday Night Football* Takes Off (1971–74)

By the second season of *Monday Night Football*, the show's increasing popularity took hold in many forms. Big name celebrities from outside the football world dropped by the booth. By the show's 10th anniversary, Milton Berle, Bobby Goldsboro, Jack Nicklaus, Burt Reynolds, Jackie Gleason, Hubert Humphrey, Spiro Agnew, Sargent Shriver, John Denver, Gabe Kaplan, Olivia Newton-John, Bob Hope, John Wayne, and Marvin Gaye all had dropped by at one point or another to plug a project or just hang as a special guest. In Los Angeles once Ernest Borgnine, Lee Majors, Glenn Ford and Richard Anderson all patiently waited to go on the air.

Promotions associated with the series also started to come out in full force. In one, a coin token by the Schick shaving company had the 1971 *Monday Night Football* schedule on one side and "Brought to you by Schick Super Chromium Blades" on the other. For kids, Aurora unveiled a talking *Monday Night Football* game with Dallas Cowboys quarterback Roger Staubach's picture on the box cover in 1972. It was a natural — the board game company was one of the biggest advertisers on the show — given its appeal to a young male audience.

The show's stars found themselves in unprecedented demand outside the booth on TV. Howard Cosell had enough clout to play himself on two ABC sitcoms in 1971, *Nanny and the Professor* and *The Partridge Family*, while Don Meredith popped up as guest host on *The Golddiggers*, a syndicated 1971 variety series featuring Dean Martin's chorus girls.

Meanwhile, for those who couldn't watch *Monday Night Football* on TV, or didn't want to hear Howard talk, the Mutual radio network carried the show with its own set of announcers beginning in 1971. It would remain on the network through 1977, then switch to CBS radio.

Finally, and most notoriously, in 1971 ABC inaugurated the sportscasters wearing bright canary yellow blazers with the "ABC Sports" emblem on them, a fashion change that looked hip at the time but became regarded as gaudy in later years. The change in color was perfectly appropriate in timing though, as *Monday Night Football* in the fall of 1971 faced the arrival of sportscasting's "Golden Boy" in the booth.

The "All-American Nice Guy" Arrives

With his chiseled build, pearly smile and matinee idol façade, Frank Newtown Gifford gave off the aura of being perfection personified, a happy-go-lucky, youthful stud who oozed magnetism. It wasn't accurate, but it was what the publicity machines and the media by and large put out about him for the first 50 years of his life.

"After reading everything that's been written about him for over 25 years, I found that the worst that's been said is that he has spent over a quarter of a century playing the All-American nice guy," wrote Frederic A. Birmingham in one typical piece on Gifford for *The Saturday Evening Post* in 1978.

The reality was much harsher. Born on August 16, 1930, in Santa Monica, California, Gifford grew up the son of a struggling oil worker whose temporary employment gigs during the Depression forced the family to relocate more than 20 times, mainly in southern California. He, his dad, mom, sister and brother survived the turmoil before they finally settled in Bakersfield, California, when Frank was a teenager.

Even with a regular place to live, the Giffords remained a poor family, and Frank was adrift in his own world. He had a lisp that embarrassed him, and little interest in school. He cut classes frequently during his junior year in high school until his football coach, Homer Beatty, forced him to attend them.

Beatty thought Gifford showed enough potential in several different positions on offense that he encouraged his student keep up his grades and his practice so that he could go to a major school, perhaps even the University of Southern California (USC) in Los Angeles, Beatty's alma mater. Gifford did so, and with Beatty maneuvering to let Frank be eligible to play for USC by his sophomore year, Gifford went to Los Angeles to become a football star at various positions, most notably tailback. He also found love there too.

In his junior year at USC, Gifford met Maxine Ewart, an arts major, homecoming queen and Phi Beta Kappa. Her accomplishments impressed Gifford. She in turn inspired him to take more interest in his studies. He found himself intrigued by what he learned, as well as with Maxine herself. When she told him she was pregnant at Christmastime, Gifford did the honorable thing and married her shortly thereafter on January 13, 1952.

Meanwhile, after he lettered in football three years at USC (from 1949–51),

Gifford became the number one draft choice of the New York Giants. During his tenure there from 1952 to 1964, he was an All-Pro halfback for six seasons, including winning MVP honors when he led the Giants to the league championship in 1956. Not surprisingly, he won induction into the National Football Foundation Hall of Fame for his college years in 1975 and the Pro Football Hall of Fame in 1977.

While making his accomplishments in the NFL, Gifford's looks and ambition helped him carve out an entertainment career at the same time. He made several commercials endorsing a wide range of products from orange juice to hair tonic. He dabbled in movies, acting opposite Tony Curtis in *All American* (1953) and James Garner in *Up Periscope* (1959) but more often serving as a stunt double, including for Jerry Lewis (!) in *That's My Boy* (1951). He also did two TV pilots in 1958 and 1959 that failed to sell. Dissatisfied with both of them, he gave up on acting.

A different venue of show business proved more fruitful for him. Gifford made his sportscasting debut on KERO-TV in Bakersfield during the off-season in 1957, hosting a sports show Friday nights after *The Fight of the Week* boxing matches from NBC (the same ones that ABC later bought in order to get the AFL sponsored in 1960). CBS radio gave him a regular five-minute sports show later that year.

By 1959 CBS added Gifford to TV to do pregame work with Chris Schenkel. He became a part-time sports reporter for WCBS-TV in New York City in 1962, then the station's sports director a year later before he retired from football. The network also employed him as a sportscaster in various roles, including color man for its coverage of the Giants games starting in 1965, and he even hosted one series, *NFL Countdown to Kickoff*, on Saturday afternoons in the fall of 1966 discussing the picks for the next day's games by the Great One himself, Jackie Gleason. Cementing Gifford's status as a sports icon by the late 1960s was the 1968 publication of *A Fan's Notes*, a novel by Fred Exley based largely on the author's impression — some might say deification — of Gifford at USC.

Yet family man Gifford grew increasingly uncomfortable at CBS Sports, feeling it had a frat house atmosphere (he and wife Maxine had two sons, Jeff and Kyle, and a daughter, Vicki). When Arledge asked him to join *Monday Night Football* in 1970, he wanted to do so, but his contract ran one more year. His recommendation that Don Meredith do the series instead proved to be magical though, and Arledge stayed high on the prospect of adding Gifford, which he did when Frank's CBS contract had ended.

The battle lines in the ABC booth were drawn almost as soon as the announcement of Gifford's hiring. "I love and respect Frank," Meredith told Frederic A. Birmingham, obviously indebted to the sportscaster for having recommended him for his job. Meredith and his later wife Susan (they wed in 1974) often hung out with Gifford after the *Monday Night Football* games, and they had an easy rapport in the booth on and off the air.

As for Cosell, well… Let's get back to when Gifford first became an integral participant in *Monday Night Football*.

Being Frank with Frank

If Gifford expected a warm, accommodating welcome like Meredith received for his first time doing *Monday Night Football*, he certainly did not get it. Cosell already seemed to resent him taking his WABC nighttime news spot, and Meredith, while friendly, remained fairly centered on what he himself was doing rather than his booth mates.

And though Gifford had done sportscasting before, it was as an analyst, not as a play-by-play announcer. The latter role required a different skill, to know the names and numbers of players automatically as they were involved in the unfolding action, plus do promos for other ABC series during the game and know when to lead into and lead out from commercials. Unlike the seasoned Keith Jackson, these tasks did not come easy to him.

Thankfully, not all went wrong for Gifford initially. On a preseason NFL Hall of Fame game in August 1971, Gifford interviewed guest pro football fan President Richard Nixon, and he carried off the job well. His announcing on other preseason games failed to meet this mark, however, and Gifford found it challenging to get the knack of doing his job without making gaffes.

"Frankly, I feel like I'm facing a firing squad," he told Edwin Shrake in *Sports Illustrated* two days before his official *Monday Night Football* debut in September 1971. "It's not what I have to do on Monday nights that's so hard, it's who I have to do it with!"

"With whom you have to do it," Cosell corrected him.

"See what I mean?" Gifford shot back.

The tension between the two grew more palpable the next day, as a Colts-Jets game played during a production meeting and Cosell said the Jets' quarterback handed off so slowly that the Colts' defense could (and did) easily knock down the Jets' running backs. "I wish Baltimore would play with your butt for a while. You'd find out how easy it is," ex-player Gifford growled back to Cosell. Sensing a possible fight about to emerge, director/co-producer Chet Forte broke up the meeting.

Later on Sunday night, Gifford, Cosell and Meredith went to the studio to tape a four-minute introductory piece for the next night's show, but all three kept blowing their words at various points that it took three and a half hours to complete the task. It was not an encouraging sign.

There was better cohesion among the crew during the debut game, even though Gifford incorrectly announced both a quarterback change and said the first half had ended while in reality it was not even midway through the second quarter. Still, some reviewers thought he did OK, including one for *Variety* who wrote that "Frank Gifford … acquitted himself very well. He should improve as he continues."

Gifford finally found some room to shine in the second game when Phil Wise of the Jets received a long kickoff and kneeled down to signal he would not run it back. "Wise wisely stays in the end zone," Gifford quipped. "Little play on words there, Frank," Meredith said. "I don't get a chance for many," Gifford responded. "That's an even better one," Meredith followed.

As usual, Dandy Don inserted the last word, but the interplay was something missing from the first season. Gifford, it turned out, would work out just fine for *Monday Night Football* for on-air chemistry, but there would still be many verbal gaffes by him and a general state of increased rancor among Cosell and his booth mates. While Cosell dubbed him "Faultless Frank" on the air, he called Frank less affectionate terms off it.

Not all at ABC felt the same way as Cosell, of course, and in fact some were strong defenders of Gifford. Peter Heller, a producer with ABC News, told Frederic A. Birmingham that "Frank gets the least attention of the three, yet he is the cohesive element there. Meredith and Cosell are two very strong personalities, and there has to be a buffer guy. Sometimes he takes an unfair rap for being too straight and too bland. Of the three, Frank has the most difficult job, highly underestimated by the public."

So where exactly did Gifford stand in *Monday Night Football*? A review of three games with him and Cosell and Meredith, one in 1971 and two in 1973, shows that both Cosell and Heller were right in their own ways about the show's newest member.

"At Least Frank and I Have Respective Teams"

Cosell introduced the October 11, 1971, contest between the New York Giants and the Dallas Cowboys with an obvious angle. "Welcome to a night of NFL football, and tonight, the atmosphere is as tense in this booth as it is on the gridiron. We have coming to vocal grips the ex–Giant Frank Gifford and the ex–Cowboy Don Meredith. Hopefully, I shall serve as a provocative catalyst during the course of this evening."

Meredith shook his head after Cosell threw the air time to him, obviously distressed by Howard framing the game as a battle between his and Frank's former employers. "Let's hope that we don't let the activities of this booth overshadow the activities of the Cotton Bowl, because we are here to bring you a very good football game," he said.

Weakly trying to follow through with Cosell's setup, Gifford began his turn by saying "We'll try and get along." But though he and Meredith did so, Cosell could not resist needling them after both teams failed to get their offenses going with two fumbles, dropped passes and no first downs in the first three minutes.

"Well, gentlemen, so far your respective teams are performing a comedy of errors," Howard declared.

"Howard, we're only underway," Gifford immediately protested. But Dandy Don came up with a whopper of a response. "Howard, Howard, never forget that at least Frank and I have respective teams."

That comment produced a chuckle among all concerned and reduced any tensions regarding the standoff. After officials nullified another play due to a penalty, Gifford conceded, "Howard, I'm starting to agree with you." Naturally, Cosell responded, "It's about time."

Through it all, Gifford acquitted himself well during the 1971 game, making only two glaring errors. One was telling viewers "I believe that was lateraled" when the ball clearly was indeed passed backward. The other was failing to note the end of the third quarter — Cosell had to do it for him. But he still had not conquered all his announcing demons, and that remained clearly evident two years later as well.

On September 17, 1973, Gifford botched several elements in the early going. In his introduction, he made mention of "two great wide receiver" (no "s" at the end) and said "the Jets running game is a little lack," not "lax." He also called the New York Jets offside when obviously it was the Green Bay Packers, announced that the Packers were out of timeouts in the first half when they actually had one left, and barely cut himself off from saying incorrectly that they were going to a commercial in the second half.

Worse was the December 11, 1973 face-off when the Pittsburgh Steelers visited the Miami Dolphins. Gifford said singing the national anthem would be Loretta Lynn, then Meredith speedily corrected him by saying it was Lynn Anderson instead. After Anderson finished, Gifford compounded his error by begging forgiveness from her, since he had done a TV show with Anderson last year and should have remembered her name. He went on during the game to say one run ended on the 14-yard-line when everyone could see it being marked at the 17 (no apology there), and he called the wrong tackler on one play too. In comparison with Keith Jackson as a play-by-play man in these games, Gifford barely merited mention with his predecessor in terms of clarity and accuracy.

The other men handled themselves in their usual manner in the games. Meredith, sporting a moustache and bow tie in the 1973 season opener (!), got off two good lines that night. Seeing a shot of Joe Namath on the sideline wearing a headset, Meredith said it was "Joe calling one of his honeys. Whoops, not home!" He also mentioned reading Cosell's newly published memoirs and called it "a cross between Edgar Allan Poe and Jack Paar." Even Howard laughed at that one.

As for the game three months later, when Meredith mercifully had shaved off his moustache, he responded to Cosell quoting William Wordsworth by archly noting, "Wordsworth never saw a football game."

Cosell also quoted Shakespeare during the games and used his typically highfaluting vocabulary, dropping words like "truculence" and "doleful" in his regular conversation. There was some hostility evident from him, though. In the December 11 game, Cosell mentioned an incident involving Dallas during the Cowboys' game on Thanksgiving to Meredith. "I didn't see that game," Meredith said. "Should've," Cosell shot back. "Not necessarily," Meredith icily replied.

It's clear from those games that Gifford, while not a disaster, was not as strong a play-by-play man as his predecessor Keith Jackson. Meanwhile, friction increased between Cosell and Meredith. One wonders especially why Cosell felt that way. Already he told reporters that he no longer needed to do sports except for his radio show, that he would be fine without *Monday Night Football*. There was some worth to that opinion.

Cosell Branches Out

Empowered by his success on *Monday Night Football*, Cosell continued to expand his influence on TV outside of sports. He yukked it up on *Rowan and Martin's Laugh-In* in 1972, allowing comic actress Patti Deutsch to play his whiny soundalike in one sketch. The fact that NBC would let the series put Cosell on as a guest while *Monday Night Football* competed directly against the variety series on the West Coast speaks volumes about the latter series' power, as well as the declining popularity of *Rowan and Martin's Laugh-In* itself. He also did another variety guest shot on CBS's *The Sonny and Cher Comedy Hour* in 1973, getting laughs while mouthing the words to the 1957 doo-wop hit "Little Darlin'" in one sketch. He did so well there that NBC offered him a chance to host his own variety show. Cosell laughed it off as a ridiculous notion — at least at that time.

For those not watching series TV, Cosell popped up in two TV-movies in 1973 too, *The 500-Pound Jerk* on CBS and *Connection* on ABC. For those who went to the cinema, Cosell played himself brilliantly in *Bananas* (1971) and *The World's Greatest Athlete* (1973). Then there were talk shows, specials … it was nearly impossible to escape Howard, even if you wanted to do so.

Cosell's best acting moment was on *The Odd Couple* in 1972. Playing himself, he fought with Oscar (Jack Klugman) during a photo shoot Felix had with Cosell, and he stalked off in return. Oscar then went to apologize to Cosell during a *Monday Night Football* game, only to have Felix inadvertently insult Cosell. Felix made it up by doing a play-by-play for Cosell instead.

It was amusing stuff, but not to all people. Some went the other way, growing so disgusted by the very existence of Cosell that they threatened to do away with him altogether. By the third year of *Monday Night Football*, the possibility of actual harm to Cosell was so strong that it is a wonder he did not follow through with his boast and just quit the show altogether for his safety.

Howard's Death Threats

According to FBI files on Cosell, the first threat on Howard's life came from a postcard addressed to him that was intercepted by postal authorities in Lackawanna, New York, and sent to the agency's Buffalo office on October 26, 1973. With the words "NO JOKE" printed twice on the border, the message side read, verbatim: "Howard Cosell — the MOUTH. Why don't you drop dead you Homo-Fag Big Mouth and your Book sucks like you Do. I'll help you, there's A Bomb in the Rich Stadium. It will blow you up at 10:00 Monday 10/29/73 at Rich Stadium — Buffalo, N.Y."

While investigating who made the threat, the agency notified Cosell and had three officials posted in the booth during the Buffalo game. No bomb went off amid the tense atmosphere. Viewers had no knowledge of the situation.

Meanwhile, the FBI finally arrested a suspect in the incident on January 17, 1974, unemployed 27-year-old Lackawanna resident Michael G. Batko. The trial date dragged into the fall, and FBI agents thought Batko's defense attorney possibly would take advantage of the circumstances and serve Cosell a subpoena at the September 16, 1974, *Monday Night Football* game being held in Buffalo. The attorney did not do so then but did ask to serve Cosell a subpoena when the first trial date arrived on October 7, 1974. (An FBI agent had called Cosell prior to the trial date to see if he could appear in court. Cosell nixed the idea due to his broadcasting and business commitments.)

The trial continued to be delayed for more than two years despite urgings from the FBI to resolve the matter. The district judge insisted that Cosell be subpoenaed for trial whenever it started. Cosell did appear when the trial began on March 9, 1977. Two days later, a jury found Batko guilty of mailing a threatening communication. A month later, on April 18, 1977, U.S. District Judge John T. Curtin placed Batko on probation for a period of one year.

That was the last Cosell heard of Batko, but not the final encounter for Howard with an attacker. Two and a half years later, the Brown County Sheriff's Office in Green Bay received a typewritten letter which read: "If Howard Cosell comes to Green Bay on October 1, I'm going to kill him. And your sheriff's department can't stop me." As there was a *Monday Night Football* game slated for the date given at Green Bay, the office notified the U.S. Attorney's Office, who in turn told the FBI about the threat on September 24, 1979, and gave the material to the agency's laboratory in an effort to identify who sent it.

The Las Vegas division of the FBI then contacted Cosell and gave him the name and phone number of an agent working in Green Bay. An appreciative Cosell told FBI officials he would be in Las Vegas until departing for New York City on Saturday, then go to Green Bay the next day in preparation for the game. The contest (Green Bay versus New England) went on without a hitch. A week later, the U.S. Attorney's Office advised the FBI that given no harm occurred to Cosell and the subject had not been identified, they would decline prosecution on the matter.

Cosell later received a threatening letter from a Butte, Montana, man in 1982. And on June 18, 1986, he received a handwritten letter requesting help from a Milwaukee man seeking $42 million from other celebrities. The writer disturbingly decorated his missive with the numbers "666" (the mark of the anti–Christ, according to Revelation in the Bible) inside Jewish stars. There was no prosecution in either case.

No No to Nanny, But Yes to Rookies

Getting back to lighter matters at the start of the second season on *Monday Night Football*, with the Prime Time Access Rule in effect in the fall of 1971, ABC now only had to cover an hour slot before the start (eastern half of America) or end (western half) of the game. It unveiled an unusual strategy of filling only a half hour for *Nanny and the Professor*, a sitcom that had done only middling business first on Wednesdays and then Fridays a year and a half before moving to its new location. In the east *Nanny and the Professor* ran from 8 to 8:30 P.M., then ABC gave the remaining half hour back to its affiliates to install their choice of show.

Officially, ABC claimed that some stations had dropped *The Silent Force*, which had been on Mondays 8:30–9 P.M. the previous fall, in favor of doing their own local pre-game show before *Monday Night Football*. The 1971 programming strategy would allow them to continue to do such shows without pre-empting a network show. The truth was that ABC wanted an exception to the Prime Time Access Rule and keep its strong Tuesday night lineup of *The Mod Squad, ABC Movie of the Week* and *Marcus Welby, M.D.* starting at 7:30 P.M. rather than 8 P.M. and run through 11 P.M., as it had done in 1970–71, so the FCC allowed the network an exemption if it gave another half hour in its nighttime schedule back to the affiliates. According to Martin Starger, ABC vice president of programming at the time, the network's sales department had a hard time getting ads for the Monday 8:30–9 P.M. slot, so it became the one sacrificed to local stations — there really was no big demand among them to do their own pre-game shows.

As for the show preceding the slot, Starger admitted he grasped at straws at how to fill it. "*Nanny and the Professor* was so incompatible," he said. "It was not the proudest programming I did."

That sitcom was not a strong show to lead off an hour, and its audience consisted predominantly of women and young children, not the young and middle-aged men who favored football. And of course, it ran against the still strong Monday competition on CBS and NBC, respectively *Gunsmoke* and *Rowan and Martin's Laugh-In*. Ratings were so poor that ABC pulled the plug on *Nanny and the Professor* by the time *Monday Night Football* ended its second season in December 1971. For the third year in a row, the network had to find another program compatible to go before and after its football series.

Luckily, the network finally hit the jackpot in the fall of 1972 with *The Rookies*, a cop drama from TV impresario Aaron Spelling. Though hardly a quality series, *The Rookies* did do well enough to outrate *Rowan and Martin's Laugh-In* in 1972–73, causing the latter to go off the air. Its seasonal rating of number 23 in 1972–73 remained the same in 1973–74, and in 1974–75 its seasonal peak was number 18, outdoing *Gunsmoke* and leading to that show leaving the air as well. With *The Rookies*, ABC finally had a show that performed almost equally as well as *Monday Night Football*, or in the case of the 1974–75 season, even better. It was one fewer worry for the network while it still struggled to break out of third place on other nights through the mid–1970s.

However, on the other end of the broadcasting day, there was less encouraging news. As had been feared, few viewers stuck around to watch *The Dick Cavett Show* following *Monday Night Football* and local news. After three years of declining audiences, ABC stopped airing *The Dick Cavett Show* Monday nights starting in the fall of 1973 through December to let their affiliates use their own programs (or sign off after news). By that time, ABC actually had included Cavett as part of an overall rotating series of movies and specials titled *ABC Wide World of Entertainment* (later called *ABC Late Night*). The "no ABC late programs on Mondays every autumn" policy remained in place until the arrival of *Nightline* in the early 1980s, a setup which discouraged regular viewing and could explain why ABC stayed in third place in late night during this time.

Football Fever Hits TV

While ABC dithered over its football lead-in/lead-out in the early 1970s, there was much less indecision regarding the show itself. It was up to an impressive number 25 for the 1971–72 season, finishing less than a million viewers shy of its CBS competition, *The Doris Day Show*, and not too far from its new leadoff challenger, *Here's Lucy* on CBS, at number 10. The next season *Monday Night Football* finished even higher, at number 18, outrating *The Doris Day Show* (which went off that year, officially because Day's TV contract had ended, and was replaced by *The New Dick Van Dyke Show*) and coming close to toppling the slipping *Here's Lucy*, which finished at number 15.

This rise of *Monday Night Football* mirrored that of pro football in general on

TV. For example, when CBS got its turn to host Super Bowl VI on January 16, 1972, it moved the game into the nighttime and scored a huge 44.2 rating, making it the fifth-highest rated TV program ever up to that time since 1960. (The others were the finale of *The Fugitive* in 1967, two Bob Hope Christmas specials in 1970 and 1971, and the Beatles on *The Ed Sullivan Show* in 1964.)

Meanwhile, in 1973 *Monday Night Football* increased its audience by 4 percent over 1972 to average more than 14 million viewers weekly. It was ABC's highest moneymaking series, collecting $100,000 for every minute-long commercial on it. (In contrast, NBC's Sunday NFL series netted just $46,000 for a 60-second ad.) To keep the show fresh, by 1973, its opening titles typically had Cosell narrating film highlights of the projected key players of the night's game, then a shot of the control room cutting to graphics of a spinning football with groovy shots in negative of game action within the "football" while production credits were superimposed on it.

The innovations in sports coverage by *Monday Night Football* influenced other networks notably by this time. There was an upgrade in the use of camera angles and graphics by NBC and CBS. Also on CBS, the network dropped carrying the stadiums' halftime shows in 1974 in favor of taped highlights of games already in progress, with Jack Whitaker narrating the action from New York City.

Yet as *Monday Night Football* grew in popularity, there grew tension between NFL and NCAA leaders about the presence of each others' games on ABC, even between ABC personnel who worked on them. For its part, the NCAA loosened up somewhat when in 1972 it started letting ABC select the last nine dates of the football schedule to air just 12 days ahead of each kickoff, so they could get the most exciting games of the moment.

Also, those games would not count towards a university's quota of appearances on national TV that season, meaning there no longer was a limit on, say, Auburn or Michigan playing. To top it off, the NCAA gave ABC another minute of commercials to sell per game to 19 minutes total, just one less than ABC received from pro football.

With its changes ABC managed to hold its competing interests at bay during this increasingly competitive period. The one element it could not alter was how *Monday Night Football*'s success affected the other networks. It definitely impacted the creation of one series on NBC, which paradoxically would impact ABC too.

Pro Baseball Joins the Nighttime Fray

"Imitation is the sincerest form of television." With that statement in mind, the popularity of *Monday Night Football* made NBC consider doing a similar series of its own with its baseball package. The network made inroads initially October 13, 1971, where for the first time the World Series held a game in the nighttime (the fourth game, specifically). Its 34.8 rating not only won the week but was huge for the season; *All in the Family*, the number 1 series of 1971–72, averaged a 34 rating. Its success convinced NBC it ought to do the game in the nighttime as a series, just like *Monday Night Football.*

In a four-year deal (1972–75), following two successive three-year ones with pro baseball (1966–68 and 1969–71), NBC decided to add nighttime baseball as a regular season attraction every summer. To make the series more attractive, NBC received a ban on having local games air on TV opposite its nighttime network coverage (it was not until 1984 that pro baseball finally stopped the same practice on Saturday network games).

On June 12, 1972, the network debuted *NBC Major League Baseball* on Monday nights, preceded by *The Baseball World of Joe Garagiola* from 8 to 8:15 P.M. The fact it was on the same night football aired on ABC in the fall made it obvious to all that NBC was attempting to steal its rival's thunder. However, it did not have three announcers, just two, Curt Gowdy and Tony Kubek, although there was in 1973 and 1974 a weekly celebrity guest who dropped by the booth and added some spice.

There was one problem with the series. While the contract forbade other TV coverage of Monday night games beyond the series, it did not end baseball's black-out rule, which since 1953 forbid games to air in markets in which the teams competed, because the teams wanted to protect their attendance and radio broadcast deals as they had done over the years. So, if a New York teamed played Los Angeles, viewers in both markets did not get to see them play, regardless if the game was sold out. The restriction probably was the main reason ratings hovered at an average of 12 in 1973 and 1974 (a low score when the average network hits of the time generated a 19 rating or better).

The good news for NBC, however, was that the new exposure of having the World Series air in the nighttime made for excellent ratings. The best performance came in Game 2 of the World Series on Sunday, October 14, 1973, which scored a 35.1 rating and became the highest rated special of that year except for the Academy Awards.

Such popularity did not go unnoticed by Roone Arledge. As much as he and others in his department denigrated baseball on TV as too slow in the wake of ABC's 1965 fiasco with the sport, he also recognized a hit property in the field. That envy would lead him to get the series on ABC a few years later and attempt to do to baseball what *Monday Night Football* did for its sport. Alas, all it did was prove that the magic of *Monday Night Football* was not something easily transferred.

Here Goes Lucy, and Van Dyke

By the 1973–74 season, *Monday Night Football* remained a top 20 entry on TV. The biggest gauge of how strong *Monday Night Football* had become came with the announcement that *Here's Lucy*, its first half-hour competition on CBS, was going off the air at the end of the 1973–74 season.

Officially, the reason was that Lucille Ball wanted to retire from network TV after decades of being its top comedy draw. In reality, CBS cancelled it. Its strained slapstick with an aging star was irrelevant amid its contemporaries and seemed light years away in quality and content from the top 10 comedies of the time —*All in the Family, Sanford and Son, M*A*S*H, Maude* and *The Mary Tyler Moore Show*; thus, many of its former viewers now preferred *Monday Night Football*.

At the end of the season, *Here's Lucy* finished number 29 in the ratings versus number 19 for *Monday Night Football*. The sports program had done the unthinkable in finally giving ABC a show to beat Lucille Ball.

What happened to *Here's Lucy* afterward deserves a brief mention, as it was a truly bizarre odyssey for a hit sitcom, especially one starring Lucille Ball. It did not appear in repeats until 1977, running six months on the CBS daytime schedule, then disappeared another four years before being sold to local stations in syndication, where it flopped and went off the market until a 2004 DVD release. That *Here's Lucy* DVD included the 1981 sales presentation tape, recorded partly while Ball taped a Bob Hope special that aired in January that year, and it had the audacity to claim that *Here's Lucy* outperformed *Monday Night Football* in the ratings. Not so.

Meanwhile, any hopes CBS had of moving *The New Dick Van Dyke Show* up a half hour from its 9:30–10 P.M. slot to replace *Here's Lucy* disappeared when its star announced he was quitting the series. The only thing CBS had returning opposite *Monday Night Football* was *Medical Center*, which like *The New Dick Van Dyke Show* finished outside the top 30 in 1973–74. These events on CBS, coupled with NBC's continual ineffectiveness with its Monday movies, lined up to give ABC an apparently indomitable lead when *Monday Night Football* would come back in 1974.

Unfortunately, there was one major glitch to spoil ABC's potential victory. Don Meredith was leaving the show.

So Long, Dandy Don (for Awhile)

Though the animosity between Cosell and his booth mates, particularly Meredith, brewed in the first few years of *Monday Night Football*, there still were moments of levity on air where everyone could enjoy themselves. The most memorable of these occasions occurred during a 34–0 blowout in Houston by the Oakland Raiders on October 9, 1972. Surveying the stands, one ABC camera caught a sleeping fan and focused on him as the broadcasters attempted to use him as a symbol of what the game had become. Unfortunately for them, the man awoke and "flipped the bird" (extended his middle finger) to the camera, shocking them with his obscene gesture. Meredith, prompted by a producer, broke the tension by say-ing, "Howard, he's telling us we're Number One."

That humorous event faded away though, and the old tensions rose up again. In his autobiography Roone Arledge claimed that by 1973, Meredith and Cosell would not talk to each other between *Monday Night Football* games.

Even a change in producers could not end the acrimony. While *Monday Night Football* was successful, Arledge felt there was room for improvement in the pro-duction of the game, so in 1973 he replaced the team of Chet Forte and Dennis Lewin with Don Ohlmeyer. Ohlmeyer came to ABC Sports straight from Notre Dame in 1967 as a "go-for" assistant and moved up rather quickly to be a director and, by 1973, producer of *Monday Night Football*. He held that position until he left ABC for NBC Sports in 1976. Forte remained as just the director for the show, while Lewin would come back to replace Ohlmeyer as producer of *Monday Night Football* in 1977.

While everyone seemed to get along with Ohlmeyer, including Cosell, he could not bridge the increasing gap between his analysts. That was because there were fac-tors beyond his control affecting the relationship between Meredith and Cosell.

One was Meredith's increasing appeal as an actor. He received a chance to star in two episodes of the critically acclaimed NBC crime anthology series *Police Story* during the 1973–74 season. The favorable critical reception to them boded well for his chances in acting and encouraged him to explore that field more in depth.

Moreover, after *Monday Night Football* started, Meredith wed actor Keir Dul-lea's ex-wife Susan and got interested in poetry, painting, reading and a guru who thought NFL football was corrupt. Under that advice, Meredith had announced to Arledge he was quitting in week six of the 1972 season, but Arledge talked him out of it at the time. Yet the impetus to leave remained, and his new wife did noth-ing to dissuade that position.

What finally tipped Meredith's hand was the cajoling and dangling of gifts by NBC President Herb Schlosser in early 1974. In a $200,000 deal, Schlosser guar-anteed Meredith a lead role in a TV-movie, the right to star in pilots (test shows for potential series) for on the network, and opportunities to contribute to the net-work's morning show *Today* and guest host *The Tonight Show*. In addition, Mered-ith would join Curt Gowdy and Al DeRogatis as the third announcer doing Sunday NFL games for the network. No other NBC sportscaster had such broad clauses in his contract as did Meredith with this one.

Arledge tried to match Schlosser's offer once he heard about it. "We finally offered Don very nearly the same deal as NBC, with movies and pilots and so forth, and he told me four different times he'd take our deal, but then he went with NBC," Arledge told Edwin Shrake in *Sports Illustrated*. He said he even met Meredith in person twice, but that extra effort was not enough to stop him from leaving *Mon-day Night Football*. Don had said to Arledge at the last game of the 1973 season he'd be back on the show, but by late February, despite a personal visit from Roone, he said that "I'm not 'Dandy Don'" and departed the show.

When the news came out about Meredith leaving, many observers thought the reason why he left for NBC in the wake of a similar offer from ABC laid squarely on Cosell's shoulders. Some thought Cosell beared his grudge against Meredith starting when the latter won the only Emmy given to talent for the show back in 1971, but he denied it.

"I never gave a damn about the Emmy," Cosell snapped to Robert Daley in *The New York Times Magazine* in 1974. "I was nominated this year and didn't win it. The thing's a farce. I don't think televising a football game rates an Emmy." Meredith told Daley that Cosell did congratulate him graciously on winning the statuette.

Cosell told Daley the truth was Meredith leaving was that Don was envious of him, not the other way around. "He couldn't stand being second banana to me. Dandy Don doesn't want to be Dandy Don anymore." The sportscaster pointed out that Meredith's NBC contract specifically said he was not to be called Dandy Don on the air.

But Meredith told Daley the Dandy Don and Danderoo nicknames did not bother him, nor was he leaving due to a bruised ego. "I'm not really hung up on being a star," he said.

However, he said he did have an unhappy relationship with Cosell. "To say that Howard never offended me, never hurt my feelings, would be wrong. Because he has."

Talking to Daley, he specifically cited when Cosell once said on air about Meredith's former NFL coach, "Everybody knows how you feel about [Tom] Landry, but I think he's a nice guy," thus implying that Meredith had a grudge about his old boss. Meredith in fact did have issues, so to speak, with Landry, so much so that Gifford said he was one of the few people on which the two disagreed.

This situation contradicted what Meredith told Edwin Shrake in *Sports Illustrated* a few months earlier when he said, "I was pretty snippy to Howard last year" and added he thought it was frustration at himself that led him to take it out on Cosell. "I like Howard, I really do," he told Shrake. "I mean, he's very weird, but I respect him."

By now, though, even the respect was gone. Meredith thought Cosell was one of the most intelligent men he knew and defended him during the first few years. But now, he really did not care to dwell on the man and looked forward to moving ahead with his career.

Whether they wanted to do the same or not, the crew at *Monday Night Football* had to look to the future as well, and hope that the new third man would create as strong a chemistry on air as Meredith had with Gifford and Cosell. The results did not make viewers forget their love for Meredith, much to the chagrin of several on the show, including Cosell, the same man who said he could do without *Monday Night Football*.

6

Meredith to Williamson to Karras to Meredith (1974–77)

Though nowhere nearly as mythic as the search for the right actress to play Scarlett O'Hara in the 1939 movie version of *Gone with the Wind*, there was considerable discussion as to who would be right to replace Don Meredith on *Monday Night Football.*

In television, the final decision on major personnel matters rests with the executive producer, and Arledge spent four fruitless months reviewing possibilities. Roone considered and rejected NFL stars O.J. Simpson and Joe Namath, NFL veterans Paul Hornung, Willie Davis, Sam Huff, Bart Starr, Jimmy Brown, Dick Butkus and Bill George, and even actor and ex-college football player Burt Reynolds.

The oddest candidate had to be Bill Cosby, whose CBS variety series *The New Bill Cosby Show* went down in flames opposite the second hour of *Monday Night Football* in the 1972–73 season. Cosby was a friend of Cosell's, who always felt the comedian and actor would make a perfect addition to the booth.

Arledge refused the notion, as did his successors, but Roone did integrate the booth, at a time when black sportscasters still were a novelty, especially on the network level. The few African Americans to make the leap as of 1974 included Jackie Robinson on ABC's baseball coverage in 1965 and Irv Cross on CBS's NFL coverage in the early 1970s.

In his autobiography, Arledge claimed it was Cosell who brought Fred "the Hammer" Williamson to his attention; other sources say it was from a list of candidates from Pete Rozelle. Regardless, Williamson had impressed Arledge with his wit and demeanor when the former appeared on Cosell's radio show, as well as Arledge's assistant Dick Ebersol during a weekend with Williamson in Los Angeles. Arledge had the Hammer come to New York to eat dinner with him, Cosell and Gifford. They followed it with a game of pool at Arledge's residence, then Arledge announced that Williamson had the job — even though Williamson had not announced a game before in his life.

Arledge was happy with the decision, and so even was Cosell; not so were producer Don Ohlmeyer and director Chet Forte, who had no say in the matter. It was a hint of divisions to come from the hiring.

Hammer Time

"My lifestyle has always been ahead of my time," Fred Williamson boasted to me when we talked. It was classic Williamson — outrageous, opinionated, yet credible. It is also his explanation as to why he has been a maverick through much of his life, including his blink-and-you-missed-it tenure on *Monday Night Football*.

Born in Gary, Indiana, on March 5, 1938, Williamson attended Northwestern before going into the NFL. In the 1960s he was a defensive back for the Kansas City Chiefs, the San Francisco 49ers and the Oakland Raiders. His 6-foot-3, 220-pound frame may not sound too impressive in today's nutritionally and chemically enhanced world of athletics, but it intimidated opponents at the time. He earned the nickname "the Hammer," which he still used into the 21st century, for using his arms to stop passes to receivers. He played for the NFL through 1968 and then Canada a year later.

Following the path of fellow NFL star Jim Brown, the Hammer went to work in Hollywood. He secured results rather briskly and notably — he showed up in two major 1970 films, *M*A*S*H* and *Tell Me That You Love Me, Junie Moon* and played Diahann Carroll's occasional boyfriend on the TV series *Julia* in 1970–71. But unlike Brown, who worked in smaller roles in major films for five years before becoming a lead, Williamson dropped doing supporting parts quickly to star in his own parts.

Williamson required three elements to do a movie: his character never would get killed, he won every fight and he got the girl at the end. Most producers balked at such stipulations, so by the mid–1970s Williamson involved himself in the writing, directing and production end of the movies as well. His early efforts included the now politically incorrectly titled *The Legend of Nigger Charley* (1972) and *Black Caesar* (1973).

To cement his reputation of doing his own thing, he posed naked in the October 1973 issue of *Playgirl* magazine, the first celebrity to do so. The nudity was modest (no shots of his penis), but as the first black celebrity to appear in the fledgling publication, showing off his wide smile and solid torso, it only enhanced his sex appeal and notoriety. Incidentally, Jim Brown did a more explicit layout in the magazine a year later.

Obviously, there would be no mistaking Williamson with his predecessor Don Meredith. However, any worries about how the audience would react to him never really surfaced because Williamson disturbed others instead, namely his fellow production team.

Williamson agreed to do the series only because ABC promised him he could star in three TV-movies for the network in exchange for his announcing services. That was what sold him on the job. "I had no interest in *Monday Night Football*," he said frankly.

That attitude should have been enough to stop the deal right there. But it was not the only element that doomed Williamson on the show. In a bizarre breach of protocol, Arledge and Ohlmeyer decided to install the Hammer without any off-air tryouts, even as they knew that Williamson had even less experience than Meredith did in the broadcast booth. But, as the Hammer noted, "Roone Arledge was my supporter."

Williamson bragged about his lack of preparation to reporters at a preseason press conference in New York, saying he would just swim and dance prior to showing up for the show. He announced he would be the show's sex symbol (not too hard against Cosell) and proclaimed how big a star he would be on it. Such pronouncements unnerved several on the *Monday Night Football* production staff, but with Williamson now signed for the show, there was no turning back.

Freddie's Dead on Monday Night Football

On August 19, 1974, the Hammer made his debut on *Monday Night Football*. Before halftime on the first show, Williamson created a stir among the production staff when he noted that one runner went through a hole so big that he told Cosell, "Even an old cripple like you" could have done it.

Williamson defended the remark. "It was in the moment of the game," he said. The Hammer claimed that while Howard was off on a tangent, he was trying to show how big the hole was. He did not apologize for using the word "cripple."

But according to Williamson, it was not that incident that prompted problems for him on the show, but rather the failure to get a rapport going with his co-analyst due to Cosell talking about matters Williamson felt were extraneous. "I was quicker than Howard and made more comments to the game at hand," he said. "He wouldn't talk to me."

As for the other man in the booth, the Hammer received no help at all. "Frank was too concerned about getting the names and numbers right," Williamson said. "He was preoccupied. He wasn't interested in any bonding."

Williamson believed Cosell was instrumental in getting him off the show, a claim he has held since 1974. Cosell denied it several times, such as when he told *Ebony* flat out in 1976 that "I had nothing to do with his dismissal." But several sources in 1974 backed Williamson's version, such as *Newsweek*, which insisted that Cosell told ABC officials "It's him or me" for them to pick to keep on the show.

With no support for him anywhere nor any incentive to change, Williamson knew soon he would be off the show. Realizing his situation, the Hammer put caution to the wind and did something in his final appearance that only Muhammad Ali had been daring enough to try on air. "I did my little Mexican hat dance around Howard's toupee," he said. If there was any hope of trying him longer, it vanished with that maneuver.

Williamson's third and last show was September 2, 1974. He made a clean break with the *Monday Night Football* staff after his firing. "I never saw any of them after that," he said.

He had no regrets about his performance, only about the way he was not used on the show. "I went in as the Hammer and went out as the Hammer," he said. "You didn't fit me in. I could've been even bigger than Howard Cosell, but they wouldn't understand."

The aftermath of ridding Williamson from *Monday Night Football* was considerably messy. Cosell had written a chapter in appreciation of the Hammer for his book *Like It Is* that due to press time constraints could not be removed when it came out. And at least one major newspaper, *The Chicago Daily News*, had to apologize for the outdated cover with him on its listings insert *TV News* for the week of September 28–October 5, 1974. "A third member of the team, Fred Williamson, started the season but departed after the covers for *TV News* had been printed," it was meekly noted in an item on page 3.

As for the TV-movies starring Williamson that ABC promised him, he found upon meeting network executives that they were not interested in fulfilling their part of the deal. "Every time, it was like, 'We are not interested right now,'" he said. They paid him off instead. Nevertheless, Williamson claimed that didn't stop ABC from buying all his theatrical movies to show on the network in later years. The network had a short memory about the whole affair, for in its 25th anniversary special on *Monday Night Football* in 1994 it proudly mentioned Williamson as one of its announcers in its promotions.

Williamson became the first of several black sportscasters to have limited exposure on the series, with O.J. Simpson, Lynn Swann and Chris Dickerson later getting no more than two years with it. Yet even given this record, Williamson does not believe there is a color barrier among decision makers surrounding *Monday Night Football*, but rather there were personal flaws that hurt each man on the show. "I can't say it's racial," he said. "You have to look at each individual."

As for the series, he said, "I only watch *Monday Night Football* because it's a ritual." He griped that Al Michaels and John Madden made only obvious comments about the action, and that he often just viewed the show with the sound off.

After his *Monday Night Football* stint, Williamson continued to have a busy film career starring in his own low-budget films, although he was willing to do a comic supporting turn in the hit movie *Starsky and Hutch* in 2004. He said his upcoming leading films will be sequels to his 1970s ones, with of course him coming out as a hero in each of them.

The Hammer also allowed that if *Playgirl* asked the then 67-year-old to bare it all for another pictorial, he had no qualms about doing it. "I ain't got anything on me that wasn't hanging then," he said seriously.

Clearly, Williamson did not nor has not dwelled on *Monday Night Football* and how it has affected his career, thus letting it become a minor footnote. It's that attitude of refusing to let what looks like a setback actually become one that has helped Williamson stay active in the entertainment world for more than three decades now.

"I'm bulletproof," he said. "They've been shooting at me for years."

Meredith Replacement, Take Two

As it became obvious that Williamson had to go, Roone took another look at his previous list for replacements for Meredith earlier in the spring and settled on one name in his pressing circumstance. Alex Karras, a beefy 39-year-old ex–All Pro defensive tackle, had been suspended for the duration of the 1962 season for betting on games, came back in 1963, then was cut from the Detroit Lions in 1971 and lent his name to a betting sheet called "Pro in the Know." That tip sheet included recommendations on how to gamble on *Monday Night Football*, which, combined with the 1962 suspension, concerned Roone that NFL executives might oppose Karras for his connections with wagering on games. Even so, NFL officials let it slide, given the need for a quick replacement in the booth.

There was one advantage Karras also had over most of the other candidates — actual experience as a TV football analyst. "I was doing Canadian football, which I was having a grand time doing," Karras recalled. (In fact, Karras found Canadian football a better game to watch than the American version.)

But Arledge remained concerned that he not flop with his third member of the booth again, so he asked Detroit Lions owner William C. Ford his opinion about Karras. "I told Arledge that if they could get him to control his mouth, he should be good," Ford told *Newsweek*.

With that bit of advice, and no one better around immediately, Arledge contacted Karras while the latter participated on a sports series in Chicago. "Roone asked if I was interested and I said, 'Hell yes, I would be interested,'" Karras said. The men never discussed the debacle surrounding Williamson in their negotiations for the job. As Karras put it, "I never even talked to him about it."

Karras said he did make one thing clear to Arledge up front — he intended to continue his burgeoning acting career in Hollywood away from the series. After a winning job of playing himself in the 1968 movie *Paper Lion* (based on George

Plimpton's experience as a player with the Detroit Lions), he found himself in demand on movies and TV after retiring from pro football. In 1974 alone he gained attention for a guest shot on *M*A*S*H* and a hilarious portrayal of a dumb cowboy in the Mel Brooks movie comedy *Blazing Saddles* (he was the one who punched a horse in a fight).

With those successes, Karras did not want to lose his momentum, and he advised Arledge that while he looked forward to working on *Monday Night Football*, his time with the show would be a limited one. "I was just getting involved in motion pictures, and I told them I was going to leave them in two or three years," he said.

Considering that Fred Williamson lasted only three weeks in the booth, the condition set by Karras was fine with Arledge.

Karras Goes Into Action

When viewers of *Monday Night Football* got their initial look at Karras, he was easy to identify. Besides his chunky 260-pound physique, he suffered from myopia, so he sported thick glasses often while on camera. While his vision was limited, however, his appreciation for the show was boundless. "I had a lot of fun on that show," he said. "I had one of my most pleasurable times with those people."

Karras already had been interviewed by Cosell several times prior to the series. Each enjoyed and respected the other person's wit and company then, and it only increased when they did *Monday Night Football*. "We were very good friends," Karras said. "We would have dinner and get together. Whatever he says goes with me." Likewise, Karras had nothing but praise for Frank Gifford. "Frank is a superb human being. I've always liked Frank. He was very good to me."

The result of such friendliness in the booth produced a different dynamic on air. Karras was not antagonistic toward Cosell as Meredith had been, nor as talkative. As a result, Cosell had more latitude to speak on the air, and unsurprisingly he took it and ran with it.

One typical incident occurred on the December 14, 1974, contest between the Oakland Raiders and Kansas City Chiefs. Earlier in the season, Otis Sistrunk of the Raiders had played on *Monday Night Football* and sported an otherworldly appearance that led Karras to say he was from "the University of Mars." Karras repeated that sentiment again in the opening segment. Otherwise, Karras was strangely silent in the first 10 minutes of the game, saying no more than four sentences and rarely starting a conversation on his own.

Taking up the slack for Karras was Cosell, who yammered even about the dinner guests he had the previous night. In the few times when Gifford or even Karras was able to say something insightful, Cosell had the irritating habit of saying

"Exactly," as if he had to submit the last word on the play. Watching this episode, I felt now more than ever compelled to yell out, "Oh, shut up, Howard!"

There was one nice exchange between Karras and Cosell regarding a duo of Oakland Raiders defenders on the field in the first half. "There's two guys who are uglier than I am, Howard," Karras said. "That's arguable," Cosell responded, amid guffaws from Karras.

Indeed, Karras yukked up a few laughs at what he thought were Howard's funny quips, something that Meredith rarely did. Karras actually had little interesting to add to the game throughout the contest even when he spoke. For viewers used to Meredith's commentary, it was a considerable shift to handle this new interplay, which no doubt explained in part the ratings being down slightly when Karras arrived.

At least one element stayed the same — the gaffes from Gifford. In this game, he managed to misidentify one defender, incorrectly awarded a penalty to one team, claimed a player was out of bounds when he was not, credited a receiver with catching the ball at the 30-yard line when it was the 20, and most embarrassingly of all, mispronounced "ABC." Luckily for his sake, Cosell made a joke out of the misstep. But overall it was a performance that would have had a lesser broadcaster canned by the end of the season.

However, he certainly did not fall apart the way a potential competitor to *Monday Night Football* did that same season.

The World Football League

Three years after its merge with the AFL had been completed, the NFL faced a new competitor when the official announcement of the World Football League (WFL) came in October 1973. It would start earlier in the summer months than the NFL and feature franchises in many big cities not already served by the NFL, as well as some that had an NFL team. WFL games would air nationally on Thursday nights in a syndicated deal, while some WFL games would go out locally on Wednesday as well.

Since the new league would not compete directly with the NFL, much of the early focus on the WFL was on the TV overexposure it lent professional football and how it could cripple the sport. "It means you're going to have televised football in many parts of the country on every day except Tuesday and Friday," Pete Rozelle told *U.S. News and World Report* in 1974. "That's an awful lot of any one product to be on television."

Undaunted by that concern and troubles lining up financing in time, the WFL opened its first season in the third week of July 1974 and boasted it averaged 43,000 spectators in its first few games. However, an investigation by *Sports Illustrated* discovered those figures were inflated. For example, of the 120,253 people who saw the Philadelphia Bell's first two games, 100,000 of them were admitted free because the game aired on TV, and WFL officials realized the stands would look barren without them in attendance.

At the same time, WFL games received limited TV penetration nationally thanks to having a smaller number of teams than the NFL (12, to be exact) and the reluctance of network stations to give up time for the competitions Thursday nights when each of them had hit shows they would have to pre-empt that theoretically competitors could carry instead (e.g., *The Waltons* on CBS, *Ironside* on NBC and *The Streets of San Francisco* on ABC). Also, the networks were publicizing their new fall shows, which would require affiliates to tell their viewers that the new Thursday shows would not be seen due to that week's WFL game — a duty many station managers did not relish performing. Thus, most WFL games aired on lower-rated independent stations, or not at all in many markets.

Given these circumstances, word came back soon about financial difficulties the WFL faced. For one, by October the Detroit Wheels team filed for bankruptcy. The most humiliating report, however, came at the end of the WFL championship game between the Florida Blazers and the Birmingham (Alabama) Americans. With the league facing a cash crisis, the winning Americans found their jerseys being confiscated by creditors during their celebration. All totaled, the WFL lost $3.2 million its first year of operations.

With the humiliating blunders being publicized, TV stations began dropping clearances for another season of WFL in 1975, causing more money shortages and operations being in disarray. The league bravely (or maybe foolheartedly) commenced a second season, but it was hopeless. On October 22, 1975, WFL Commissioner Chris Hemmeter officially announced the WFL was out of business.

Less than three months later, on January 9, 1976, Birmingham and Memphis leaders officially asked the NFL owners at special meetings to consider their entry of their old WFL franchises into the league. But Rozelle was reluctant to add them, having already planned to add Seattle and Tampa Bay to the league to make it 32 teams to split nicely into four divisions, so they were turned down.

If nothing else, the WFL proved that if you were going to do professional football, you needed a solid TV contract in order to get anywhere near the success of the NFL. It's a lesson that would not be heeded by future failed challengers, though — see the USFL in Chapter 8 for the first of several of those types.

The 1974 Season Fumbles

While the WFL wilted in the fall of 1974, ABC looked to have a better future with *Monday Night Football* as a nighttime sports attraction. The only problem was that CBS gave the show tough competition with *Rhoda*, a spin-off of the critically acclaimed and popular sitcom *The Mary Tyler Moore Show* that aired Mondays from 9 to 9:30 P.M. Eastern and Pacific Time. The highly anticipated show drew a huge number of viewers, and with the loss of Don Meredith, viewers had more reason to check it out.

From its debut, *Rhoda* easily outperformed *Monday Night Football* in the ratings. Then came the wedding episode. CBS programming head Fred Silverman heard about plans from the show's producers to marry the title character and told them to do an unprecedented special hour-long show concerning it. When she wed on October 28, 1974, in a well-written, hilarious episode, the ratings went through the roof, and few people bothered to watch *Monday Night Football*.

To his credit, Cosell full well sensed the publicity for the competition and the excitement surrounding it. As the visiting Pittsburgh Steelers punished the host Atlanta Falcons after *Rhoda* had aired, he decided to have fun with the CBS show, since the field game was a disappointment. "Do you realize that we were not invited to Rhoda's wedding?" he asked Karras. "Now it's over, and the hors d'oeuvres are being served."

"I can taste them now," mused Karras.

"Let's not waste our time with this disaster — let's go," Cosell responded, and both men stood up in the booth as if they were ready to leave. Naturally, their actions confused and unnerved Gifford, who needed a moment before recognizing it was a joke.

But one viewer got a laugh out of it instantly. Valerie Harper, the actress who starred in *Rhoda*, dropped Cosell a note saying "You are the greatest! You're the only man alive who would have dared to do that."

Even so, the 9–10 P.M. *Rhoda* show flattened *Monday Night Football* and seemed to take some of the life out of the latter program's season. *Rhoda* also reinvigorated *Medical Center*, which followed the former series at 10 P.M., pushing that show's ratings up to finish in the top 30 as well.

As a result of the competition and uneasiness with the new booth arrangement, *Monday Night Football* lost a considerable share of its audience and finished the season at number 32. That was disappointing, but in light of what else was happening at ABC at the time, the network probably was thankful the show was doing as well as it was.

The Big Collapse of 1974–75

ABC did not note the changeover in personnel on *Monday Night Football* in its 1974 fall presentation film to affiliates and the media, merely stating in the sports section of the program that "And ABC's a winner again with NFL *Monday Night*

Football." What the network did proclaim several times was the slogan "What you see on ABC this fall, you'll be talking about tomorrow." Whoever "you" was turned out to be not too many viewers, as ABC had one of its worst seasons ever in 1974–75.

Of 10 new series the network introduced in September 1974, only two survived for a second season — *That's My Mama* and *Harry-O.* Neither was a hit; both went off in 1976. As for the other entries, ABC's Friday night lineup with two similar sounding title characters, *Kodiak* and *Kolchak the Night Stalker,* bombed so badly that they were mocked both by Chicago TV critic Gary Deeb and within a sketch on *The Carol Burnett Show.* Returning programs did not do much better either, with *The Odd Couple* and *Kung Fu* ending their runs and *Marcus Welby, M.D.* coming close to joining them.

When the Nielsen tally settled, ABC had just one series in the top 20 for 1974–75. That was the midseason replacement *S.W.A.T.,* which faced heavy criticism for the amount of violence it aired per show and thus received pressure to reduce it when the show returned the next season (and ended up cancelled). *S.W.A.T.* finished at number 16, the lowest seasonal peak for ABC's top series since *The Donna Reed Show* also topped out at number 16 in 1963–64. It also marked the first season ABC had only one top 20 show in the seasonal ratings since 1962–63, when *Ben Casey* at number 7 was the network's sole representative entry.

ABC did not want to go back to the dismal days more than a decade earlier, so ABC President Fred Pierce, installed in 1974 to replace Jim Duffy as head of network TV while Elton Rule remained as ABC's overall president and CEO, wooed CBS programmer Fred Silverman over to the network to save it in 1975. Silverman did his job masterfully. In the next season (1975–76), for the first time ever, ABC finished number 1.

There were some flops, of course. One of the first new programs Silverman received emerged from when Pierce met with Arledge in 1974 about having Howard Cosell become a variety series. This was during the days when variety series were all the rage, and given how Howard had guest starred on most of them, it made sense for those reasons. When approached with the notion, Howard liked it too, having visions of being the next Ed Sullivan to show off the best entertainment to the nation live from New York.

Pierce felt with Cosell's ego and Arledge's production talent that the show could be a smash, particularly on Saturday nights, where ABC had compiled a grand total of one series ever to crack the top 30 in its history — *The Lawrence Welk Show* in the 1960s. Cosell and Arledge also would be co-owners of the series and thus could make profits from the show, plus it assured ABC neither man would leave the network unexpectedly.

The result was one of TV's more notorious bombs. "It was a near disaster," claimed Martin Starger, who approved the concept as head of programming before leaving ABC in the summer of 1975 (he became a major producer of TV-movies, miniseries, films and Broadway shows and currently is head of Marstar Productions in California). Others argue there was no "near" about it at all.

Saturday Night Live with Howard Cosell: The Genesis

Putting the show together in 1975, Arledge realized he lacked the needed experience in producing a nighttime entertainment series, so he interviewed people who had done so, such as Bob Precht, former producer of *The Ed Sullivan Show*, according to the ultimate producer of *Saturday Night Live with Howard Cosell*, Rupert Hitzig. (Ironically, the series would come live from the Ed Sullivan Theater, so named after the host who presided over his TV show there from 1948 to 1971.) The meetings with candidates started at 9 P.M. and ran about two hours as Arledge presented his vision for the show.

"No one was acceptable to Roone and Howard," Hitzig said. Then Arledge remembered how Howard hung out in Las Vegas at tennis tournaments with comedian Alan King and Hitzig, who was King's business partner. Hitzig had produced several of King's well-received comedy specials on ABC, so he received the offer to do the show, and Arledge in turn would draft King to serve as "Comedy Consultant" for the series.

Though not ecstatic with the offer, Hitzig thought the series had potential and so became its producer. King helped him write the openings, while Hitzig wrote some himself along with Walter Kempley, formerly a writer and supervising producer on the ABC sitcom *Happy Days* in 1974. Another writer Hitzig found was actor/comedian Christopher Guest, who introduced him to comic actor brothers Bill Murray and Brian Doyle Murray. Hitzig designated them to be part of a regular comedy troupe for the show.

"I called our guys the Prime Time Players," Hitzig recalled. At the same time over at NBC, Hitzig's buddy Lorne Michaels worked on getting his own live variety series together on Saturday nights in the fall of 1975. Learning that he could not use his original title *Saturday Night Live* due to Cosell's show already employing it and thus had to call it *NBC's Saturday Night* instead, Michaels kept the continuing gentle competition between the programs going and dubbed his regulars "The Not Ready for Prime Time Players," since his show ran late at night.

For the director's chair, Hitzig hired Don Mischer, a 13-time Emmy winner primarily for live TV entertainment shows. Mischer's need for Cosell to stand at certain areas on the stage perplexed the host and Arledge during early rehearsals, as they were used to having the cameras go to the action like in sports rather than vice versa. "They didn't understand that they had to hit the mark to be seen," Hitzig said.

That dilemma was minor and easy to correct ahead of time. So was planning the show around *Monday Night Football.* "Howard did nothing till the day we aired," Hitzig said. He and Arledge worked on the games while Hitzig planned the guest lineup and rundown of shows. However, that did not mean they were detached totally from what Hitzig did.

According to Hitzig, Arledge would call him very late at night to discuss projected ideas. "I had the distinct pleasure of talking to Roone on the phone until 3 A.M.," he said. He didn't get much sleep after that, as Cosell would call as he prepared for his radio show at 5 A.M. and ask Hitzig, "What did the redhead have to say to you?" Somehow, Hitzig managed to say enough to please both sides and get some sleep during the workdays.

Hitzig's real discomfort came Saturday afternoons. The show held a runthrough (rehearsal) with the acts from 2:30 to 4 P.M. At 4:15 P.M. Hitzig and his assistant met with Arledge, Cosell, Alan King and new ABC programming head Fred Silverman to get everyone's opinions on what needed to be kept, dropped and added for the night's show. "That was four of the biggest egos in show business telling me what to do," he said. Somehow he reached common ground with them by 5:30 P.M. to get a rundown of what acts would do and when, and to finalize cue cards for Cosell's introductions.

As it turned out, getting the show together was not the hardest part. Hitzig found talent all around, including giving a break to a young comedian named Billy Crystal drawing praise for his Muhammad Ali impersonation. His biggest obstacle was exaggerated expectations for the series from its executive producer and host, both of whom thought it would propel them into the entertainment stratosphere and thus plugged it to the limit.

"We want people to feel, 'Boy, I better not miss this tonight because Lord knows what will happen,'" Arledge told *Time* in one typical pre-debut comment. He and Cosell crowed to the press about how they would avoid having the typical guests seen on other variety series at the time and how it would be event television.

Arledge should have realized from experience that when a producer announces plans that big, his series rarely lives up to the hype, and it backfires on the production. Especially when you do a live show from the Ed Sullivan Theater, named after the man who set the standard for live TV variety. Unfortunately, he had to find it out the hard way.

Saturday Night Live with Howard Cosell: The Terminus

Premiering September 20, 1975, *Saturday Night Live with Howard Cosell* came on ABC from 8–9 P.M. Eastern Time (and Pacific Time, albeit on tape delay). There were plenty of top stars, from a walk-on by Frank Sinatra (who did not sing) to a live shot from London of the band then being promoted as "the next Beatles," the

Bay City Rollers, to sing their emerging and appropriate hit "Saturday Night." Directing the latter was none other than Don Ohlmeyer. Hitzig said he suggested videotaping the segment to be safe, but Arledge insisted that all the show's entertainment be live.

Hitzig had confidence in the series before it debuted. "I thought it would be a big hit," he said. As always, though, it's up to the critics and especially viewers to deliver the verdict. Surprisingly, the critics were not as negative as one might imagine, though their main complaint was the same one Hitzig had of the show.

"I think expectations were that Howard would be Howard," Hitzig said. In that vein, "I wanted him to do something not Ed Sullivan–like. I wanted him to be extremely critical of everything." Hitzig gave the example of Cosell saying after a comic's appearance that the latter was not as funny as he could be, and so he will spend a week with Alan King coaching him to polish up his monologue and perform it on next week's show.

Cosell's reaction to the notion was "I can't do that! No one will come do the show!" It then became obvious to Hitzig that Cosell wanted to project a warm image unlike the one he had on *Monday Night Football* to make viewers love him. "He felt insecure outside the sports world," Hitzig said.

But a cuddly Cosell was not what people expected, and ratings started to fall as reviews pointed out this shortcoming, as the man known for being honest on TV suddenly was pandering on it. *Time* noted that "even Cosell's talent for sardonic invective was dulled. Obviously reading from cue cards, he made his finest hour seem 90 minutes long." The magazine singled out as an example during the episode when tennis player Jimmy Connors made his network TV singing debut accompanied by Paul Anka. Ignoring the inanity of the occasion, Cosell said at the end, with a straight face looking into the camera: "That was a great magical moment in musical history."

The show also soon sunk to where it broke its pledge to not use overexposed guests when it featured Charo, the Latin American songstress whose tiresome "kootchy kootchy" broken English and hyperactive personality had been seen on virtually every other variety show then on the air. Typical of its approach, Cosell introduced her as "that electrifying vivacious bombshell." This obsequiousness irked *TV Guide* reviewer Cleveland Amory, who wrote that "On this show, nothing exceeds like excess."

Also, one important point seemed to have been forgotten by the personnel on the show — the series ran opposite *The Jeffersons* on CBS. A spin-off from the number 1 series *All in the Family*, *The Jeffersons* already was the number 4 series during its introductory season in 1974–75 airing Saturdays from 8:30–9 P.M., and there was little reason to think the audience would fall off much when it started a half hour earlier in the fall of 1975. There was a little erosion among viewers for it — it dropped down to number 21 for the 1975–76 season — but it still remained the top choice in its period.

"I think the first eight shows, we were exhilarated," Hitzig said. But then the working relationship between Cosell and Arledge on the series was strained, precisely because of what Hitzig said was the different approach each man had on the show. He became the go-between for the men as they gave their thoughts, with him being chummy enough with Cosell that the latter let him attend two *Monday Night Football* games outside of New York City and fly back home with him on a Lear jet while Cosell drank a considerable amount of vodka, according to Hitzig. Meanwhile, Arledge felt uncomfortable about contacting performers he knew to do the show as a favor for him, thus showing his inability to grasp the needs of running an entertainment series.

It was at that point that Hitzig realized the show had no future. The announcement of its cancellation came shortly thereafter in November, although it stayed on the air until January 17, 1976. ABC canned the series even though its ratings were not as bad as some of its other new shows, and it had improved upon the ratings the network had with its dramatic series offerings in the same slot in 1974–75 (*The New Land* for the first six weeks, then specials and finally *Kung Fu* from January through June 1975). Its replacement, the hour-long game show *Almost Anything Goes*, ran only from January 24 through May 2, 1976.

Happily for most talent involved in the series, they survived the debacle and prospered in show business thereafter, with the biggest irony being that Christopher Guest, Bill Murray, Brian Doyle Murray and Billy Crystal all wound up as regulars later on *Saturday Night Live*, which is what Michaels got to call his late night NBC show after *Saturday Night Live with Howard Cosell* went off. ABC wanted to pretend the series never happened, so they erased all tapes of it. "That's the only show I know of that they completely destroyed," Hitzig said.

For his part, Arledge dismissed the program in just two paragraphs in his autobiography. He called his decision to produce the series a "detour of rationality," but blamed its failure in part due to the time slot and not the content.

Saturday Night Live with Howard Cosell was gone but not forgotten, however. Bud Shrake confirmed that for his 1976 comic novel *Limo,* co-written with Dan Jenkins, Arledge inspired the lead character Frank Mallory, who produced a three-hour live Wednesday night program like *Saturday Night Live with Howard Cosell* called *Just Up the Street* under the directive of CBC network honcho Harley O. Chambers (a/k/a "The Big Guy"). Unlike *Saturday Night Live with Howard Cosell,* however, *Just Up the Street* became a hit as it caught various families across the United States in their "real lives," including a bigoted family, a neighborhood fireworks demonstration gone awry and a man admitting his infidelity to his livid wife in its debut.

Later, in 2003, probably due just to the idea of Cosell being a variety host, *TV Guide* listed *Saturday Night Live with Howard Cosell* at number 37 among its "50 Worst Series of All Time." "They were wrong, because we were entertaining," Hitzig said of the selection.

Hitzig did have one happy recent event connected to the series. In 2004 he left a message with Billy Crystal about a possible movie project. The comedian returned the call to Hitzig by impersonating Cosell telling Hitzig that "You ruined my career!" It gave Hitzig a nice laugh about a project he remembered in positive terms despite its brevity and notoriety. Hitzig said he and Cosell ended on good terms.

The failure of *Saturday Night Live with Howard Cosell* deterred Arledge from pursuing any further projects in the entertainment field. It also dampened Cosell on doing any work outside of sports on TV except mostly for talk shows thereafter.

It did not lessen its host's ego at all, of course. A year after its demise, Cosell had the audacity to tell Bill Rhoden in *Ebony* magazine that "I have reached the point of visibility in this country that is little short of phenomenal."

In the same article, former football great Jim Brown agreed with Cosell, up to a point. "Howard wasn't the same Howard after he became a celebrity—which is fine—but he doesn't stand up for the little man anymore."

Cosell thought otherwise, to the point where he seriously considered running to be the Democratic nominee to the U.S. Senate in 1976. He ended that quest when his wife Emmy wisely warned him not to do so. Going through a failed variety show was one thing—enduring a failed candidacy before the press and public was quite another.

Arledge Goes to News

The cancellation of the Cosell show did not mean Arledge had given up on pursuing projects outside ABC Sports. Getting word about Roone's desire to stretch his talents, NBC enticed him in 1976 with an offer to take over its sports division plus do some entertainment programming.

But the stench of *Saturday Night Live with Howard Cosell* made Arledge doubt his ability to handle entertainment production, which lessened the appeal of NBC's offer. Besides that, ABC President Fred Pierce had a better counteroffer for him to take over news as well as sports, which he proposed in November 1976. It was a no-brainer. On May 1, 1977, the appointment of Roone Arledge as the new president of ABC News was official. (A little-known fact: In 1964 Arledge rejected ABC President Tom Moore's suggestion to leave sports and take over as head of ABC programming.)

Arledge proved to be as innovative with ABC news as he had been with sports, and despite a few notable missteps (a multiple anchor format, a condescending debut for *20/20*), he helped move ABC out of its perennial third place status in that field. But there was a huge downside with this new activity. Several in the sports division felt their president no longer put as much interest into their work, causing resentment and dissension. Some also believed that his expanded concentration on news and sports caused him to drop the ball in realizing the growing problems between on-air talent on *Monday Night Football*.

Those issues were not in Arledge's mind at the time of the announcement he was news president, of course. He was more concerned with other activities involving both news and sports, including ABC's newest addition, nighttime baseball. But whereas *Monday Night Football* became an audience favorite, *Monday Night Baseball* stalled as a dubious entry. It wasn't another *Saturday Night Live with Howard Cosell*, but neither was it a sterling item for Arledge to put on his credits.

Let's Play Baseball

The NFL's dominance on being on all three networks nagged at major league baseball officials, who decided in 1975 that spending their last nine years exclusively with NBC might have been to their sport's detriment. To that end, baseball's media director John Lazarus made a $12.5 million deal with ABC to alternate coverage yearly with NBC through 1979, with one network having the World Series while the other had the league playoffs and All-Star Game each year through 1979. ABC would get the World Series for 1977 and 1979 in the deal, which was the main reason Arledge approved it.

Oh, and ABC would get Monday night baseball starting each April too, thanks to talks with Lazarus, who coincidentally had been a salesman for the network in 1974 prior to working for major league baseball, and then returned to ABC as a vice president in 1976. Nothing fishy there.

Regardless of the circumstances, the new deal did have the advantage over NBC's nighttime games of no local blackouts whatsoever anymore. This meant a wider potential audience for the series.

Yet it had the disadvantage of being on a network unfamiliar with the sport, and it showed. The first few games displayed sloppy technical work that never would have occurred on *Monday Night Football*. Cameras missed shots of hit balls, runners off base, even runners on base. Incomprehensibly, the show gave no starting lineups when each team was on offense, a standard feature on every other baseball show by this time.

"It may be unfair to say that *Monday Night Baseball*, as it has been presented by ABC so far this season, is the worst television treatment ever given a major sport, because by all odds somebody at sometime must have done something worse," mused William Leggett in *Sports Illustrated*, in just one of many bad reviews for the series. Leggett singled out Warner Wolf from the lead three-man team (the other announcers were Bob Prince and Bob Uecker) as being a main detriment, spouting off statements about players and teams that were just plain wrong.

The industry belief was that ABC installed Wolf, Prince and Uecker to be the respective baseball equivalents of Cosell, Gifford and Meredith, but the team did not jell. ABC canned Prince at the end of the 1976 season, and Wolf did only a few backup games in 1977 before being relieved.

Replacing Prince and Wolf in 1977 were two familiar names — Keith Jackson and Howard Cosell. Arledge pushed Major League Baseball Commissioner Bowie Kuhn to add Cosell on the show despite the fact Cosell had disparaged the game publicly several times previously as being out of date. It took a lunch with Cosell to convince Kuhn ultimately if not reluctantly to let Cosell cover the games.

But if Arledge wanted to draw more comparisons to *Monday Night Football* by adding those two announcers, it failed to translate in the reviews and ratings. Concerning the former, Barry Lorge of *The Washington Post* spoke for many in 1978 when he complained about Cosell (naturally) and also wrote: "Producer Chuck Howard and director Chet Forte, who have been instrumental in making *Monday Night Football* a colossal success, try to use the same velvet-covered sledgehammer techniques with baseball.... Instead of a siren song lovers of the game find so intoxicating, a baseball telecast on ABC becomes a full-scale assault on the sense, and ultimately an earache."

As for ratings, ABC's baseball on Monday night generated about the same 12 average rating that it had on NBC from 1972 to 1975 for its first five years, and ratings fell lower than that through 1983. At the same time, the show dropped from covering 16 games in 1976 to just five in 1980 before getting back to 16 in 1982 and 15 in 1983, albeit no longer covering any games in April or May, so that they would not count in the regular season averages for ABC and bring it down.

Despite this treatment, baseball went ahead and re-upped with ABC from 1984 to 1989, with the network repaying it by showing only eight games both in 1984 and 1985. It was only the power of alternating the World Series with NBC that kept the network involved with the sport, and Arledge was willing to have ABC shell out $575 million for that honor.

Yet there were some changes made to try to attract bigger and better audiences. Shortly prior to the deal in 1983, ABC dropped Uecker and Jackson and replaced them with Al Michaels (who had done backup games since 1977) and Earl Weaver to join Cosell on its lead team. Jim Palmer came on board with Michaels and Weaver in 1984 to replace Cosell temporarily, then in 1985 the lineup was Palmer, Michaels and Cosell. When Cosell's book *I Never Played the Game* made negative comments about Michaels and the duo's relationship deteriorated during the playoffs, ABC took him off World Series duty and replaced him with Tim McCarver for the 1985 fall classic. McCarver, Palmer and Michaels remained as the lead announcers for ABC baseball thereafter.

Unfortunately and unknowingly at first for the trio, they were part of a lost cause. Dennis Swanson, who replaced Arledge as ABC Sports president in 1986, actively hated the 1984–89 baseball deal because it cost ABC an estimated $100 million, as ratings were not high enough to generate ad revenues and thus cover its expenses. Swanson found no appeal of having the World Series the way Arledge did, so when the contract ended, he made no effort to renew it.

The network moved its final year of coverage to Thursdays in 1989, doing its eighth and final nighttime game of the season on July 27. By the time it ended, its ad rates were less than half of those being charged for *Monday Night Football*. Since that time, baseball has never had a regular nighttime network series.

If nothing else, *Monday Night Baseball* on ABC proved that the network's formula for its announcing lineup was not all that was needed to make any sport a success. It takes people involved to love what they are doing, and quite frankly ABC often came off lukewarm in its desire to make baseball as exciting to watch as its football. The limitations of what ABC Sports could not do for baseball was a low mark for the division during the Arledge era, and if nothing else, it warned him and others to follow to be careful to keep the *Monday Night Football* approach just to that show itself.

Football Gets Stronger

While baseball never became the draw ABC hoped, interest in nighttime football remained strong, even as ratings for *Monday Night Football* were softer in the mid–1970s than they had been a few years earlier. Advertisers remained committed to the series as it held up sturdily if not overwhelmingly to a number 30 season finish in 1975–76 playing opposite the number 1 show on TV, *All in the Family* on CBS, which moved to Mondays from 9 to 9:30 P.M. that season. When it relocated the next fall and *Maude* replaced it, *Monday Night Football* ratings increased and surpassed *Maude*, proving that it would take only the strongest of series on CBS to give it a serious challenge.

Confirming the trend at the March 28, 1977, NFL owners meeting, Commissioner Pete Rozelle announced *Monday Night Football* had its two highest-rated Monday night games ever in 1976. Also by 1976, *Monday Night Football* commanded $124,000 per commercial minute vs. $60,000 in 1970.

And most importantly, ABC no longer had to sell commercials for its NCAA games as part of a package with NFL, as the NCAA was doing well enough by itself to attract its own advertisers. Likewise, NCAA officials liked the way ABC presented its games that they awarded ABC a $105 million contract to show the football games there through 1981, the longest contract the NCAA had awarded to a network up to that time.

Amid all this good news, there was one disconcerting note. ABC decided that yet another shakeup was needed in the *Monday Night Football* booth. Incredibly, the person who went out got replaced by the person he in turn replaced.

Bye Bye Alex

While *Monday Night Football* ratings were back up into the top 25 in 1976, a major change still lurked for the series' next season. In the spring of 1977, Arledge learned that Don Meredith would be interested in returning to *Monday Night Football* even though he had a verbal agreement with NBC to extend his three-year contract with the network. Roone jumped at the chance to bring Meredith back, sensing it would be a ratings hit.

After a little legal wrangling, the deal was done, and Karras was unceremoniously out of a job. Meredith would return to *Monday Night Football* in the fall of 1977. Karras claimed the change bothered him little, since he knew his job was not a long-term one nor his true interest.

"I told Roone I would love to stay another 20 years, but I also wanted to do some acting," he said. He went on to do several movies and TV series, most notably the 1983–88 sitcom *Webster* with his wife Susan Clark featuring the adorable tyke Emmanuel Lewis.

He also wanted to do some writing as well. In 1991, he co-authored with Douglas Graham a comic *roman à clef* about his show business career called *Tuesday Night Football*. Promoted as a satire along the lines of Robert Benchley and the film *Airplane!*, most reviewers felt it fell short of being compared to those entities.

The setup was that Karras supposedly heard a fable about Lazlo Horvath, a Forrest Gump-ish idiot savant who was mute until age three, when he began to sing along with advertising jingles. Horvath's improbable rise to the top as an adult culminated when Phineas Higgins, president and CEO of a conglomerate called Everything, Inc., directed Horvath to join the booth of *Tuesday Night Football* which Everything, Inc. sponsored on the fictional CBA network (ABC backwards — get it?). Higgins groused that while ABC had the best announcers on *Monday Night Football* ("even Alex Karras, for pity's sake"), all *Tuesday Night Football* could manage was Haywood Grueller and Lance Allgood.

Though their names were unfamiliar, their types were not. Haywood Grueller spoke with an extensive vocabulary that prompted jeers and hatred from viewers, although Lazlo admired him. Grueller ended up passing out in the booth with his toupee falling off from inadvertently eating a cookie laced with marijuana, thus letting Lazlo save the day filling in for him as commentator and making *Tuesday Night Football* into a hit. As for Haywood's partner Lance Allgood, he was a handsome ex-football player "not noted for his keen grasp of current events" who spent much of his time trying to score with women between his monotonous play-by-play coverage on the Tuesday games.

"That seems to require a response," Frank Gifford wrote about the Allgood character in his autobiography. "All I can say is that Alex has written one more book than he's read."

Karras told me the novel was just meant as a goofy take on the sportscasting and media industries, not an attack on anyone, and that he had bigger plans for it. "I want still to do a movie of it," he said. "I like it. I think it would be a good hour and a half movie."

He did not follow up *Tuesday Night Football* with another novel. In fact, as Karras headed into his seventies by the time *Monday Night Football* ended, his acting career was slowing down too, though he said he was not retiring.

"I try to enjoy my life," he told me. "I've never taken a break."

Karras said he still watched *Monday Night Football* through its cancellation and remained honored by his association with the series. "I think the kind of people that did *Monday Night Football* were honest, thoughtful people," he said. "They respected me, and I respected them."

Meredith's Back, and ABC's Got Him

Respect was not exactly the reaction to the return of Meredith to the booth among the other announcers, predictably so. For his part, Cosell felt Meredith came back because he could not get a series deal with any of his NBC projects and had to return to *Monday Night Football* to regain his luster. He felt Meredith therefore owed him some respect.

On the other hand, Gifford was happy to see his old buddy return, particularly in regard to the personal turmoil he had to deal with in the years while Meredith was gone. He divorced his first wife Maxine, who suffered from multiple sclerosis, although Gifford said it fell apart because he was a workaholic who loved crowds and she was neither. He married Astrid Lindley, a Swedish-English aerobics instructor, on March 1977. It would be a stormy marriage that also failed seven years later, as they concentrated on their own jobs without doing much together. In his autobiography, Gifford included 36 pictures without including one of Lindley, who barely merited three paragraphs in the book.

The five-year contract Meredith signed with ABC included deals for acting in TV-movies and promises that he would not have to do every *Monday Night Football* game. Meredith's contract called for him to receive $400,000 year per football season, or $25,000 per game. When he first signed for the job in 1970, he earned $2,500 per game.

According to Meredith's old buddy, sportswriter Edwin Shrake, Meredith came back to do the game coverage purely due to the money and the glory he would receive from it.

With those terms in hand, Meredith returned to what he called "the traveling freak show," and all would be all right with *Monday Night Football* the next few years.

At least on the air, that is.

7

Changes Afoot (1977–82)

With remarkably little hype on air about him rejoining the team, Meredith came back to the *Monday Night Football* fold on September 19, 1977. Unfortunately, the match-up paled next to the reunion. The Pittsburgh Steelers buried the San Francisco 49ers 27–0, making it only the fourth shutout game in *Monday Night Football* history after St. Louis won over Dallas 38–0 on November 16, 1970, Oakland beat Houston 34–0 on October 9, 1972, and San Francisco topped Los Angeles 16–0 on October 11, 1976. It was so lopsided Meredith didn't even sing "Turn out the lights, the party's over."

"The first game of the season was probably the worst one we've ever had," groused director Chet Forte to William Leggett in *Sports Illustrated*. Yet it didn't matter. With anticipation high over Meredith's return, the 1977 debut racked up 35 percent of the viewing audience, decisively beating CBS and NBC. The ratings stayed strong the rest of the season, and for the first time since Meredith left in 1974, *Monday Night Football* finished the seasonal ratings in the top 20, at number 16.

Perhaps the biggest gauge of Meredith's popularity was the surprisingly strong ratings the show earned against the network debut of the movie *The Godfather Part II* on NBC on November 14, 1977. While that offering notched a 28.0 rating and a whopping 42 share of the audience, *Monday Night Football* was not too badly behind in second with a 23.8 rating and 26 share for its match-up of the Kansas City Chiefs and Denver Broncos.

Still, NBC held onto its movies, which wound up finishing just a hair ahead of *Monday Night Football* in the final 1977–78 ratings (movies were at number 15). But CBS found its new lineup of *The Betty White Show*, *Maude* and *Rafferty* sinking fast. After November 28, the latter two were banished from the Monday schedule, although *Maude* reappeared on Saturdays before ending its sixth and final season on April 29, 1978. *The Betty White Show* hung on until January 1978.

The network reloaded its slate and put on a stronger set of series from 9 to 11 P.M.

on January 30, 1978 — *M*A*S*H* followed by *One Day at a Time* and then *Lou Grant*. It was a potent schedule, and it would remain tough competition for *Monday Night Football* as it stayed mostly intact the next four seasons (CBS moved *One Day at a Time* for *WKRP in Cincinnati* in January 1979, then *House Calls* took the spot at the end of 1979 through 1982). Typically the first hour ranked ahead of football, with *Lou Grant* fighting it out to a virtual tie in the second. Meanwhile, the *NBC Monday Night Movie* fell out of the top 20 by the 1978–79 season, but it stayed in contention as well.

It was not only increased competition that led *Monday Night Football* to have a notable slump after the first year back with Meredith and for the rest of the 1970s. (In 1978–79 it averaged only number 28, while it did even worse in 1979–80, finishing at number 37. This was particularly disturbing because by 1980 ABC had more affiliates than CBS or NBC thanks to its number 1 overall finish in the ratings from 1975 to 1979.) There were two main problems for the series — a saturation of games being covered, and indecision among the production staff.

More Games = The Arrival of Fran Tarkenton

By the 1970s the NFL was the first major pro league to get most of its income from TV, with a 1978 deal giving each team about $5 million a season. The NFL also now wanted extra games to show on Thursdays and Sundays, and ABC acquiesced to them and started doing them that year. In that go-round, the show appeared on Thursday once (October 26) and Sundays thrice (September 24, November 12 and December 3).

Meredith, however, was having no part of it. He came back to do only Monday night games as his contract stated and refused to do any more no matter how much extra he could earn from the new games, for several reasons.

"Basically, I guess I'm a little lazy," Meredith said in explaining his decision to Dave Brady of *The Washington Post*. "I still kind of enjoy it; it's a fun game, but it is easier not to do all the games. This time of the year is also big in the entertainment industry, and I wanted to keep some time open for that." Meredith no longer had an exclusive acting contract with ABC as of 1978, a situation which no doubt made him less willing to do more games because the network did not give him as many roles as he had hoped to get from his new deal, but he did have offers from NBC and CBS that he pursued.

Meredith's announcement meant either going it alone with Gifford and Cosell or hiring another announcer for the Thursday and Sunday games. After using just those two men for the four extra games during the 1978 season, Arledge decided to go for a replacement.

Fran Tarkenton got the job. A professional football player for 18 years with the Minnesota Vikings and the New York Giants, Tarkenton retired at age 39 on

May 8, 1979, and announced the same day his new affiliation with *Monday Night Football*. His contract called for him to do three exhibition games, six regular season games and the Pro Bowl. He was not a novice to broadcasting; for three years prior to his new job, Tarkenton covered sports off-season for NBC.

A native of Virginia born on February 3, 1940, Tarkenton definitely had the good ol' boy air of Meredith. He even would chew tobacco while covering games. But substituting for Meredith was a thankless job, and with Tarkenton's relative inexperience he never came close to matching Dandy Don's appeal. William Taaffe of *Sports Illustrated* dubbed him "irksome," and Gifford in particular found it hard to like Tarkenton due to their differences over action on the field. Gifford, ever the defender of the player, always believed in muting criticism about any errors on the field, while Tarkenton had no reservations about criticizing and thus upset Gifford.

On the other hand, Cosell got along with Tarkenton because of that approach and, according to Cosell, because he followed Howard's advice on how to call games. In his memoirs *I Never Played the Game*, Cosell even credited himself with advising Tarkenton to take the offer to host another ABC series, *That's Incredible!* while still with *Monday Night Football*. The program, an early example of the exploitative reality genre, aired in the dreaded 8–9 P.M. Eastern/7–8 P.M. Central time slot before *Monday Night Football* starting in 1980 and surprised everyone by being the first show there since *The Rookies* in 1974–75 to win the time slot. (The failures between *The Rookies* and *That's Incredible!* were *The Barbary Coast* in 1975, *The Captain and Tennille* in 1976, *The San Pedro Beach Bums* in 1977, the last season of *Welcome Back, Kotter* paired with *Operation Petticoat* in 1978, and *240-Robert* in 1979.) *That's Incredible!* lasted until 1984, two years after Tarkenton was fired from *Monday Night Football*.

Cosell thought the dismissal benefited Tarkenton in the long run. "The last couple of years, he wasn't exactly thrilled about his working on the package, and now he had more time to devote to his vast and profitable business interests," Cosell wrote in *I Never Played the Game*. Tarkenton became a rare presence on national TV thereafter save for exposure on infomercials and a guest shot here and there.

Meredith was not the only one who disliked the new Thursday games. The players themselves hated them because it gave them virtually no time to recuperate from a Thursday night game to play a Sunday afternoon one three days later. It messed up the weekly pattern of training, rest and nourishment they had under the old Sunday-Monday routine; it already had taken them a few years to adjust to Monday games as well.

But it generated ABC and the NFL more money too, so that of course trumped any complaints the players had and forced them to live with the new setup. Thanks in part to the extra games, by the end of its first decade, *Monday Night Football* netted ABC $230,000 a minute in advertising revenue, an amount most other nighttime series of the time could only envy. Even with the ratings slipping in the late 1970s, the fact that *Monday Night Football* still drew so many more adult males than most other shows made it a hard target for advertisers to resist in getting out their message.

The Producer Merry-Go-Round

When Don Ohlmeyer left as producer of *Monday Night Football*, Arledge picked Dennis Lewin as his successor in 1977, the same Dennis Lewin who previously co-produced the series with director Chet Forte in the early 1970s. Some thought a more likely candidate was Chuck Howard, vice president in charge of production at ABC Sports and a producer on *ABC's Wide World of Sports* since 1962 after being a production assistant there and on NCAA games since 1960. But Howard was known not to get along with Chet Forte, who remained as the director, and so he had no qualms about Lewin getting the job.

Lewin did have experience with the series on his side. The series earned him Emmy nominations in 1972 and 1973, and he won three consecutive Emmys from 1974 to 1976 for his production work on *ABC's Wide World of Sports*. Nevertheless, he did have to navigate some difficult territory in being Forte's former colleague and now boss while getting less help than previous producers from Arledge, who split his time between running sports and news on ABC.

Lewin's planning routine for *Monday Night Football* turned out to be this: He first met with Forte on how the show should open, then the two of them watched the Sunday afternoon football games to note key plays to include in the highlights package they would compile from NFL Films and have Cosell narrate without a script before game time on Monday. Cosell mainly talked with key sports figures who called him before the Monday game, while Gifford did the same as well as watch game film. As to how Meredith prepared for a game, only he knew, and some even doubt he did anything, although his knowledge on the air usually belied that belief.

At the same time, the crew had done enough games from all NFL stadiums by the late 1970s to have files on where to put their trucks and cameras, thus saving valuable time setting up the equipment to check on lighting 24 hours before kickoff. It made the show come together in workmanlike efficiency, and to some critics dull and ordinary in the process. "Nothing different here," sniffed *Variety* in a review of the 1978 season opener.

The one area Lewin could not control was the growing iciness between Howard Cosell and the other announcers. In spite of nicknaming Lewin "Dendoo," Cosell soon thought the producer was not doing his job and complained often about him to anyone who would listen. A meeting in the middle of the 1979 season between Lewin, the announcers and Arledge did not resolve the animosity growing in the booth, but it did convince Arledge he needed a stronger hand overseeing his operation. He dropped Lewin as the show's producer in 1980 in favor of a 31-year-old who like Lewin had worked for ABC Sports.

Terry O'Neil had his first job with the company in 1972 as a research assistant during the summer Olympics. He assisted in the *Monday Night Football* booth that fall as well as the next two years before successfully overcoming thyroid cancer while writing Pittsburgh Steeler running back Rocky Bleier's memoirs, *Fighting Back*. He came back to ABC Sports full time in 1976 and made his mark producing showy specials that impressed his boss, Roone Arledge. He felt O'Neil's production pizzazz was exactly what *Monday Night Football* needed to get back on track.

The problem was that while O'Neil believed the show needed a considerable overhaul, he made moves so brashly that director Chet Forte soon formed an intense dislike of him. Joining him soon during the 1980 preseason games was Howard Cosell after O'Neil unwisely barred him from a production meeting and argued about a news feature for one of the games. Putting up a united front, Forte and Cosell demanded O'Neil be fired before the regular season started. With the option of proceeding forward with his new producer against two strong personalities, Arledge felt that was a battle not worth having. He replaced O'Neil with nine-year ABC Sports veteran producer Bob Goodrich, who had worked on *Monday Night Football* as a production assistant during the other years.

O'Neil quickly moved to CBS to become the executive producer of its NFL coverage in 1980 after his dispute with Chet Forte. He won several Emmys there for Outstanding Live Sports Series starting in 1982. Dennis Lewin went back to *ABC's Wide World of Sports* and likewise racked up several more Emmys for himself there.

As for Goodrich, he did not innovate the way O'Neil planned to do with *Monday Night Football*, but in 1980 the production team needed placidity among its members before improvements, so he won acceptance among all parties involved and stayed five years with the show, longer than the tenures of both Lewin and O'Neil.

Goodrich managed to get the ratings on *Monday Night Football* up to number 20 in the 1980–81 season. This was impressive not only in comparison to the previous season but also when one considers its initial competition. The show took a real beating in September 1980 when the NBC miniseries *Shogun* drew half the available audience that Monday night and the network debut of the movie *Foul Play* gave CBS a 25 share, leaving *Monday Night Football* with just a measly 18 share. Yet after these special programs vanished, the series managed to rebound and come back to the levels it had nearly three years earlier. Admittedly, an actors' strike that fall hurt the efforts of CBS to compete effectively, preventing new shows from getting on the air, but viewers always had the option of not turning on the TV rather than watching *Monday Night Football*. More preferred to do the latter.

So Goodrich could take credit for stabilizing *Monday Night Football* in general. He even managed to make an improvement by adding a camera covering the field opposite the press-box side that could record action from a different perspective. Unveiled in 1981, Goodrich's "reverse-angle replay" became a standard feature of the show thereafter and enlivened the series' overall coverage. Goodrich could not, however, mend the backstage bickering.

The Tension Keeps Rising

As it always seemed before, much of the aggravation for everyone on the series emanated from Howard Cosell. Part of that stemmed from his thwarted ambitions away from *Monday Night Football.*

For example, in 1977 when Arledge took charge of ABC News, Cosell told him he thought he rightfully ought to be there too, perhaps to deliver commentary on the nightly telecast. Then he got word about a new newsmagazine Arledge was to unveil in 1978 called *20/20,* and Howard thought he would be perfect for that too. Arledge politely but firmly nixed Howard's offers.

While failing to get those assignments, there became more moments of prolonged silence from Cosell during a few games by the late 1970s. Sometimes it came from disagreements with the others in the booth, other times by what director Chet Forte told him about something he did on the air, causing Howard to sulk during the game until Forte managed to get him back into the groove.

One "network source" told Don Kowet of *TV Guide* in 1980 that "Chet is really the only one Howard can work with at ABC. No one else understands Howard, the care and stroking he needs."

Don Meredith frequently was the cause of Cosell's distress; Cosell felt Meredith was either attacking him or detaching himself from the game. The latter charge was true for at least one game in 1979, according to Meredith's friend, sportswriter Edwin Shrake. Shrake said he and Don decided to write a song on air one night, without anyone else knowing. They did it alternating line by line, so when he spoke occasionally during the game, what came out sometimes was a short non sequitur. "What they didn't know was that was a line from a song," Shrake recalled with a chuckle.

Nonetheless, Meredith downplayed the discontent that took place. "We all know what to expect of each other, and we get along fine," Meredith told Melvin Durslag in *TV Guide* about his co-workers in 1980. When Durslag asked him if he saw Cosell outside the booth, Meredith said: "No. But then we never were social. Gifford and I are more social."

In the same article, Durslag expressed one personal wish that indicated with whom his sentiments resided. "If Howard lasts another 10 years on *Monday Night*

Football, it is hoped, but hardly expected, that he will be heard to say — just once — 'Interesting point, Don. I didn't know that.'"

For his part, Gifford told Arledge he left the show some nights "feeling like a survivor of Omaha Beach," as he put it, while Don and Howard now just sniped rather than jostled with one another. Howard also did his part in grimacing or mocking Gifford during his verbal gaffes, though rarely on the air, as he knew it would be unprofessional and would cause people attack him for going after the generally well-liked Gifford.

As the disagreements became known in the industry, one competitor tried to take advantage in a unique way. In 1978 the CBS radio network took over the audio-only coverage of the games from Mutual with Jack Buck and Hank Stram announcing. Soon popular lore among some columnists had it that many *Monday Night Football* watchers turned down Cosell, Gifford and Meredith to listen to Buck and Stram instead, but that never bore itself out in ratings for the radio show, although admittedly it would be hard to judge exactly how many people might have done that.

There was one unassailable fact about the radio show — Buck and Stram stayed partners on it until 1995, when Howard David and Matt Millen replaced them. Their tenure was longer than Cosell, Gifford and Meredith's, and much less stormy, of course.

As if all the discontent within the booth was not enough, the NFL itself began having dissension within its membership. The decisions reached would impact how Cosell would view the league thereafter and naturally affect his coverage of the sport on *Monday Night Football*.

The NFL Goes to Court

The first NFL battle of the period that involved *Monday Night Football* dealt with members' ownerships in other sports leagues. Lamar Hunt, owner of the Houston Oilers, also had a team in the North American Soccer League (NASL) and planned to work on that league's future TV policy when NFL officials objected, citing a conflict of interest. Joined by Miami Dolphins owner Joe Robbie, Hunt initiated the lawsuit *NASL v. NFL* on April 1980 to sue the football league to which they belonged. Hunt and Robbie argued that the NFL's proposed ban on cross-ownership was anticompetitive and thus a violation of the Sherman Antitrust Act. A federal appeals court in January 1982 found in favor of the NASL and banned any ownership policy amendments forever for the NFL.

Nevertheless, NASL officials could not generate enough interest among the networks to telecast soccer games on a regular basis. This no doubt grew out of previous failures of regular telecasts of the sport on CBS in 1967 and 1968 and ABC in 1979 and 1980. Each time the sport eked out only low ratings opposite baseball games in the spring and summer, and advertisers likewise turned out in only small volumes too. In fact, when ABC had a bargain basement contract of showing NASL games in 1979 and 1980 for only $1.8 million, it still managed to lose money on the transaction due to general sponsor and viewer disinterest. If ABC covered the NASL to try to appease the feelings of Hunt toward the NFL, it was a failure on several levels.

A more pressing dispute in 1980 took place when ABC let the NFL know its dissatisfaction if any *Monday Night Football* games were blacked out in Los Angeles because Oakland Raiders owner Al Davis threatened to relocate his franchise there. ABC and other network broadcasters were concerned that the Raiders would not sell out home attendance in Los Angeles because it already had another team there, the Rams, and so the Raider games by league rules would be blocked there. Davis said his Raiders would sell out.

As part of his relocation plan, Davis sued the NFL. On April 13, 1982, a jury found in favor of Al Davis over NFL for more than $50 million in damages, in the process allowing him to relocate the Raiders to Los Angeles. Davis had the possibility of making an individual TV deal for the Raiders thanks to his court win, thus threatening the longtime policy ABC had with the NFL in doing *Monday Night Football*.

It did not happen. Instead, NFL Commissioner Pete Rozelle used the leverage of demand for pro football from other teams in the league to hold out the networks and drive up prices for NFL TV rights for five years to $2 billion total in 1982. At the March 22, 1982, league meeting, officials said ABC had logged an all-time high in ratings in 1981, up 4 percent from its previous record (it in fact finished number 11 for the 1981–82 season, its best average ever). Given that success and the huge popularity of the Super Bowl (since 1972, every Super Bowl finished among the top 40 highest-rated TV shows of all time), the league now demanded a 150 percent increase in money from TV coverage — and they got it.

ABC agreed to pay $680 million over next five years to do *Monday Night Football*. Along with NBC and CBS, the TV rights generated the NFL $14 million per club per season among 28 teams, meaning they would guaranteed a profit even before counting the attendance take. For the networks, however, it was much riskier and assumed that sponsors would be willing to shoulder the increased ad rates needed cover the expenses.

That gamble haunted ABC by the mid–1980s, even though it gave the network its first opportunity to telecast a Super Bowl in 1985. The more immediate effect of it was to disgust Howard Cosell, who thought the league had become too powerful and disrespectful to certain individuals and entities. His feelings only added to the acrimony on the series. Those feelings would come back to hurt almost everyone connected to it by the mid–1980s.

Odds and Ends in the Early 1980s

There were a few other highlights on *Monday Night Football* before Cosell's growing displeasure and the costs of the games consumed the series.

One central issue to certain fans was there were biases among what teams were featured on *Monday Night Football*. For example, the San Diego Chargers were not seen on the program in 1973 and 1974, then returned on December 15, 1975, only to vanish from the lineup again until December 4, 1978. They soon joined Dallas and Pittsburgh as yearly favorites on the show. Meanwhile, supporters of the Tampa Bay Buccaneers were vocal in the late 1970s about how their new franchise did not get a shot on the show (the team finally made its debut on October 6, 1980, when the Chicago Bears shut them out 23–0).

In response to these complaints, the show allowed more parity in scheduling teams on it, even though this sometimes produced a lousy season schedule. In 1981–82, for example, the San Francisco 49ers and the Cincinnati Bengals competed in the Super Bowl without either team having made a *Monday Night Football* appearance that season. It was a tribute to the show that ratings rose in the face of that obstacle.

The saddest moment on the series took place when Cosell had to tell the nation on the December 8, 1980, broadcast, that John Lennon, a former member of the Beatles, had been assassinated. In an eerie coincidence, nearly five years to the day earlier, on December 9, 1975, Lennon had shown up as a guest on the series and was in awe. "It's an amazing event and sight," he told Cosell then. "It makes rock concerts look like tea parties."

Now Cosell delivered the following news: "John Lennon, shot twice in the back, rushed to Roosevelt Hospital, dead on arrival." He followed the announcement with an impromptu eulogy to the man he knew and loved. He quoted poetry as the game continued and Beatles fans lined up to mourn Lennon in New York City. For a generation raised on the group's music, the loss of what some considered the intellectual leader of the quartet was a heavy burden to bear, and Cosell acquitted himself admirably in the spur of the moment praising the musician. When ESPN counted the greatest happenings in *Monday Night Football* history in an August 29, 2005, special titled *MNF 36: The List*, the program ranked this event as number one.

Forgotten in the wake of this event was that the game itself, between the Miami Dolphins and the New England Patriots, resulted in only the fifth overtime regular season game on the series to date, with Miami winning 16–13. (The first *Monday Night Football* overtime contest took place on September 27, 1976, when the Washington Redskins prevailed over the Philadelphia Eagles 20–17, followed by Cleveland winning over New England 30–27 on September 26, 1977, Minnesota stopping Denver 12–9 on September 11, 1978, and Pittsburgh topping New England 16–13 on September 3, 1979.)

On a lighter note that same season, on October 27, 1980, three of the New York Jets claimed that their 17–14 victory over the Miami Dolphins stemmed in part from the aggravation of knowing that Howard Cosell was calling their game. This, mind you, even when no one could recall anything specifically negative Cosell said about the team that season prior to the game. "This will shut Howard up for a while," Jets quarterback Richard Todd told George Vecsey of *The New York Times.* "If we'd been down, he would have been making fun of us again."

The incident showed the power of Cosell on *Monday Night Football* at its best — he was an announcer who actually was able to inspire teams to win in response to his critiques. This, along with the Lennon tribute, would be the high point for the announcer on the show. Afterward, Cosell's negativity eventually would consume him and the program, and both began a sad public decline.

There would be other factors than Cosell to contribute to the messy situation on *Monday Night Football,* of course. And it's not like the show's difficulties had not become public before — remember the time with Fred Williamson temporarily taking over Meredith's position in 1974? The problem now was that changeover in the booth became an annual event, with Cosell leaving in 1983, Meredith forced out in 1984, newcomers Joe Namath and O.J. Simpson getting canned in 1985 and the show even trying a two-man setup in 1986. Nothing seemed to work, and changeover behind the scenes in response only aggravated the situation.

The Emmys witnessed the train wreck and responded in kind. After having won the Outstanding Live Sports Series statuette in 1979, the series failed to win again in the same category until 1988, nearly a decade later. Some years in the mid–1980s *Monday Night Football* was not even nominated for the award.

Once the gold standard of sports, *Monday Night Football* now was becoming an embarrassment to both its network and the NFL.

8
Capital Messes (1982–86)

Monday Night Football faced a multitude of hindrances going into its second decade on air. One was the growth of cable television, which finally was making inroads into the homes of many Americans after years of being promoted as the option that would end the stranglehold ABC, CBS and NBC had over choices to watch. The growth of specialized channels on cable, such as ESPN, contributed to the networks paying much more to the NFL in the five-year deal in 1982, just to prevent any of the other operations from getting hold of the games.

At the same time, the home video market exploded as well. With a videocassette recorder (VCR), a person could tape a show and watch it whenever he or she wanted, or watch other prerecorded matter at his or her convenience. This posed an additional threat to the Big Three networks, though less so for *Monday Night Football*; since it aired live in most markets, it virtually required a person to watch it as it happened. Still, it was another option not previously available to viewers, and it worried TV executives at every level.

As it turned out, the big difficulty facing *Monday Night Football* first in this period was what was happening with professional football itself. A pastime designed to get spectators' minds off their daily troubles ended up mirroring them as conflicts within the NFL threatened to destroy the organization. It was the start of what would be many events that coalesced to form the most topsy-turvy four years *Monday Night Football* had ever witnessed.

The Strike

With its big TV deals and other streams of large revenue, the NFL was doing fine in 1982. The only drawback was that while more money came into the league, the players themselves were getting less of a cut than pros in other major sports, such as basketball and baseball.

Playing on that discontent, Ed Garvey, director of the NFL Players Association, told league officials that his membership demanded 55 percent of the gross profits being generated as well as a union wage scale. The leaders rejected this demand as unreasonable. This left Garvey with limited, drastic options. He decided to use one of them in the hope of securing a win on his side.

On Monday, September 20, 1982, Garvey announced his group was on strike, and the football season went on hold due to the event. Luckily for ABC, the strike did not take effect before that night's contest between the Green Bay Packers and the New York Giants. It was the second game of the season on *Monday Night Football*, and everyone connected to the show worried it might be the last one that season too if the sides could not come to an agreement.

Garvey thought the owners would fold in two weeks while no games took place. He did not count on how strongly the leaders could resist his pressure and how much the players themselves preferred to work rather than wait for all their demands to be met.

To handle the absence of games, ABC could have done what NBC did and run Canadian professional football in place of NFL contests. Wisely, however, they decided against doing so, which probably prevented a disaster in the ratings, since NBC gave up covering the matches after three weeks of low ratings from September 26 through October 10, 1982, even though the strike remained in place. Movies filled ABC's time slot instead.

Meanwhile, public outcry grew on both sides of the conflict to get something resolved so that the 1982–83 season would not be a wash. By November 4, 1982, the NFL offered players a total of $1.6 billion over five years (the same amount the owners promised before the strike began) plus $60 million in "money now" bonuses, which would pay every veteran player $60,000 as soon as an agreement occurred. Players on four teams voted to accept the terms, and Garvey was forced to accept it on November 17, 1982, even though it still meant football players would draw the lowest average salaries in pro sports.

The league scrambled to set up games and get them in place so that there would be another Super Bowl. They succeeded in doing so quickly, and two months after its last telecast *Monday Night Football* was back in action on November 22, 1982. There were five more games on the series before it ended its abbreviated season on December 27.

The strike cost *Monday Night Football* an estimated 5 million viewers that year. Ratings for the program were down 5 percent in 1982 from 1981 in the few games that actually aired, but because some other top-rated shows lost significant audience as well, the series actually wound up in the top 10, one notch higher than the previous year. Still, that was small consolation, given how the network had to cover not only Monday shows but also some Thursday games planned as well (the Sunday night games from the late 1970s and early 1980s never fared as well as hoped and were dropped in the 1982 deal). It also gave ABC deserved trepidation about its participation in a new project involving pro football that would hurt it even more than the 1982 strike season did.

The USF-Hell

When Oakland Raiders owner Al Davis made rumblings about starting a new football league during his lawsuit against the NFL in 1981, he found a receptive ear in ex–Redskins general manager George Allen. Allen liked the concept and received details from Davis on how it could happen. After several months of meetings and discussion, an announcement came in 1982 about a new pro group that would start the next year — the United States Football League, or USFL.

The USFL was meant to complement the NFL, not to compete with it. With the assurance it would run only in the spring and summer months, ABC paid $20 million for broadcasting rights for the United States Football League. It hired Keith Jackson as its main play-by-play man and ex–Pittsburgh Steelers receiver Lynn Swann as its top analyst. USFL Commissioner Chet Simmons wanted Cosell to do Swann's job, but Arledge was wary of comparing the product to *Monday Night Football*, so he rejected that proposal, along with any notion of televising games regularly in the night.

The league held its first draft in the spring of 1983 to compete with NFL on signing players. USFL officials convinced some 48 current NFL players and 17 college prospects to join it in the early going, a fact that rattled some NFL owners. NFL committee members urged franchises not to get into a bidding war for talent with the USFL, thinking the latter was overpaying players, but San Francisco for one escalated its salaries to prevent future losses of talent. Eventually many NFL players' salaries escalated as the USFL competed with them to offer huge deals. Ironically, this made the players better off financially than they would have been had they made the NFL owners pay 55 percent of team gross revenues like they demanded in the 1982 strike.

The new league's games were quite profitable to ABC in its first season. *Forbes* estimated the network turned more than $15 million in profits from the series, based on ABC collecting $34 million in ad revenue from it and subtracting the $9 million broadcasting rights plus other expenses such as production costs from the revenue.

However, in 1984, the USFL's ratings fell apart, as did attendance. ABC went back to a trick it used in the old AFL days of the 1960s and aimed their cameras at action on the field while avoiding home crowd shots as much as possible. Most franchises moved or merged, prompting ABC to cover only one game a week rather than two the next year to save money (Jim Lampley and Lee Corso called the backup game for areas not served by the Jackson and Swann main game in 1983; Tim Brant and Lee Grosscup did the job in 1984). Even with this reduced, focused coverage, by 1985 17 percent of ABC affiliates did not carry the USFL games.

While the league's downturn was obvious to everyone, knowing that the networks' NFL contracts ending in 1986, some USFL leaders thought it had a shot in competing head on with the older league for the contracts then, among them Donald Trump, owner of the New York City franchise. He began convincing fellow USFL owners to move their schedule into the fall season to allow them to reap a bigger share of money.

"The networks need us as a hedge against the NFL, so when the TV contract comes up in three years, they have an alternative," Trump told John Merwin in *Forbes* in 1984. "They can pay us substantially less, and we can do very nicely."

Yet in the same article, Commissioner Chet Simmons downplayed how the USFL could compete with the older league in terms of relations with the networks. "There is still the glamour and the history of being involved with the NFL," he said.

Despite Simmons' belief, pressure grew to where the USFL announced that after its 1985 season, it would play in the fall rather than spring of 1986. ABC opposed the change, no doubt worrying about how it would impact their NFL deal for Monday night football, so after it carried the USFL championship game on July 14, 1985, the network dropped any plans to carry future league games. No other network nor syndicator made an offer to hold the contests either thereafter, seeing ABC's low ratings average of 4.9 in 1985. Without any money for TV coverage, the league knew it could not afford its salaries and thus would go out of business.

In response, USFL officials invoked the Sherman Act and filed an antitrust lawsuit against the NFL in October 1984. They hired famous (or infamous, if you prefer) attorney Roy Cohn to represent them. They even got Howard Cosell to testify against the NFL. They won the battle, but boy, did they lose the war.

On July 29, 1986, a jury charged ABC Sports and the NFL guilty for "involuntarily conspiring" to drive the USFL out of business. That was the only good news for the USFL. When it came time to award damages for the charge, the jurists awarded the USFL just one dollar. The final amount was trebled to $3 per requirements of the law; still, that amount was short of what the league needed to be financially solvent in time for a 1986 fall football schedule, so with the announcement of the decision, the USFL effectively went out of business.

More than a decade later, in an online poll on the *Time* magazine website, visitors listed the USFL in the "100 Worst Ideas of the [20th] Century." Guess they forgot about the World Football League or the World League of American Football (see Chapter 9). Both were much lower in quality.

Cosell Melts Down as Simpson Steps Up

The troubles with USFL proved to be small potatoes to the *Monday Night Football* staff in 1983–84 compared to the aggravation Howard Cosell provided to almost everyone else on the show. Howard became bored of doing the show, and he complained about such things as boxing, Commissioner Pete Rozelle's treatment of Al Davis, and of course the work habits of his booth mates Don Meredith and Frank Gifford.

He similarly soon displayed a cavalier attitude to a surprising target — the newly added *Monday Night Football* announcer Orenthal James "O.J." Simpson, who replaced Fran Tarkenton as Meredith's substitute on extra games in 1983. Born in San Francisco, California, on July 9, 1947, the handsome Heisman Trophy winner of 1968 was a star fullback first at the University of Southern California before playing for the Buffalo Bills from 1969 to 1977, where he set several records including being the first football player to gain more than 2,000 yards rushing. At the same time he engaged in a busy acting career during his offseason, making many TV appearances on everything from *Here's Lucy* to the miniseries *Roots* and even big-name movies such as *The Towering Inferno*. His appeal as a thespian was strong, so when he retired in 1979 from football, he went with a Don Meredith–style offer from NBC to do both TV roles and sportscasting, even though he had done the latter occasionally for ABC in the late 1970s.

Cosell had taught Simpson the finer points of sportscasting when Simpson first worked for ABC in the 1976 Summer Olympics. In his 1985 memoirs *I Never Played the Game*, Cosell claimed O.J. became a family friend who hung out at his apartment in the late 1970s and said he wanted to work with Cosell on *Monday Night Football*. Cosell thought he had potential and therefore accepted him when Arledge put O.J. in the booth. But Cosell soon felt Simpson joined Gifford and Meredith in teasing him on and off the air and considered it a betrayal. To Cosell, O.J. had become yet another part of the "jockocracy" that gained their employment on the air more for their reputation on the field than in the booth.

With Cosell having no Karras or Tarkenton to offer him solace, he now did his job on edge, with decreasing rapport among anyone around him. Even director Chet Forte, who made Cosell his best man during his wedding in 1976, now no longer felt up to defending his old friend in the increasing opposition to him.

Concurrently, Cosell found himself on the brunt of much public criticism, possibly even more than from the early days of *Monday Night Football*. "When the game is scintillating, Howard is superfluous," said Dick Friedman in *TV Guide* in 1983. Keep in mind that was one of the more approving reviews of Howard's work at the time.

More typical was this from John Leonard in *New York* magazine: "It often seems on ABC that there are at least three too many mouths, two of them Howard's." Leonard went so far as to compare Cosell with the current bombastic U.S. secretary of state. "Cosell, of course, is the most egregious blabbercaster, as if he were Al Haig, reporting from Mission Control at NASA, with his aspirate overemphasis, his faked emotions: every fumbled punt an aesthetic insult, every hamstring pull a loss of China."

Opinions against Cosell were nothing new. Unfortunately for Howard, his performance on air gave more justification than ever to his critics for having him removed. And it wound up doing so in the end.

Cosell Closes Shop

The first glimmer of Cosell's collapse came in the September 5, 1983, season opener with Dallas at Washington. During the game, Redskins receiver Alvin Garrett received a pass from Joe Theismann, prompting Howard to remember how Washington's coach Joe Gibbs was impressed with Garrett's abilities while the two worked for the San Diego Chargers. "Gibbs wanted to get this kid and that little monkey gets loose, doesn't he?" Cosell noted.

Upon hearing those words, the Rev. Joseph E. Lowry, president of the Southern Christian Leadership Conference, fired off a telegraph to Cosell with copies to news wire services saying Cosell had made a racist remark by comparing the black Garrett to a monkey. Roone Arledge got wind of the situation and made Howard address the comment at the start of the second half, which he reluctantly did by saying he did not call Garrett a "little monkey."

But it was not enough to end the controversy in the press that week. Even though praise for Howard from such black civil rights leaders as Bill Cosby, Arthur Ashe, Rev. Jesse Jackson and Jackie Robinson's widow Rachel, and Garrett himself never spoke against Cosell, several in the media spoke out against him and called him a racist. A tired, upset Howard took time off from three games that season to let the brouhaha die down before he came back no happier than when he left.

Upon his return to the booth on October 3, one on-air sparring gave him justification for being in such a sour mood. With the New York Jets leading 7–0 over the Buffalo Bills early in the game, Cosell interjected the following: "If the Bills can get anything going, they'll be right back in this thing!"

An on-the-ball O.J. Simpson responded: "Howard, you've proved once again you've got a firm grasp of the obvious—to use one of your lines."

"Fine! OK!" Cosell replied, disgusted that the sportscaster mocked him. Columnists, who had early watched the game to see how the analyst would handle being back in the booth, lapped up Simpson's cutting comments as a sign of Howard getting his comeuppance. (By the way, the Bills did get enough going to score 10 points, but the Jets did even better by finishing with 34 to win the game.)

In the wake of the incident, Howard repeated his threat to Arledge to quit *Monday Night Football*. The only thing was that now Arledge had had enough of him; he was hearing constant complaints about how ornery Cosell was from others in ABC Sports and seeing how ratings were down from the number 10 average in 1982–83 to number 21 in 1983–84. Add to that Howard's occasional rants to

Roone for not letting him do news commentary and holding him back from doing top assignments on the Olympics, among other matters, and Roone was ready, albeit reluctantly, to get rid of the man he first hired to do *Monday Night Football*.

The dismissal occurred oddly in July 1984 after Arledge and Cosell had spent months on individual projects with virtually no contact with each other. Cosell believed Arledge was trying to avoid him while rumors swirled about his retirement from *Monday Night Football*. When no one at ABC denied the rumors, Cosell went ahead and told inquiring *Los Angeles Times* television reporter Larry Stewart that he did intend to give up doing the show. The story upset Arledge, as ABC had not ordered any press release announcing Howard's departure, but he did not object to Cosell leaving.

In *I Never Played the Game*, Cosell said although there were numerous and complex reasons why he offered to quit *Monday Night Football,* the chief one was that he wanted to spend more time with his wife Emmy. He also cited his sense of morality (he felt the NFL had become arrogant and greedy), his boredom with the sport, and his ambivalence toward Gifford and Meredith.

Whatever the reason was, Howard was history. Many people in and out of the series thought this move would be a relief, that harmony would take place within the booth and a smoother, more enjoyable program would emerge.

But once again for *Monday Night Football*, reality had a tough time following high expectations.

As Howard Goes, So Goes the Ratings

Given the lateness of Howard's retirement, Arledge had little option but to go with having Simpson work full time as his replacement along with Meredith and Gifford. However, he did draft Jim Lampley from NCAA football coverage to narrate the halftime film highlights, knowing that anyone who did the job would face comparison with Cosell's stellar work in the field. The other regulars simply did not have the background to do the task as efficiently as Cosell had. About the only other major change that season was that the series retired the notoriously bright, gaudy canary yellow blazers worn by the sportscasters since 1971.

Still, the shadow of Cosell loomed large over the show, and when the new team began in earnest in September, most critics knocked them as being boring without having Cosell on board. The complaints were predictable — Simpson was too inexperienced to offer solid insights, spoke too quickly and failed to enunciate, Meredith was unable or unwilling to bounce off Simpson's observations and therefore seemed flat, and Gifford was as stiff as ever.

Ratings started to slide too, and for the first time in five years, *Monday Night Football* was finishing third in its time slot. CBS had shaken off the disappointment of *After M*A*S*H* and *Emerald Point N.A.S.* from the fall of 1983 to come back with a stronger Monday lineup in 1984 of *Kate & Allie*, *Newhart* and *Cagney & Lacey*, all top 30 hits in 1984–85. At the same time, NBC's Monday film series offered TV-movies that did well enough to finish at number 18 in 1984–85, its best seasonal average in seven years.

Meanwhile, *Monday Night Football* struggled just to make the top 40 each week, even though it had some exciting contests (e.g., San Francisco edged out Washington 37–31 on September 10, and the Los Angeles Raiders eked out a squeaker over San Diego 33–30 on September 24). Coupled with the failure of the military drama *Call to Glory* as the new lead-in/lead-out following the cancellation of *That's Incredible!* in 1984, ABC executives squirmed about what was happening to them Monday nights in the fall of 1984, especially as ad revenues dropped dramatically.

To quell the growing criticism, Simpson told Bob Raissman of *TV Guide* in September 1984 that Cosell still would do a couple of *Monday Night Football* games that season, plus ABC's first Super Bowl. "Whatever Howard may say, the fact of the matter is, he still loves the people involved in the sport," he said. "Even if he does cut back drastically, there is no way he cannot be in the booth for the Super Bowl." If Cosell did not take part in the bowl game, Simpson cautioned, "It will be a major mistake on everyone's part."

The "major mistake" took place, even after the chorus grew against the Simpson-Meredith-Gifford trio. In its October 6–12, 1984, issue, *TV Guide* offered "Cheers" to Cosell in its "Cheers 'n' Jeers" section to point out how important his contribution had been in making the series above the usual football game on TV. "Howard, we never imagined how much we'd miss you," the periodical stated.

Two months later, ABC Chairman Leonard Goldenson had lunch with Howard and his wife Emmy and offered him the chance to cover the Super Bowl in place of O.J. Simpson, whose performance on *Monday Night Football* disappointed him. Howard relished it, but Emmy thought it would be a step back for him, and he agreed. Even after that rejection, Goldenson insisted to Arledge that Simpson could not do analysis of the game. Arledge agreed, but let him appear before and after the game and at halftime. He was replaced by Joe Theismann, who was quarterback for the non–Super Bowl contenders the Washington Redskins. Putting on an active player with limited broadcasting experience was a dicey call, and one that did not impress many critics. Theismann did not become a regular announcer for the series in its wake.

While that transpired, Cosell's appearances on ABC, and on television in general, fell off soon after he left *Monday Night Football*. For his network, he participated in the coverage of the 1984 Olympics and in the entertainment special *Night of 100 Stars II* on March 10, 1985. A month after the special, he was the final guest host for the 1984–85 season of *Saturday Night Live* on NBC. That summer of 1985, he did his last tour of duty announcing for *Monday Night Baseball*.

Later, in the fall of 1985, he released a book that Howard apparently thought would settle his scores against all his old enemies. To most readers, though, it just emphasized what a mean, grumpy old man Cosell had become and reminded them why many of them wanted him off *Monday Night Football* just a few years earlier.

Cosell: The Final Years

With the publication of *I Never Played the Game*, Cosell laid bare his grievances with all the key executives and booth mates at *Monday Night Football* in recounting what events had bothered him over the last five years or so in professional athletics. That was his right. But he did it with words and phrases so hateful, it came out as a vindictive rant, character assassination rather than thoughtful rumination.

Here's a typical sample from the book: "When push came to shove, Gifford and Meredith were as thick as thieves. They would never take sides against each other, and somehow I always was cast as the bad guy. I could never really trust either one of them."

Cosell's screed also took on fellow broadcasters and their supposed shortcomings, plus NFL Commissioner Pete Rozelle, the boxing industry, and a few other random topics that ticked him off. It appalled book critics, who gave it overwhelmingly negative reviews, and it naturally lowered his profile at ABC. The network denied him a chance to cover the World Series upon its printing, and then a few months later he completed his last regular series job at ABC-TV when his stint as host of the Emmy-winning investigative series *Sportsbeat* ended on December 15, 1985, after four years on the air. By mutual agreement, he parted with ABC Sports on TV by the start of 1986.

Two people on *Monday Night Football* mentioned extensively in *I Never Played the Game* professed to have ignored it. "I never read the book," Frank Gifford said in an interview on the 1999 HBO documentary *Howard Cosell: Telling It Like It Is*. "I had enough agitation with him, traveling with him for *Monday Night Football*."

Roone Arledge had not read *I Never Played the Game* when he met with Howard at lunch after the book came out (much to Howard's amazement) and insisted in his own autobiography that he never had looked at it. What he heard about it from others was enough to dissuade him. Besides that, Arledge still held Cosell in high regard, despite all his faults and affronts.

After the book controversy died out, Cosell largely disappeared altogether from TV, even on guest shots and specials. Among the exceptions were a visit to Louis Rukeyser's financial series on public television, *Wall Street Week*, on January 19, 1990, and a touching tribute to his old boxing pal in the special *Muhammad Ali: 50th Birthday Celebration* on March 1, 1992.

He did try one more series, a syndicated late night talk show called *Speaking of Everything* in early 1988. Most reviewers and viewers ignored the offering. It went off in 13 weeks. Four years later, Cosell officially retired from ABC radio, where his commentaries had been the bulk of his broadcasting work after *Monday Night Football* on a weekly series. Several major news outlets carried the news of his departure, which might have startled some people who thought the seldom-seen Cosell already was dead.

In a sense, he was, as his beloved wife Emmy had passed away by the time he left ABC, leaving him largely a shell of a man. Following her death in 1990, Cosell eulogized her with these words on his radio show: "My heart aches. I thank whatever gods may be, Emmy, for your unconquerable soul."

On April 13, 1995, Howard Cosell died from a heart embolism in New York City. It happened a month after his 77th birthday. Nearly every major sports columnist submitted a story in his honor, in varying degrees from deifying to denigrating him. All of them, however, made mention of his contributions to *Monday Night Football.*

Don Meredith's reaction to all these events went unrecorded. Meredith was off *Monday Night Football* a year after Cosell left, and he walked away from the spotlight afterward, rarely talking to the press or doing much of note. The last time he sang "the party's over," he apparently meant it for himself in terms of public appearances.

Dandy Don Is Gone

As much as O.J. Simpson and Frank Gifford faced criticism for their work on *Monday Night Football* in 1984, it was the third member of the team who many on the staff knew would be marked first to go. Don Meredith's contract for the show ended after 1984, and his increasingly lackadaisical performances only got worse as the season progressed, while Simpson and Gifford at least tried to improve theirs. It was a feature noted by both show insiders and the critics.

To William Taaffe of *Sports Illustrated*, the Don Meredith of 1984 was "Not So Funny Anymore." "So far, his whimsical humor and wonderful timing just haven't clicked," he wrote. *Variety* agreed, noting that "Meredith was perceived as uninterested in the games and spent more time projecting his personality than he did the game."

Having shed Cosell, albeit with some regrets, and feeling there was nowhere to go but up, Arledge had no fears in letting Meredith loose from *Monday Night Football* for a second time. But unlike 1974, there was no contract waiting for him to act or announce on NBC, CBS or even a cable network. That was fine by him.

Meredith returned to live with his wife in Santa Fe, New Mexico, where they had lived since 1980. He rarely acted or announced afterward and had little contact with Hollywood, although he did participate in a symposium tribute to *Police Story* at the Museum of Television and Radio in Los Angeles in 1992. He also did virtually no interviews with the media, preferring to try to slip into obscurity. To that end, he no longer has any contact information on file at the Screen Actors Guild, unlike most major performers even in retirement.

"Don's a very private guy," noted his pal, sportswriter Edwin Shrake. "He doesn't like his laundry to be hung out in public."

When *Sports Illustrated* reporter Richard Hoffer caught up with Meredith in 2000 for a "where are they now" feature, he had to negotiate the interview via fax. Despite this relative inaccessibility and his lack of public activity in later years, Meredith did not consider himself a recluse. He said he and his wife Susan hosted visiting friends at the house and traveled often, and he stayed busy playing golf every Thursday.

Hoffer found Meredith had little interest in looking back at the past. He had no artifacts of his football days at his home, and he had no regrets when ABC dropped its option on him in 1984. By then, he was weary of the different towns and crowds he faced every week with *Monday Night Football*. "It was a great time, but it started to change when we needed security to get in and out of stadiums," he said. "That was just stupid."

As for his old series that brought him his greatest fame, Meredith said that he had to force himself to watch *Monday Night Football* at present. He wasn't the only viewer to feel that way, even as early as the mid–1980s, when he left. Particularly if that viewer was a potential advertiser.

Money Troubles

When *Monday Night Football* ratings fell 12 percent in 1983 from the previous year (it went down from 21.1 in 1982 to 17.8), it set an ominous tone for getting ads for the show the following year. Add to that the increased competition for ad dollars from the 1984 Summer Olympics, the USFL and individual universities (the Supreme Court ruled in June 1984 that the NCAA could no longer hold a monopoly on giving TV rights to college games, thus letting each school set up their own deals), and perhaps even the departure of Howard Cosell, and *Monday Night Football* suddenly found itself no longer the automatic cash machine it used to be.

By the start of the 1984 season, *Monday Night Football* was not sold out for the run as it customarily had been in the past. Nervous ABC officials began offering 30-second ads for $100,000 apiece by October rather than the $150,000 charge they had given in upfront sales a few months earlier. The drop in ratings that season did not help matters either. The average rating of *Monday Night Football* fell from 17.8 in 1983 to 16.1 in 1984. Suddenly, ABC wondered if it would ever at least break even on the $680 million it paid the NFL for five-year TV rights back in 1982.

The show did make up its ratings in 1985, improving nearly 20 percent over the previous year, according to *Fortune*. Yet at the same time, advertisers of big-ticket items normally placed in commercials for *Monday Night Football* such as automobiles shifted their emphasis toward the growing big-money female market at that time. Thus, even with ratings up and 30-second commercials on *Monday Night Football* costing $10,000 less than in 1984 for $175,000 apiece, the show's ad space remained dry in an unprecedented way leading up to each week's game in the fall of 1985.

In desperation, ABC executives began offering bargain basement deals at the end of the work week to agencies referred to as "Friday night buyers." Some of them haggled ABC down to as little as $75,000 for a half-minute ad. Losing up to $100,000 per ad naturally cut into profits, and at year's end ABC had lost at least $25 million on *Monday Night Football* that season.

What made ABC hopeful that the situation could turn around in 1986 was that the season included the highest rated *Monday Night Football* game ever, the undefeated Chicago Bears losing to the Miami Dolphins at the latter's field on December 2, 1985. It scored a 29.6 rating with a 46 share of the audience, meaning nearly half of all the TV sets in use at the time were on the game. On the *Monday Night Football Mania* special of 1996, former Dolphins coach Don Shula said he liked his old team's victory for a personal reason: "That preserved our 17–0 season of 1972."

Calling that game was ABC's third *Monday Night Football* booth lineup, this time consisting of Gifford, Simpson and newcomer Joe Namath. And as in the previous two times, the lineup changed again after the season ended. Only this time it would be two personalities fired instead of just one.

Broadway Joe Is Monday No-Go

The selection of Joe Namath to replace Don Meredith was a brilliant move to make — if it had happened when Meredith left the first time in 1974. The decision to do so in 1985 was antiquated and shortsighted.

Namath, born in Beaver Falls, Pennsylvania, on May 31, 1943, was a charming, easygoing football star on the gridiron in the late 1960s and early 1970s as quarterback with the New York Jets, with a showy style on and off the field that earned him the nickname "Broadway Joe." He attempted to transfer his appeal and good looks (he had a killer dimpled chin) in Hollywood during the offseason while with the Jets, but movies such as *C.C. and Company* and TV guest shots on the likes of *The Brady Bunch* made people realize that as with Frank Gifford, just being a personable athlete is not enough to become a top acting attraction.

When Joe retired from pro football in 1977 after 12 years of service, he still tried to carve out an acting career, but could not cut it nationally (his best effort, a sitcom on NBC called *The Waverly Wonders*, was one of the first casualties of the 1978–79 season). His draw faded considerably going into the 1980s, yet Roone Arledge felt enough appeal existed for him among the general public that he signed him under a two-year deal. Unfortunately, Arledge neglected to take into account that Namath had had the least amount of sportscasting experience prior to *Monday Night Football* since Fred Williamson in 1974, an oversight that proved to be costly in many ways.

ABC forked over an estimated $850,000 annually for Namath to join the booth. It paid off in terms of ratings going up 18 percent for his first five games, but as previously noted, the advertising industry remained reluctant to do business with the series, so the rise in audience did not correspond with a similar one among sponsors.

According to reviewers, this was a smart move on the part of Madison Avenue. As lacking as Meredith's last games were on the series, they were not nearly as denounced as what Namath brought to *Monday Night Football*, or maybe what he did *not* bring to it.

For one, Namath's analyses were so weak and apparent that one almost wondered if they deserved to be termed as commentary. One notable example: When the Chicago Bears led the Minnesota Vikings 30–17 during a preseason game, Namath actually said on air, "It looks like the Vikings will need two scores to pull this game out." Where was Simpson with his "firm grasp of the obvious" line when that came out?

Meanwhile, Namath and Simpson rarely brought out anything insightful from each other or Gifford, leaving one with the impression there was no real chemistry among any of the announcers. Namath just came across as a casual observer of the game, in some ways even more distant from it than Meredith had been.

In an October article, William Taaffe of *Sports Illustrated* explicitly stated, "Artistically, *MNF* is going down the tubes," and blamed it largely on Namath. "Namath ... is O.J. cloned," he wrote. "They're the same person, saying the same things."

Taaffe laid it on more later in the piece. "Namath doesn't know if he should be a star, a teacher or a Mr. Nasty who puts down 'lousy' passes. [Many reviewers noted how often Namath used 'lousy' to sum up a botched play.] Unsure of himself, he becomes redundant."

Though the ratings were up (the show finished at number 15, its best seasonal average in three years), comments such as Taaffe's were the norm for the Namath-Simpson-Gifford combo. Knowing what had happened on the show recently, and the reluctance of advertisers to splurge on the series, plus a takeover in ownership of ABC (more on that shortly), should have concerned all parties about their future.

Even so, both Simpson and Namath reportedly were stunned to learn in 1986 that ABC no longer needed their services for the next go-round on *Monday Night Football*. For his part, Namath went back into sportscasting for NBC's NFL coverage in the late 1980s before settling down in Florida to semiretirement in the 1990s. He embarrassed himself on TV in 2003 when ESPN sideline reporter Suzy Kolber interviewed him during a football game after Namath had had a few too many drinks. "I want to kiss you," the buzzing ex-superstar said and smiled to Kolber. She managed to extricate herself from his tipsy pass at her, while Namath went into detox and made few public appearances in its wake.

And then there was the saga of O.J. Simpson.

Freed from *Monday Night Football*, Simpson concentrated on commercials for the Hertz auto rental company and acted on the HBO sitcom *1st and Ten* the rest of the 1980s. In 1989, he went back to sportscasting as a sideline reporter for NBC's NFL coverage. He held that position through 1993.

In 1994, Simpson was charged for the murders of his wife Nicole and her friend Ron Goldman. Police questioned his alibi during the time of their deaths, and his attempt to elude arrest via a freeway chase in Los Angeles. A trial with high-profile lawyers became a media circus, as did the jury's vote to acquit him. Despite that decision, no one in broadcasting hired Simpson, as a cloud of suspicion remained over him while the murders remained unresolved. He moved to south Florida and lived off his NFL pension while claiming to be looking for the "real killers" in his case. If anyone from *Monday Night Football* remained in contact with him, it was not publicized.

Of course, no one could foresee the future for Simpson or Namath when they left the series. At *Monday Night Football*, more probably worried about how the new management would affect an already weary and worried staff. The answer in the short term was that it gave even more drastic changes to a series already in considerable flux.

Enter Capital Cities

When Ronald Reagan took office as the 40th president of the United States in 1981, one of his administration's earliest accomplishments emphasized deregulation of government oversight. Along the same time, investors gained a new tool in leveraged buyouts through junk bonds. Put together, the two factors made hostile takeovers of major corporations a reality in the decade. ABC was among one of the targets by the fall of 1984, with the network needing money due to its extravagant sports deals and losing nighttime lineup — ABC had now sunk back to third after being number 1 or number 2 overall for nearly a decade until NBC managed to go to the top.

In response, ABC Chairman and CEO Leonard Goldenson set out to find a friendly operation to which he would sell his company (Goldenson turned 79 on December 1, 1984, and realized he did not have the time nor power to fend off any outsider wanting to raid his network). He found one with a conglomerate called Capital Cities Communications that owned and operated seven TV and 12 radio stations, most of which were ABC affiliates. Since it already was a broadcasting entity, Goldenson felt Capital Cities would be the best outfit to which to entrust the future of ABC.

The ABC board of directors approved the sale on March 16, 1985. Two days later, word became public that Capital Cities Communications had bought ABC in a $3.5 billion deal. Everyone on staff at ABC knew this meant new personnel in charge once the changeover was official and complete in 1986.

One person in particular, Roone Arledge, worried greatly about the transition. He hated hearing about the new company's reputation for pinching pennies at every chance, and he thought it could really impact ABC Sports in particular, given its travel budget and large staff. He was right about his feelings.

On January 27, 1986, as Capital Cities management prepared to take over handling the network, Arledge received a new title — group president of ABC News and Sports. It sounded impressive, until one realized that there would be a new president of ABC Sports as well, and that person inherited much of Arledge's job functions, including being executive producer of *Monday Night Football*.

Dennis Swanson, 47, had spent less than a year as head of ABC's owned and operated stations, following long stints in front of and behind the scenes at several local TV outlets, chiefly Chicago in the 1980s. He gained fame nationally for having been the one to hire Oprah Winfrey to host a morning talk show at ABC's Chicago affiliate WLS in 1984, where her show became an immediate sensation locally and then nationally through syndication by the time he was the new ABC Sports president.

Swanson impressed Capital Cities leaders as a man who could handles expenses for their new acquisition responsibly. Capital Cities was not thrilled about their financial forecasters telling them ABC's projected $70 million profit in 1985 would not be met in 1986 — quite the opposite, in fact. With ABC Sports alone projected to lose at least $50 million in 1986 (later estimated to more than $80 million), Swanson was essential in Capital Cities' plan to cut down losses there, and he did not disappoint them.

As previously mentioned, Swanson oversaw Joe Namath and O.J. Simpson being dropped from *Monday Night Football*. An estimated 50 employees in ABC Sports received their walking papers from Swanson upon his arrival. Under the pressure of these changes, including getting word that there would be fewer cameras used to cover *Monday Night Football*, producer Bob Goodrich decided to leave his post as well. Replacing him was Ken Wolfe, who worked his way up in various capacities at ABC Sports for a decade to be a producer of NCAA football games and who received several Emmy nominations for that duty in the 1980s.

Seeing these developments, Roone Arledge dropped his in-name-only ABC Sports president designation in disgust to do just news. He claimed in his autobiography that *Monday Night Football* never recovered from the changes.

Marvin Schlenker, Arledge's colleague from the 1960s NCAA football days who worked with Roone at ABC News (and would stay there until he retired in 1992), said his boss regretted having to withdraw from the program due to the circumstances.

"That was his baby," Schlenker said. "He loved it. I think overall he was disappointed that sports was put on the back burner when he left."

Swanson backers would argue that he was not trying to bring down the Sports department but rather eradicate most traces of the Roone Arledge followers at ABC Sports, whom Swanson regarded as profligate and pampered while the network was hurting. Among those in that category whom he really wanted to see leave ABC Sports were longtime *Monday Night Football* head of production Chuck Howard and director Chet Forte. Feeling the heat, Howard departed in the middle of the 1986 season.

Forte managed to stay put. But in Swanson's defense, he actually had a more legitimate reason to fire the director than Howard, because Forte was a gambling addict, and everyone at ABC Sports knew it.

Bye Bye Forte

By the mid–1980s, Forte earned more than a half-million dollars annually from ABC, and yet he still wanted to gamble a considerable amount of it on the outcomes of the Monday games he covered. It was an open secret at ABC, as Forte's bookie regularly came out of the office. Swanson told Forte in no uncertain terms he had a problem with the money the director was making in the first meeting, without acknowledging any creative contributions the man had made to *Monday Night Football.*

"Things between Chet and Dennis started out bad and never got better," observed Chuck Howard to Geoffrey Norman of *Sports Illustrated.* Eventually fed up with his new boss, and knowing that his contract ended in the near future of 1988, Forte took a buyout from ABC at the end of 1986, only to suffer a heart attack two months later that required a half-year for him to recuperate fully. After that, he directed the syndicated *Roller Games* TV show — and he kept gambling.

With a friend, Forte established a talent agency called Starkives and enticed others such as his first cousin Anna Perrin to invest in the property. In 1989 federal authorities investigated him for using investors' funds for Starkives for his gambling activities, prompting Anna and her husband to sue him for $280,000 he owed them for their investment. Forte used a public defender in Newark, New Jersey, named Larry Lustberg to assist him amid the charges. Lustberg learned how severe his client's monetary problems were when Forte's house in Saddle River, New Jersey, was sold at a sheriff's office on April 15, 1990. Twelve days later, while living in a rented house in Midlothian, Virginia, with his wife, mother and daughter, Forte pleaded not guilty to nine charges against him, then started attending Gamblers Anonymous.

Lustberg succeeded in getting six charges against Forte dropped. Still, the notoriety of his activities haunted Forte's attempts to get back into directing TV series. In May 1991 he finally returned to broadcasting in a minor way by accepting an offer to co-host an afternoon sports commentary and call-in radio show on XTRP in San Diego, California. He still held that job when he died of a heart attack on May 18, 1996, at age 60.

Taking Forte's place in 1987 was Larry Kamm, a veteran director with ABC Sports since the early 1960s who received his first Emmy nomination for his direction on *ABC's Wide World of Sports* in 1975. He won his first Emmy the next year as one of six directors for the Winter Olympic Games on ABC, followed by 12 other statuettes, usually for the Olympics, *ABC's Wide World of Sports* or NCAA football. Even so, insiders realized that with the changes going on throughout *Monday Night Football*, as well as what Forte had achieved as director there, Kamm faced an uphill battle for respectability on the program.

Frank Survives with New Partner Al Michaels

While ironing out his *Monday Night Football* crew in 1986, Swanson also needed to replace O.J. Simpson and Joe Namath in the booth. With his assistant Dennis Lewin — yes, the same Dennis Lewin who had produced the series in two brief terms during the 1970s — Swanson proposed to Frank Gifford that the latter now move into being a color commentator for the series as part of a revised two-man arrangement. Joining him as the new play-by-play man would be Al Michaels.

A role on *Monday Night Football* would be the perfect culmination for Michaels in nearly a decade of service for a network he felt did not always give him the plum spots he deserved. The swarthy, curly-haired 41-year-old had come to ABC in 1976 following several years in the 1970s as the local announcer for the Cincinnati Reds and then the San Francisco Giants baseball teams, plus at least one year (1975) as backup play-by-play announcer for NFL games on CBS.

As part of ABC's backup crew on baseball, Michaels had a somewhat low national profile even while he attempted to expand his presence on other sports events, such as ABC's *World Series of Auto Racing* held every January through March on Saturdays from 1978 to 1980. He finally achieved recognition in 1980 with his emotional coverage of the "Miracle on Ice" hockey game where the underdog United States defeated the Russians on the U.S.'s way to a gold medal (most people forgot in the excitement that it was not the final match for first place that America eventually won). Capturing the mood of the frenzied home crowd in the rink at Lake Placid, New York, Michaels shouted at the end, "Do you believe in miracles?! Yes!"

Yet even with that memorable moment, it would not be until 1983 that Michaels would become the lead play-by-play man on ABC's nighttime baseball, and he remained a supporting player on NCAA football coverage with Keith Jackson still leading the network there. To assuage him, Swanson and Lewin figured the offer of handling *Monday Night Football* would keep Michaels right in line with the network.

To Swanson and Lewin, the Gifford-Michaels team made sense. They would save costs with two men in the booth rather than three, use talent ABC already had under contract and prevent criticism about drastic makeovers in the booth once again by retaining longtime member Gifford. Michaels knew it would give him the biggest regular platform before a sports audience he ever had outside of the Olympics and signed up for it.

But Gifford had his doubts. It had been more than 15 years since he had been an analyst, and he was not sure he wanted to revert to it. He also was uncertain whether this new task was a subtle demotion for him as a play-by-play man. Other factors were in play as well.

Though it was not publicized at the time, Gifford received an offer to host the umpteenth incarnation of *The CBS Morning News* following his relatively smooth handling of *Good Morning America* on ABC as a guest host during the early and mid 1980s. It was on *Good Morning America* in November 1982 that Gifford first met his future third wife, Kathie Lee Johnson, as a fellow co-host. The two clicked despite the facts that she was 23 years younger than Gifford, and he still was married to his second wife Astrid until their divorce was finalized in 1984. What made *The CBS Morning News* hosting offer especially tempting was that his fiancée started co-hosting her own morning talk show with Regis Philbin, *Live with Regis and Kathie Lee*, in 1985 locally on WABC New York, and therefore they would both be working at roughly the same hours and could spend quality time together versus Frank having to be away at least one workday while staying with *Monday Night Football*.

Even in the face of such incentives, Swanson managed to win over Gifford with a five-year contract paying him $1.1 million annually to stay with *Monday Night Football*. But Gifford did find time during the show's schedule to wed Kathie Lee on October 18, 1986.

That wedding may have been the only positive note for him surrounding *Mon-*

day Night Football in late 1986. As before, Gifford still made plenty of boners on the air (he announced that season one time that "Joe Walton succeeded Al Michaels as coach of the Jets"), while Michaels himself, while solid in the eyes of most reviewers, developed little chemistry with his new partner.

Yet the ratings dropped only slightly from the previous season (number 18 in 1986–87) and it finished with virtually the same amount of audience as its competition on NBC and CBS. As it also was costing ABC less to produce, the network could handle that performance for the time being.

Still, longtime viewers must have wondered what was happening to their beloved show. So did some of the personnel. Never before had *Monday Night Football* come across appearing as if it were in freefall, and no one was certain when or even if it might end.

The Four-Year Nightmare Ends

As 1986 came to a close, Swanson braced himself for one more battle — the next NFL TV rights contract. Though he swore in public ABC would bid for lower fees, the reality was that there was now a new fourth network named Fox whose owner, Rupert Murdoch, had pockets deep enough to threaten to usurp ABC's control of Monday night games for his own affiliates. Facing this very real threat, and knowing the possible ridicule and hatred he would get from network and local staff and critics if he lost the games to the fledgling Fox (it had just begun operations one year earlier) while ABC remained in third place among the networks, Swanson gulped and raised his ante to secure the rights.

Swanson succeeded, but he wound up having to pay $500,000 more for each *Monday Night Football* game in a deal finalized in February 1987. The NFL would receive more than $360 million from ABC alone over the next three years. As part of the negotiations, the NFL gave the rights to Thursday games to ESPN, in which ABC now owned a majority interest.

During the same talks, facing less competition for their Sunday afternoon slots, CBS and NBC lowered their football costs from their previous contracts by an average of 7 percent at the same time. Regardless of that fact, Swanson now knew he had to take stronger steps to make sure *Monday Night Football* would perform better than ever for his network and, of course, his own reputation.

Longtime fans hoped as well too. In the space of four years, *Monday Night Football* had lost two of its original announcers, its executive producer (and arguably founder), its director, and its producer. Its status as a moneymaker for ABC disappeared as well. Any lesser series on the network may well have folded under all these circumstances.

But *Monday Night Football* finally got a solid team the next year with the addition of a new announcer who would give the show a lineup that lasted a decade, as well as long serving as executive producer, producer and director. Unfortunately, the chaos that took place in the mid–1980s would take place once again when that period ended, and incredibly, it may have been even more of a debacle than the first time.

9

Stability Leading to a Meltdown (1987–98)

In the fall of 1987, *Monday Night Football* went back to its three-man configuration with the addition of Dan Dierdorf as another analyst along with Frank Gifford, complemented by Al Michaels at play-by-play. Even though the series ended a point lower in its seasonal average that year than the 18.4 compiled in 1986, the show actually finished slightly ahead in the ratings standings (number 16 in 1987–88 versus number 18 in 1986–87) thanks to an overall decline in people viewing broadcast network TV series.

More importantly, ad rates were up, even with a strike of a few weeks early in the 1987 season that used replacement players for picketing NFL stars. Couple that with encouraging reviews, and ABC was happy with the show. There would be no more on-air tinkering with the series for at least seven years as ratings remained strong and the series became a recurring top 15 (sometimes top 10) hit.

The Gifford-Dierdorf-Michaels team now was a fixture for the series, a credit to the men's talent. But in the process, the trio found themselves compared to the Cosell-Meredith-Gifford combo and inevitably came up lacking. Contrasting that with their popularity, the three men had to deal with the overall impression that while they were good, they were not as great as their predecessors.

Even an advertising promotional section in *Sports Illustrated* in 1989 acknowledged this belief obliquely. "*MNF* still is an important part of the television landscape, even though it doesn't attract the attention and provoke the controversy that it did in, say, 1981, when its average rating was 21.2," the copy read.

In his 1993 autobiography *The Whole Ten Yards*, Gifford admitted that people still wanted to hear about Don and Howard from him, even though it had been a decade since all three of them worked together. "I knew it was difficult for Al and Dan in the beginning, because the early years of the show haunted them," he wrote.

Eventually, though, viewers began to tolerate the crew, if not fully embrace them the way they did with Cosell-Meredith-Gifford. If their commentaries weren't as memorable or able to generate much buzz the day after a game, neither were they too offensive or stupid either. Considering what ABC had been through with *Monday Night Football* prior to Gifford-Dierdorf-Michaels, that was fine with them.

Hello, Dierdorf

The third piece of *Monday Night Football* from 1987 to 1997 was Dan Dierdorf, a 38-year-old, 6-foot-3, 290-pound former offensive lineman for the St. Louis Cardinals. Ironically, the first *Monday Night Football* game he played in 1971 also was the first one Frank Gifford covered.

Raised in Canton, Ohio, Dierdorf went pro in 1971 with the Cardinals after leaving the University of Michigan. He had been an All-American player there but also was a mediocre student majoring in history. He played there 13 years and became an All-Pro player six times, but when he dislocated his right knee against the New York Giants in 1979, his glory days began to wind down.

Dierdorf made his initial foray into broadcasting by co-hosting a Saturday afternoon radio call-in show in St. Louis with Cardinals quarterback Jim Hart in 1974. (The two men also partnered in owning four restaurants in St. Louis by the time Dierdorf joined *Monday Night Football.*) Ten years later, after retiring from pro football, he began doing commentary for college and pro games on St. Louis radio. The following year, CBS found itself without a play-by-play man for its NFL game with the unexpected death of Frank Glieber. Even though Dierdorf had only done radio commentary, the switch to TV and coverage of game activity worked fine for him in 1985.

The next year, CBS put Dierdorf back into being a game analyst on its "second team" along with Dick Stockton (the lead team was John Madden and Pat Summerall). Dierdorf also became a sports director and sports reporter for a St. Louis TV station that year. Amid this increasing popularity, ABC Sports executives learned that Dierdorf had not signed a contract to work with CBS beyond the two years he had been there, as he felt it would not pay him what he deserved. At first they offered him a spot doing college football, which disinterested him, then they came back with *Monday Night Football.* Dierdorf bought it eagerly.

The beefy, mustachioed Dierdorf signed a contract to make $600,000 annually, $185,000 more than he made as NFL analyst at CBS. It also was $200,000 less than what ABC had been playing the previous number 3 guy on *Monday Night Football*, Joe Namath. Both sides were happy with what they were getting.

When Dierdorf debuted on *Monday Night Football* on September 14, 1987, critics praised his contributions to the show, and most took some swipes at fellow commentator Gifford. The comments of William Taaffe of *Sports Illustrated* were typical. "By joining the rapidly slipping Gifford, who has become a chatterbox and an apologist for the players, as an analyst for the show, Dierdorf is boarding a leaking boat. Although ABC Sports president Dennis Swanson says that Dierdorf was not hired because of any dissatisfaction with *MNF*, his addition is, in effect, a slap at Gifford."

Dierdorf addressed the situation with Taaffe. "I think Frank feels victimized. He hasn't aired this to me, but I think he'd still rather be doing play-by-play. But Frank has nothing to fear from me ... Let's face it. I've been hired to make Al look good, I've been hired to make Frank look good."

He indeed did that task and did it well. Still, there was a certain precarious post Dierdorf held in relation to Michaels and Gifford, both of whom had been with ABC many times longer than his tenure with the network and covered more sports for it. Thus, they faced less pressure for losing a spot on *Monday Night Football* than did Dierdorf. This was borne out when there was a move in 1994 to replace Dierdorf with John Madden when CBS lost the rights to its Sunday afternoon NFL games to the Fox network.

Madden had been doing commentary for NFL games on CBS since 1979 after retiring as coach of the Oakland Raiders. There, Madden made his presence known as an intense, yelling, perspiring, big-boned hulk pacing on the sidelines to inspire his team, which appeared on *Monday Night Football* 13 times under Madden's leadership. At CBS, he became known for diagramming plays on screen thanks to a device called a Telestrator, a video graphics machine that allowed him to "draw" electronically lines, circles, squiggles and anything else he felt onto the monitor to illustrate certain plays. He explained those diagrams with humor and basic language, making him a most engaging presence. He soon became the top color man on CBS, paired with Pat Summerall in the 1980s. The network did have to make one unusual concession for him, however — Madden was afraid of flying following a panic attack he had flying home from a Thanksgiving game in Tampa in 1979, and thereafter he only used land transportation to get to game venues.

Roone Arledge had tried to get Madden onto *Monday Night Football* as early as 1985, but Madden was under contract to CBS the first time and then wanted too much money in a second negotiation. Then in 1994, with the NFL switching to Fox, ABC executives believed that their network's higher prestige than that still struggling fourth network and the chance to become a nighttime star would sway Madden to their corner.

However, Madden decided to go with Fox as well, so Dierdorf stayed on the show. Dierdorf said he held no grudge for ABC's publicized effort to recruit Madden in his place. He went on to have perhaps his most memorable quote that season. On October 17, 1994, with the Denver Broncos having a 28–24 lead over the San Francisco 49ers, the latter's quarterback, Joe Montana, led his team to a victory with eight seconds left with a dramatic touchdown pass. "Lord, you can take me now, I've seen it all!" exclaimed Dierdorf in delight.

Still, it had to have been damaging to Dierdorf's ego to realize that despite all his years of fine reviews and solid ratings, ABC considered him an expendable part of the *Monday Night Football* picture.

Kamm Is Super Bowled Over

The future of Dierdorf on the show back in 1987 was of less concern to *Monday Night Football* than its upcoming second broadcast of a Super Bowl in early 1988, three years after its first time on the network. Always the biggest audience grabber for American television every year, the Super Bowl was the crown jewel in sports that only seemed to get bigger hoopla surrounding it every year. ABC was all too willing to hype what it had.

To make a pitch for viewers to watch Super Bowl XXII, Frank Gifford wrote an article for *Popular Mechanics* crowing about how much gadgetry would be in play when the *Monday Night Football* crew took their shot at it. There would be 20 cameras, including some on motion picture cranes; 10 tape machines for replays (including "Super Slo Mo," which *Monday Night Football* added in 1987); and two parabolic microphones to record sounds from the sidelines (usually just one was in use).

Additionally, Dierdorf would use a Telestrator. Yes, it was the same device Madden had employed on CBS, but the article portrayed it as some sort of breakthrough for broadcasting at the time. Well, it was for *Monday Night Football* at least.

The emphasis on gadgetry showed the increased pressure faced by new director Larry Kamm regarding his handling of the series. Though his shots were not a disaster, they were not seen as innovative either. Also in 1987, Kamm endured embarrassment when he managed to miss the winner crossing the finish line during ABC's coverage of the New York City marathon. Adding to that, new producer Ken Wolfe also was unimpressed by Kamm. The director needed to redeem himself soon in the face of these obstacles.

Sadly for all concerned at *Monday Night Football*, the 1988 Super Bowl was a super flop for ABC. The network scored a 41.9 rating for the event — the highest rated broadcast of the year, yes, but the lowest score for a Super Bowl since Super Bowl VIII on CBS on January 13, 1974, which received a 41.6. For a show known for spicing entertainment into its sports coverage, the lack of appeal of the Super Bowl hurt badly.

On the heels of that disaster, Larry Kamm received his dismissal from the series, though he continued to work at ABC Sports on other events, including NCAA football. Incredibly, despite all the notoriety surrounding the series, at the awards ceremony for sports Emmys on July 13, 1988, *Monday Night Football* won in the category of Outstanding Live Sports Series. As part of the production team, Kamm won a statuette for his maligned directorial work.

Kamm stayed with ABC for more than 36 years and also was the coordinating director for Turner Sports from 1995 to 2000. He held the same title for the Yankees Entertainment and Sports (YES) Network in 2003, the same year he directed the special *A Wedding Story* for the Learning Channel. He died on February 13, 2004, of lung cancer at age 64.

Replacing Kamm was Craig Janoff, another veteran ABC director who worked alongside Kamm in the 1980 Winter Olympics and on *ABC's Wide World of Sports*, winning his first Emmy on the latter in 1982, and ironically with his future *Monday Night Football* producer Ken Wolfe around the same time in their Emmy-nominated presentation of the New York City marathon. Perhaps because the Gifford-Dierdorf-Michaels lineup now was in place solidly as well as most changeover off the air, Janoff was able to guide the show more steadily than Kamm. He would remain its director for more than a decade.

Lead-In/Lead-Out Blues

While the directors changed for *Monday Night Football*, there was relatively good news for Capital Cities about what it slotted in the problematic hour before the program (or after, for West Coast viewers and beyond). The action adventure series *MacGyver* starring Richard Dean Anderson did respectable enough business when switched to Mondays from 8 to 9 P.M. Eastern at the start of its second season in the fall of 1986 that ABC kept it there through December 1991, apart from moves during the summer. It was no ratings blockbuster by any means (the sitcom *Alf* on NBC outrated it most of the 1980s, and in 1991 competition from the sitcoms *The Fresh Prince of Bel Air* on NBC and *Evening Shade* on CBS forced it out of the period), but it did outdraw most of the fare on CBS in the 1980s, and that was well enough for ABC.

But after *MacGyver* departed, the hour reverted to being a nightmare for ABC to program each fall. They tried *The Young Indiana Jones Chronicles* in 1992, a failed effort to exploit the titular 1980s movie character by illustrating his days as a juvenile. Then came *Day One* in 1993, a failed newsmagazine that like *The Young Indiana Jones Chronicles* had run unsuccessfully in another time slot during the spring before going to Mondays.

Next up in 1994, ABC tried a more logically themed intro by moving its five-and-a-half-year-old hit sitcom *Coach* to start the 8–8:30 P.M. block. As its title suggested, it starred Craig T. Nelson (who 10 years earlier was in the same slot as lead of the flop drama *Call to Glory*) as a football coach, albeit a college one. The remaining half hour featured *Blue Skies*, a sitcom about two young men that had so little appeal ABC yanked it after seven weeks and replaced it with another episode of *Coach*. The back-to-back episodes failed to make much headway against the

CBS sitcoms *The Nanny* and *Dave's World*, not to mention Fox's soap opera *Melrose Place*, so *Coach* left to continue in another slot while ABC endeavored once again to try something else there.

Yet neither *The Marshal* (crime drama, 1995) nor *Dangerous Minds* (school drama, 1996) nor *Timecop* (sci-fi crime drama, 1997) attracted enough of an audience to last more than half a season on Mondays 8–9 P.M., frustrating programmers at ABC about what to try next in that stretch of TV time. The dilemma of trying to find a show that could strongly attract viewers on one half of the country before *Monday Night Football* and the other half after the show ended appeared to be an insurmountable obstacle.

An easier decision for ABC in the same period revolved around what to program at the end of each football season for the 9–11 P.M. Eastern/Pacific slot. The network kept the policy it had since 1982 of replacing *Monday Night Football* with movies, at first until May or June to make room for baseball, then until August after losing baseball in 1989. This rule continued virtually uninterrupted through 1999, even though movie ratings eroded considerably.

For example, after peaking at number 12 in the 1984–85 season, ABC's Monday movies had a drastic drop-off in audiences compared to *Monday Night Football*, unable to get a higher average than number 25 in 1991–92 (whereas *Monday Night Football* averaged number 12 that season). NBC's Monday movies regularly beat it, sometimes by huge margins (it peaked at number 14 for the 1995–96 season), so it seemed rather shocking when NBC decided to drop it at the end of the 1996–97 season, after having been on almost unendingly since September 1998. In fact, the NBC Monday movie ranked an impressive number 23 for 1996–97 when the network canned it.

Still, ABC regarded the Monday film series as one of its lesser problems on the schedule. The idea of a series being a regular midseason replacement had not taken hold among programmers as it would in the early 21st century, and with the network being a comfortable first or second place in the ratings overall in the late 1980s and early 1990s, it could stand a relatively weak performer in place of spending more money on at least two shows to fill the slot.

The Up and Downs of the Early 1990s

There were some notable alterations to the *Monday Night Football* telecast once new director Craig Janoff and producer Ken Wolfe had time to do some planning. The most recognized one occurred in the show's opening. It now had a theme song with words that put an already energetic show onto a higher plane.

"Are You Ready for Some Football?" grew out of Hank Williams Jr.'s 1984 top 10 country hit "All My Rowdy Friends Are Coming Over Tonight." With lyrics reworked weekly to reflect that week's contest and Williams, who was a *Monday Night Football* fan, singing them amid a staged raucous bar crowd, "Are You Ready for Some Football?" became an easily identifiable element of the series.

Wolfe also re-emphasized the importance of celebrity guests visiting the booth, something that had been decreased during the transitional mid–1980s years while the series attempted to establish its own continuing lineup. The best of these arguably was when David Letterman made a rare appearance outside his nightly talk show, which competed sometimes for audience attention against *Monday Night Football* every fall. Letterman cracked up Dan Dierdorf by saying of the announcer, "Every Monday night, when he gets ready to do one of these telecasts, he still wears a cup!"

There was also more variability in the halftime shows, with more emphasis on interviews and less on weekend game highlights. A standout talk that made headlines occurred on December 14, 1992, when Al Michaels interviewed player Marcus Allen on tape. Discussing his stormy relationship with his boss, owner Al Davis of the Los Angeles Raiders, Allen pulled no punches by stating flatly, "He told me he was going to get me. I think he's tried to ruin the latter part of my career, tried to devalue me. I think he's tried to stop me from the Hall of Fame."

There also was a big explosion in memorabilia for the series that made earlier efforts looked restrained. Now viewers could get *Monday Night Football* CD-ROM games to play on their computers, along with changing shirts, plastic cups, phone cards, jackets, backpacks — you name it, if you could sell a product, chances are the show's name would be on it for sale from ABC or affiliated partners.

While these activities added to the appeal of the series, there was some concern in the early years about a dip in ratings. In 1990 Mark Candler reported in *Business Week* that *Monday Night Football* lost 1.7 million households from a year earlier, and the lower ratings forced ABC to discount up to half the network's standard ad rates for the show in order to get reluctant companies to participate. Thus, the normal $250,000 charge for a 30-second commercial on *Monday Night Football* became just $125,000 for some lucky last-minute advertisers.

Luckily, there would be no more falloff in audience for *Monday Night Football* the next few years — its 16.6 rating from the 1990–91 season remained virtually and remarkably the same the next three years, and it actually increased a full point in the 1994–95 season. Coincidentally or not, the show added its first new regular in seven years to the mix.

The First Sideline Reporter and His Swann Song

In 1994, as *Monday Night Football* celebrated its 25th year on the air, the series spiced up its coverage by adding a sideline reporter as a regular. Selected to do the job was another NFL veteran, Lynn Swann.

Born on March 7, 1952, in Alcoa, Tennessee, Lynn Swann was an All-American at the University of Southern California before going pro as a wide receiver for the Pittsburgh Steelers from 1974 to 1982. He became a national star during Super Bowl X on January 18, 1976, when he received the game's MVP award for making four catches for 161 yards of offense and helping the Steelers win that championship. He also was a three-time Pro Bowl selection.

After retiring from playing, Swann directed his energies to being an announcer for ABC Sports, where he had done sports reporting as early as 1976 during his offseason. He served as analyst for ABC's *USFL Football* from 1983 to 1985 alongside Keith Jackson and also indulged a little in the entertainment side of TV, hosting a NBC daytime revival of *To Tell the Truth* for three months in 1990–91.

The addition of Swann to the roster as the first sideline reporter on *Monday Night Football* would add variety to the proceedings during the game, but also quietly address the lack of a black announcer on the show. But Swann's reports were not seen as particularly distinguished either.

Still, with the series' ratings remaining solid (17.1 in 1995–96 versus 17.7 in 1994–95, which nonetheless kept *Monday Night Football* at number 5 each season), there was no talk about replacing Swann in this period. Instead, the word around ABC centered on its new owner.

The Walt Disney Company, creator of one of the biggest entertainment enterprises in history in movies and theme parks, had bought the network.

ABC Becomes the House of the Mouse

If longtime ABC employees thought Capital Cities was a stingy owner when it arrived in 1986, they had yet to acquaint themselves with what was known in Hollywood as the Ebenezer Scrooge of movie studios. Under the leadership of former ABC executive Michael Eisner since the mid–1980s, Disney prided itself on making money for the company above all else. That included but was not limited to driving hard bargains for rights and fees in contracts for creative personnel to get the maximum bottom line. The approach did get results by bringing Disney back to the top of the film industry after laying dormant for much of the 1970s and 1980s, but it left plenty of residual ill will.

Composer Randy Newman encompassed the general feeling Hollywood had about Disney when discussing his scoring the motion pictures *Toy Story II* (1995) and *James and the Giant Peach* (1996) for the company at the Film and Music Composer's Conference in Los Angeles in February 1997: "Working on the two animations for Disney was my best experience. They are hands-on people, and they actually know music. But they are the scariest people to deal with since Torquemada."

Under Disney management, taking effect in the spring of 1996, ABC employees would be subject to the same intense scrutiny used in budgeting movies. "The House of the Mouse," so nicknamed because the company grew under the success of the Mickey Mouse character when creator and founder Walt Disney unveiled the character in 1928, was ready to use its hands-on approach to fix everything at ABC to save money, even if it did not need mending. One of the first targets was one of its biggest expenditures — sports, naturally.

Swanson's Swan Song

To save money quickly, Disney management decided to merge most operations of ABC Sports with ESPN, since it now owned both properties. Dennis Swanson, who had been president of ABC Sports since Capital Cities took over ABC in 1986, and had been with Capital Cities since 1976, received the offer of being a "co-president" of the new division along with ESPN President Steve Bornstein. Judging it to be a demotion, Swanson took up a resignation package offer from Disney and left ABC.

"These people paid $19 billion to buy Cap Cities/ABC, and they're making changes. That's life in our business," Swanson told Rudy Martzke philosophically in *USA Today*. Though his resignation became known on April 11, 1996, he did not officially "retire" from ABC Sports until May 4.

A month after his departure, Swanson's former rival, NBC Sports President Dick Ebersol, recommended appointing Swanson to be president and general manager of WNBC, NBC's New York affiliate. Swanson loved the idea and began at his new post June 26. "The most fun I've ever had was in the station business," he told *The New York Times* on his first day of work.

Swanson stayed with WNBC until being appointed as chief operating officer for the Viacom Stations Group (including CBS affiliates) in 2002. In October 2005 he left that post for a similar one at the Fox Television Stations Group.

That Swanson pursued management over involvement in sports after his tenure with ABC is quite telling. Indeed, when one looks back at what Swanson did at ABC, he seemed better fit as a bureaucratic station manager rather than a visionary leader. Under Swanson, cost cutting took priority over innovation at ABC Sports, with Fox taking the lead over ABC in pioneering such flourishes as adding an onscreen corner box giving the score and time remaining throughout each pro football game it aired.

Incredibly, one of his self-proclaimed proudest achievements was to get the Olympics committee to start alternating the winter and summer Olympics every two years. Fine enough, but the fees of these "separated" events were too high for ABC to win even one bid anytime he was the network's sports president. Compare that with his predecessor, Roone Arledge, who had nearly all the Olympics shown on ABC during his tenure from the mid–1960s through mid–1980s, and Swanson's contribution to TV sports in this field looks small indeed.

Other missteps by Swanson included losing the rights for baseball and the NBA. True, he strengthened ties the network had with college and pro football, but if he had not done so, there probably would have been no sports at ABC at all. In addition, during his watch, ratings for two sports programs created in the 1960s, *ABC's Wide World of Sports* and *Pro Bowlers Tour*, fell drastically, and both were cancelled not long after he left ABC.

In short, there are very few highlights to spotlight for Swanson, unless you consider he made his division profitable and well-managed. Not surprisingly, while some people still wax rhapsodically over the "Arledge era" at the sports department, few do the same for the Swanson administration.

Replacing the 58-year-old Swanson was 33-year-old Steve Bornstein, an employee with ESPN since 1981, two years after the cable channel began operating. He soon learned that the ennui settling on one of the division's top properties, *Monday Night Football*, would be a chief concern.

Are You Ready for Some Changes?

Because *Monday Night Football* had been doing so well for ABC by the time Disney arrived (it was the network's highest-rated program in 1995–96), there was less momentum for management to make sudden alterations. Also, to be fair, it was not only the new ABC management who clamored for some kind of change at *Monday Night Football*. Some critics felt that after nearly a decade of working together, the creative unit now was stale in its presentation, or perhaps even condescending.

In an article for the Canadian magazine *Saturday Night* in late 1996, writer Mark Kingwell decried the "aggressive jingoism" he viewed in the series' opening animated segment with thundering fighter planes zooming overhead and passing by the Statue of Liberty, prompting the statue to raise her arms and signal a touchdown. Kingwell also derided the analysis of Frank Gifford ("He is consummately enviable to the sort of guy whose annual highlight is the arrival of the *Sports Illustrated* swimsuit issue") and found the team's banter uninspiring.

Kingwell concluded that "*Monday Night Football* is a world where the civil rights movement, gay radicalism and postmodern feminism never happened.... It's Monday nights, it's back to the simple certainties — and certain simpleminded-ness — of Fifties America."

It wasn't this cultural critique that led ABC to change *Monday Night Football* the next season. Instead, it was what gets the attention of any executive — a downturn in the audience. While still in the top 10 in the 1996–97 season, the show lost around a million viewers to finish with a rating of 16.0. It was still ABC's top show, though, so there remained some reluctance to freshen its personnel or presentation with that in mind.

Even so, by December 1996, *Boston Herald* columnist Jim Baker complained that the *Monday Night Football* announcers refused to do interviews about the new leadership at ABC and the show's dip in its ratings. In the wake of those events, at least one columnist took that as an opportunity to pounce on the series the next year.

"When was the last time recently that anyone stood around the water cooler discussing what *Monday Night Football* announcers Al Michaels, Dan Dierdorf and Frank Gifford said the night before?" fumed Dan McGraw in a *U.S. News and World Report* article titled "Send Michaels, Gifford and Dierdorf Packing."

McGraw noted how *Monday Night Football* ratings were down 10 percent in 1997 from 1996, and he used that fallout to justify his complaints. In particular, he groused about how Gifford continued to mispronounce names after a quarter century with the series, yet ABC management kept saying Gifford could stay as long as he wanted.

"The current crew has become lazy and comfortable, their play-by-play a weekly dose of warmed-over sports clichés," McGraw nagged. To remedy the situation, he half-seriously proposed ABC use guest hosts to announce games instead, such as comedian Chris Rock.

ABC didn't take that advice, but McGraw was right about the ratings going down, though *Monday Night Football* still was a top 10 show and ABC's highest-rated one. Adding to the misgivings of management was bad publicity for the show's star announcer.

On May 13, 1997, Frank Gifford was entrapped into a rendezvous with a blonde named Suzen Johnson set up by *The Globe* tabloid. The publication then reported all the details. For a man who had shown up occasionally on his wife's daytime series (*Live with Regis and Kathie Lee*), one where his wife Kathie Lee constantly updated the public on the activities of her husband and their son Cody (born in 1990) and daughter Cassidy (born in 1993), it was a humiliating transgression. Gifford apologized in public for the incident, and Kathie Lee stood beside him, but the damage to his reputation made him much more expendable now to the Disney management at ABC.

It happened at the worst possible time for Gifford too, as ABC faced new contract negotiations for the next few years of rights to NFL Monday night games. As expected, costs kept rising, so to pay for them, expenses would have to be removed from other areas. What was a better target to remove than an aging sportscaster caught in controversy? True, Gifford had a contract through 1999, but that did not mean ABC had to employ him on *Monday Night Football* in the future.

New Rights, New Expenses

During the 1998 TV rights negotiations, the NFL had the networks where they wanted them. CBS especially was desperate to gain pro football back after having lost it in 1994 to Fox. That event prompted eight of its affiliates to defect to that network and pumped Fox up into being a major network contender along with CBS, NBC and ABC.

In the end, CBS paid for a package that costs twice as much as what NBC had been paying, yet the network did not flinch, believing the expense would be offset by enthusiasm from its affiliates and an increase in morale among network staff. ("You can't describe how unpleasant it was for employees of CBS," the network's sport president Sean McManus told Mark Hyman of *Business Week* in recalling the years without NFL football.) CBS was happy with what it got, but ABC was not.

ABC's $5.5 billion deal with the NFL in 1998 required the network to pay $550 million every year for rights for the show. With the additional costs of setting up the show in a different city every week, plus budgeting for veteran talent, the bean counters at the network soon realized it was not possible for the show to finish even, much less make a profit, unless there were some major changes in 1998.

One of them was simple: Move the show's starting time back an hour, thus ending the nightmare of having to find another new show or two to fill the 8–9 P.M. slot on the East Coast and making it air in prime time in all regions of the United States, thus allowing for potentially higher ad rates. The trouble with that, of course, was the old argument given for placing it to start at 9 P.M. originally — viewers on the West Coast would have to watch the show starting at 5 P.M. versus 6 P.M. now, given the three-hour delay. Many of those West Coast viewers did not get to leave work until 5 P.M., much less get home.

So to compensate for that change in time, the series would use a 20-minute pre-game segment to allow time for the audience west of the Rockies to get home to watch the opening kickoff. To promote "synergy," the segment would take place at the ESPN Sports Zone bar in Baltimore. To host it would be Chris Berman, upped from the halftime highlights show he had been doing earlier and would continue to do along with the pregame show.

Another was the addition of Boomer Esiason, a former quarterback who was named the NFL MVP in 1988. Born Norman Julius Esiason on April 17, 1961, in West Islip, New York, he received the nickname "Boomer" before he was even born when a friend of his father noticed how he kicked around his mother's womb.

Boomer was similarly feisty as an adult, reportedly being upset at being picked 38th in the NFL draft after having played quarterback successfully for the University of Maryland. Nevertheless, the 6-foot-5, 240-pound lefthander held a successful tenure as the Cincinnati Bengals' quarterback from 1984 to 1992. He played in four Pro Bowls and led the Bengals to Super Bowl XXIII on January 22, 1989, where the team lost a heartbreaker to the San Francisco 49ers 20–16. He went to the New York Jets from 1993 to 1995 and then the Arizona Cardinals in 1996 before returning to the Bengals for his last year in action.

Esiason had no national announcing experience prior to *Monday Night Football*, but given his familiar name, handsome looks and relative youth, he was considered a draw in appealing to younger viewers and women. ABC actually wanted John Madden as its third analyst and offered him, for at least a fourth time, a chance to join the booth, but Madden wanted a deadline for making the deal out of concern for his contract with Fox and ABC refused to accommodate him. Producer Ken Wolfe suggested using Esiason in his place, and so the latter got the job instead.

And where was Frank Gifford in all this? Well, ABC had designated him to be a special pregame contributor starting in the fall of 1998 as an effort to get Madden in his place, then kept him in that post when they went with Esiason instead. Gifford's contract with ABC ran out in June 1999, so the network was telling him he could serve out his deal, but only under the limited condition for the one remaining season in 1998. Gifford would still be part of *Monday Night Football*, only now a very minor one.

Visser Is Here

Also happening in 1998, Lesley Visser replaced Lynn Swann as sideline reporter on the show, the latter leaving after three years in the job. The 44-year-old was a veteran sportscaster, having started her network TV duties doing features for CBS back in 1980. She began as an intern sportswriter with *The Boston Globe* in 1974 after graduating from Boston College, working there for 10 years and covering the New England Patriots for eight of those years starting in 1976.

In January 1983, Visser married her fellow sportscaster Dick Stockton, 10 years her senior and employed with NBC at the time (he later went to CBS). She started working for CBS Sports in 1984 and became a regular member of *The NFL Today* pregame show on CBS in 1988, replacing Irv Cross as a studio host. She moved to ABC in the 1990s as a sideline reporter for the NCAA football games before moving over to the NFL.

On *Monday Night Football*, Visser showed up in places beyond the sidelines, such as in the stands with the fans or in the owners' boxes in the stadium, to get more of the story of the game. She found one group was easier for her not to use live on the air on her job. "There are a lot of times, to be honest, when it's better to paraphrase what the coach says rather than talking to him on the air.... There are going to be coaches too who won't want to talk, which is fine," she told John Walters in *Sports Illustrated*. She saw her ultimate goal as to explain the situation on the field better than what was known in the booth.

She was grateful that in 1999 the NFL loosened its restrictions and let her interview coaches going off and coming onto the field at halftime (the NCAA already allowed that). Little did she realize that a year later, ABC would not have her do anything for *Monday Night Football* at all — or Boomer Esiason either.

Bye Bye Frank, Hello Chaos

The changeovers in personnel in 1998 signaled the beginning of the most disorderly turnovers of talent on the series ever. Over the next four years, *Monday Night Football* would have a bad repeat of what happened around the time of the Capital Cities takeover in the mid 1980s — going from three men in the booth to two, then back to three, having new personnel show up nearly every season, including producers and directors, and becoming the focal point of negative criticism among the sports media.

As Yogi Berra once put it, "It's déjà vu all over again." Except now, the first years of *Monday Night Football* under Disney would be even messier on screen than those under Capital Cities, because the show was costing ABC much more than ever in rights. As a result, network executives wanted to get profitability from the series in the worst way possible.

With the questionable moves they made in the late 1990s and early 2000s, relying on inexperienced regulars and flashy coverage over substance, they at least got the "worst way" part right.

10

Mouse Attack (1998–2002)

Al Michaels and Dan Dierdorf could not believe their eyes and ears.

It was the 1998 fall preseason, and they were watching the start of Sunday night football on ABC's sister corporate cable network ESPN. The odd thing was, the show shared the same theme music as *Monday Night Football*. And the graphics too.

The men always had believed the phrase "Are you ready for some football?" was the inviolable property of their own show, along with its opening accoutrements. Now they found out it would be shared with a different series on a different network, even though the personnel barely overlapped for both shows.

This new "branding" could have been much worse. Some ABC executives wanted to rename the network's 28-year-old property *ESPN Presents Monday Night Football* to exploit the supposed popularity of the cable network. The notion appalled longtime staff members, who saw it as the ultimate effort to make ABC Sports now be subservient to ESPN. For their side, the newer ABC executives thought the title would exploit the "synergy" between the companies, but anticipating a negative backlash in publicity, they dropped the proposal.

Even having done that, it was obvious to anyone familiar with the production that the new bosses at ABC did not get the appeal and uniqueness of *Monday Night Football*. Indeed, when it came to the show the next few years, ABC leaders' approach was like that of the man in the joke where a person asked him whether ignorance or apathy was the greater problem in the world. "I don't know and I don't care," the man shot back.

Neither, it seems, did the brass at ABC.

A "Blast" on Monday Night

"ABC, why have you betrayed us?" That sentence closed a review by Susan Slusser in *The San Francisco Chronicle* of the revamped *Monday Night Football* debut on September 7, 1998. Her comments were one of a slew of negative reviews the program faced, with most criticism focused on the annoying new opening segment and the overkill of cross-promotional activities.

Concerning the opening segment, when *Monday Night Football* moved up an hour to start at 8 P.M. Eastern Time, producers accommodated the needs of West Coast viewers by actually beginning the game at 8:20 P.M. Eastern/5:20 P.M. Pacific Time. To fill up the 20 minutes, the show inaugurated "Monday Night Blast," wherein ESPN sportscaster Chris Berman hosted festivities from the recently opened ESPN Sports Zone bar in Baltimore. The rowdy crowd cheered him along while Berman introduced a few taped interview features, as did a displaced Frank Gifford beside him, stuffed into a glass booth at the bar that made him resemble an animal at a zoo.

The intention of "Monday Night Blast" was to rev up audience enthusiasm for the upcoming game, but instead it dampened that impression, with the frenzy behind the announcers at the bar forced and annoying. With most patrons drunk or at least buzzing from alcohol and boisterous beyond belief, they detracted from whatever Berman or Gifford said before leading into the pregame features. Worse than that, the interviews were none too probing. Berman said one regular feature, "Outside the Zone," would provide a "little-known aspect of a player's life." So who the sources of these supposed scoops? Well, on the first show it was Denver quarterback John Elway's high school coach, and on the second the mother of San Francisco quarterback Steve Young gave the 411. These sources were so pedestrian even high school reporters could have thought up interviewing them. To pawn them off as some kind of exclusive was pathetic and indicative of the low level of presentation provided by "Monday Night Blast."

Not surprisingly, critics blasted back this pregame show. Leonard Shapiro of *The Washington Post* flat out called "Monday Night Blast" "the worst NFL pregame show in television." Norman Chad of *The Boston Globe* compared its atmosphere to a fraternity mixer and said this of Berman: "He always has been a cheap lounge act. With 'Monday Night Blast,' he finally gets the live, lathered audience he deserves."

Richard Sandomir of *The New York Times* was more forgiving than his colleagues about it later in the season, but even he had to admit that its third outing was "a strange amalgam of football chat from the announcers; noise from an ESPN Zoneful of masticating patrons; a feel-good feature (Cowboys quarterback Jason Garrett and his father, Jim) introduced by Gifford from a quiz show's soundproof booth and a feature with an ABC star (*Spin City*'s Michael J. Fox at the Giants' camp)."

Fox showed up as one of seemingly innumerable plugs on the show for ABC/ESPN/Disney-related products. *Monday Night Football* suffered through this in the past, of course, but now the efforts were downright embarrassing, to the point where a cameo included Mrs. Munger, an animated teacher character seen between programs on ABC's Saturday morning cartoon lineup. She showed up on the first two shows (September 7 and 14, 1998), to virtually everyone's bewilderment, along with promos for other new ABC shows, Disney movies, ESPN sports events, and on, and on, and on....

"The bottom line is that Disney, in creating this new pregame show (complete with a heavy commercial load), has produced a 20-minute segment more suited to its amusement parks than television," concluded a disgusted Dusty Saunders of *The Rocky Mountain News*. Nevertheless, "Monday Night Blast" remained the pregame show for *Monday Night Football* the rest of the season.

Boomer Thumbs Up, But Ratings Down

Yet while bombarded with brickbats for its pregame show, *Monday Night Football* did receive kudos overall for having Boomer Esiason take Gifford's place in the booth. Many observers were just were grateful ABC no longer used Gifford as a color man; still, most had positive words for the ex-player's talent on air and his interplay with veterans Dan Dierdorf and Al Michaels.

"Esiason's presence is a welcome relief from the banalities offered up for so many years by Gifford," wrote Leonard Shapiro of *The Washington Post*. "He also has improved dramatically from his early starts in the preseason when he talked in volumes, not sound bites. His quarterback's perspective has been illuminating, and his self-deprecating approach so far has been refreshing, complete with more anecdotes in the first two weeks of the season than Gifford offered in a career."

The only problem was that ratings did not bear out Esiason as having a positive impact on *Monday Night Football*. After the first three games, *Monday Night Football* averaged a rating of 13.6, down 11 percent from the 15.0 average rating for 1997. Oddly, even though they now had to catch the games earlier than anyone else, West Coast viewers tuned out the show the least among time zones — its audience went down only 4 percent from 1997. Even Esiason hosting the Miss America beauty pageant in September did not translate into more eyeballs giving *Monday Night Football* a look.

Pundits proffered a variety of explanations for the decline. Naturally, the 8 P.M. start was a prime culprit often cited, as it threw off the rhythm viewers had grown accustomed to in viewing *Monday Night Football*. Some held it was due to the increasing success of the competing *Ally McBeal* on Fox and *Everybody Loves Raymond* on CBS, both top 25 hits this season. As before, an ABC official blamed the drop-off mainly on dull contests.

"It's early and we've had a couple of games that weren't competitive," Brian McAndrews, executive vice president of ABC Sports, told Richard Sandomir of *The New York Times* (actually, only two of the three games were blowouts — the September 7 season opener between Denver and New England ended at 27–21 in favor of the Broncos). "We're winning our time period, but we'd be happier if we were up."

There was no indication that anyone at ABC feared making Gifford leave the booth would be a detriment to the ratings. Gifford himself told Michael Hiestand of *USA Today* that the demotion did not disturb him, as he only now had to do the pregame show in Baltimore and could catch a plane and be home to Connecticut within two hours, leaving him more time to be with his family while still getting national TV exposure. "If I got bothered, I wouldn't have lasted through 27 years and some of the basic insanity that went with it," he told Hiestand of his *Monday Night Football* experience over the years.

Gifford did have one celebrity who held out for him, however. Winding up a guest shot on *Live with Regis and Kathie Lee* in October 1998, Bill Cosby whispered to hostess Kathie Lee Gifford this special message for her husband: "Give my best to Frank, and tell him I'm so happy that they're not doing that well … because Frank was the best." Unknown to Cosby, his mike was open and his words went out on the air. When *New York Daily News* gossip columnist Mitchell Fink asked Ms. Gifford about Cosby's statement, she said she valued the comedian's comments and added that he was not upset about it being known, as he "would never say anything privately that he couldn't say publicly."

Coincidentally, another open microphone incident affected *Monday Night Football* itself two months later. On December 28, 1998, during preparations for the halftime interview on the last game of the season, Dierdorf asked Michaels what questions the latter would ask Buffalo Bills quarterback Doug Flutie, who attended Boston College. "Are you going to tell him how you're sick of all this B.C. [Boston College] stuff?" Dierdorf wondered. "No shit," Michaels answered, thinking that their mikes had been off during the exchange. Unfortunately for the men, they had not been so, forcing Michaels to apologize for the profanity afterward.

That happening was not as worrisome for the *Monday Night Football* crew as were the final overall ratings for the season. The series ended with an average 14.0 rating, down more than a million viewers from 1997, and its lowest rating ever. However, that gave *Monday Night Football* its highest seasonal finish ever, at number 4, because all network TV series went down significantly in the ratings from the previous season (the number 1 show of 1997–98, *Seinfeld*, drew a 21.7 versus the 17.8 garnered by the number 1 show of 1998–99, *ER*). That would have been cause for celebration, were it not for the fact that ABC had paid $550 million per season for the show, and with a 14.0 rating, the network could get nowhere near the advertising dollars it needed to cover the production costs. To top it off, pro wrestling shows on cable showed signs of making inroads with the 12- to 34-year-old male viewers that made up a considerable bulk of the *Monday Night Football* audience.

ABC leaders felt the show needed more changes if it were to be profitable. The first of them came in the booth.

Dierdorf and Gifford Are Out, and
We're Back to Our Old Time Slot

On February 4, 1999, Dan Dierdorf announced he would be leaving *Monday Night Football* after 12 years when he and ABC could not come to terms over renewing his $1.75 million-a-year contract. Actually, ABC Sports President Steve Bornstein had fired him a couple of days before the Pro Bowl, the last pigskin event ABC had to air that season.

"Sure, I'd like to continue, but ABC has decided to go in a different direction, but I'd be silly to sit around and complain about it," Dierdorf said. "It's been a heck of a ride. If anybody would have ever told me when I was a player that I'd be in the *Monday Night Football* booth, I never would have believed them."

The splitting was amicable, at least in public, with both sides wishing each other well. Dierdorf felt relief after having realized the increased scrutiny the show faced among the new ABC executives. He moved over to covering NFL games for CBS.

Ernest Hooper of the *St. Petersburg Times* felt it was appropriate for Dierdorf to part from *Monday Night Football* due to the new dynamics on the show when Esiason replaced Gifford as a co-analyst with Dierdorf.

"Gifford, who seldom had an enlightening thought in his latter years, left Dierdorf with a wide canvas to paint," wrote Hooper. "Gifford often just piled on to Dierdorf's better observations. Esiason was the opposite. He challenged Dierdorf constantly. Realizing he was getting exposed, Dierdorf was often defensive.

"The initial thought may have been that having Dierdorf and Esiason mix it up would have made for good television, but in the end it was annoying. Esiason has a new deal, and, although he had some rough spots, he showed potential."

Experts believed several ESPN sportscasters were under consideration to replace Dierdorf, such as Tom Jackson or Sterling Sharpe. Later came word that ABC was not going to replace Dierdorf but go solely with Esiason and Michaels in the booth. This struck at least one critic as a big misstep.

"As good as Esiason is in explaining what quarterbacks see and what choices they should make, he needs a different analytical voice to bounce off or argue with — or even sing with — to make the games more entertaining," wrote Alan Pergament in *The Buffalo News*. "At the very least, the decision to go to two men on Monday night is television blasphemy." Apparently Pergament forgot about the 1986 season with just Michaels and Gifford in the booth, as did ABC officials, who were repeating the mistakes of the past.

Speaking of Gifford, he received an official dismissal from ABC after Dierdorf's prior to his contract expiring in June 1999. Delivering the news to Gifford was Brian McAndrews, executive vice president of ABC Sports. McAndrews was so new in the position (he only started in it in March 1998 with virtually no other

TV sports experience on his résumé) that Gifford claimed he had never heard of the man before.

In early April, ABC also confirmed that *Monday Night Football* would return to starting at 9 P.M. Eastern Time in the fall of 1999 due to the drop in ratings in 1998. The show likewise would return to starting the game by 9:07 P.M., which defused "Monday Night Blast" from coming back on the show as well. (ABC replaced the 8–9 P.M. slot that fall with a separate edition of *20/20*—yes, the same newsmagazine Roone Arledge helped create more than two decades earlier.) It was one of the first of many decisions involving *Monday Night Football* made by a new leader of ABC Sports.

Katz in the Cradle

After just three years as president of ABC Sports, Steve Bornstein left his post in 1999 to become the new chairman of Disney's website go.com, an ill-fated venture meant to challenge Yahoo!, Google and other search engines as the top portal for visitors to use on the Internet. Replacing him effective March 25, 1999, was Howard Katz, formerly a production assistant with *Monday Night Football* starting in 1971 when he came out of college. He became president of Don Ohlmeyer's sports production company in 1983. When ESPN bought the company in 1993, Katz became executive vice president in charge of global and domestic operations there before his job at ABC.

Unlike his predecessor, Katz became the head of ABC Sports only and not ESPN as well under a new setup by Disney to promote each brand. Katz realized the glory surrounding ABC Sports had slipped considerably when Disney merged it with ESPN, and he planned to rectify the obstacle.

"It has got to get better," he told Richard Sandomir of *The New York Times*. "The perception of ABC Sports is not what it should be. There was a time when ESPN felt totally inferior to ABC. Now it's flipped."

His decision to go with just Esiason and Michaels was a shaky one to make. Having just seen his two longtime booth partners forced out of a job, Michaels naturally felt like he had to defend his turf should ABC decide to complete the hat trick and hand him his walking papers after the next season.

Moreover, the two men had very different working strategies on air. Michaels had the reputation of being a stickler for facts and demanding the right information from those around him. Esiason had a looser approach, preferring to go with his gut instinct. Thus, any rapport the duo had would be forced at best, and it showed.

Also plaguing the 1999–2000 season were plenty of blowouts that did not help the show. The capper for provoking changes within the series came with the season ender on January 3, 2000, when the San Francisco 49ers and the Atlanta Falcons, former great teams now reduced to facing off while each sported a lousy 4–11 record, battled to a snoring finish. To add insult to injury, the St. Louis Rams, which would win the Super Bowl later that month, never appeared on *Monday Night Football* in 1999–2000.

However, ABC did have the rights to that Super Bowl XXXIV, so Michaels and Esiason finally would get the chance to cover the Rams. The only problem was, by that time the two men barely spoke to each other off camera, and their hatred of each other came to surface by the fourth quarter, after Michaels became fed up with Esiason's predictions of plays that never happened and musings about his Cincinnati Bengals days (a recurring irritant for Michaels in the 1999 season). As the Tennessee Titans drove the field for a possible score, the two men argued strongly over whether the team needed to call a timeout to get on the board. The disagreement was so obvious that executive producer Howard Katz felt he had to take action, so he did.

Katz instructed producer Ken Wolfe to tell Esiason he was done for the day once the game ended and that since the game ran so late, there was no time left for a recap at the end. Yet Boomer noticed the same instructions did not go to Michaels, and to his dismay Michaels alone wrapped up the coverage of the Super Bowl while Boomer stormed out of the broadcast booth. Ironically, Wolfe, the man who encouraged hiring Esiason, would be the last one to talk to him during a game on ABC.

Given those circumstances, it may have been a pleasant surprise for ABC to see the series remain in the top 10 and lose only a few hundred thousand viewers to finish at number 7 for 1999–2000 with a 13.5 rating. But Katz knew budget-minded ABC officials did not care about that figure. They only knew that ratings needed to go up to attract advertisers big enough to cover the $150 million or so it cost the network every year to do the show, and a 13.5 rating would not cut it for them.

Most distressing of all, one survey found that 47 percent of young men watching cable or satellite-equipped TVs preferred watching the pro wrestling *Monday Night Raw* series on the USA network rather than *Monday Night Football*. If those viewers were leaving the latter series in that number, the show's future had nowhere to go but down if it did not alter course. And so it did.

"We've Got to Make It Special Again"

On March 9, 2000, ABC Sports President Howard Katz stunned the sports world by canning three key members of the *Monday Night Football* staff— Esiason after two years as announcer, Craig Janoff after 12 years as director and Ken Wolfe after 14 years as producer.

The only replacement Katz had ready at the time was his former boss, Don Ohlmeyer. Don returned as producer, a job he held with the series 24 years earlier, after Katz broached the idea to him in December 1999. Ohlmeyer, now 55, took the job only after Katz and ABC President Robert Iger agreed the newcomer would have complete freedom to reshape the show. That included hiring the new director, Drew Esocoff.

"We've got to make it special again," Katz said in announcing the changes. "It," of course, meant *Monday Night Football*.

Katz assigned no blame to the men he fired, including his beleaguered analyst. "Boomer did everything we asked him to do," he said. "He is a terrific person. I just think [the broadcast] could be better."

That statement had to shock Janoff and Wolfe, as both had received notes of congratulations from ABC President and CEO Michael Eisner for their efforts on Super Bowl XXXIV just two month earlier. Additionally, Wolfe had won several Emmys for his input on the series, while Janoff already won the 1997 Lifetime Achievement in Sports Direction Award from his peers on the Directors Guild of America.

"I've never worked with a better producer than Kenny or a better director than Craig," Al Michaels said in response to the announcement, while making no mention of Esiason. "This is very emotionally difficult for me."

Esiason later claimed that Michaels stifled him and wanted to be the sole star of *Monday Night Football*. He said while he tried to please his superiors, Michaels offered no help to him whatsoever, and in fact campaigned against him.

"I imagine Howard and Don Ohlmeyer spoke about me, and Ohlmeyer said, 'I couldn't work with him' or 'He's no good'— and I'm sure Al had something to do with that," Boomer said of his dismissal to S.L. Price of *Sports Illustrated*. He threatened to write a book on his *Monday Night Football* tenure titled either *They Told Me So* or *The Making of ABC—Al's Broadcasting Company*. For whatever reason, it never became a reality.

Others disagreed with Esiason's claim, including the free weekly paper in his hometown of Cincinnati, *CityBeat*. There, reporter Bill Peterson claimed Esiason failed simply because he was not the outspoken man he had been while being a player.

"His tepid criticisms of players and coaches were viscerally boring," Peterson wrote. The sportswriter felt putting Esiason on *Monday Night Football* with virtually no experience in broadcasting a game inhibited his ability to generate coherent criticism. "He tried too hard not to upset anyone — precisely the wrong approach generally and, especially, the wrong approach for him," Peterson concluded.

Esiason bounced back by going to CBS Sports. Besides joining the network's *NFL Today* pre-game show on Sunday afternoons, he added another duty in 2002 — ironically, covering Monday night football games on CBS radio with Marv Albert, as the duo replaced Howard David and Matt Millen.

Meanwhile, new producer Don Ohlmeyer brought some baggage along with his name. Working as an executive at NBC in the 1990s, he upset colleagues by criticizing how NBC News covered the O.J. Simpson trial, claiming reporters were unfair to the murder suspect, and by demanding that Norm Macdonald be fired as host of the "Weekend Edition" segment on *Saturday Night Live*, believing him to be unfunny. With that notoriety, plus the fact he had not been with ABC Sports since 1977, some doubted he would be up to the task of refashioning *Monday Night Football*.

Adjustment wasn't as difficult for others who had found fault with the series in recent years, however. John Walters of *Sports Illustrated*, who was not impressed with the hiring of Ohlmeyer ("Get over the 1970s," he advised the show), nevertheless suggested the show look for more flexibility in scheduling, return to having three sportscasters in the booth, and consider as part of the booth either ex-coach Jimmy Johnson (who had done the Fox pregame show), former player Sterling Sharpe or veteran Paul Maguire.

Besides Johnson, the other candidates most mentioned by columnists initially for *Monday Night Football* were ex-coach Bill Parcells and ex–Denver quarterback John Elway. However, Ohlmeyer thought that the show could and should have appeal beyond the former sports figures set, and while he knew it would be impossible to find another Howard Cosell, he did want someone humorous and edgy to attract audiences. He seriously considered comedians Billy Crystal and Chris Rock for the spot. But within a few months, he threw observers for a loop with another finalist most never considered.

The "Rush" for a New Commentator

In the spring of 2000 Ohlmeyer held 20 auditions after considering 40 candidates for *Monday Night Football*, with one being conservative radio commentator Rush Limbaugh. By May following the auditions, Limbaugh was Ohlmeyer's top choice.

Arledge and other ABC executives immediately warned Ohlmeyer against hiring Limbaugh. They felt his outspoken right-wing views on his daily national show would be a considerable turnoff to much of the audience, even though a *USA Today* survey about who should be the next host at the time had him receive 59 percent of the vote. The results were taken with a grain of salt, as they were not scientific and could have been stuffed by Limbaugh's fans.

One notable voice dead set against the idea was liberal commentator and former *Saturday Night Live* writer and performer Al Franken, who already had a bestselling book called *Rush Limbaugh Is a Big Fat Idiot* and claimed to be a *Monday Night Football* fan. He wrote in *The Nation* that "it's not so much Rush's politics" that bothered him than was the fact that Limbaugh had no experience in pro football and was "a liar" and "a lout."

Franken pointed out how the closest Limbaugh came to the game was playing high school football and how he got a Vietnam draft deferment due to a knee injury, only it was really a cyst that made Limbaugh 4F. He also cited the usual litany of liberal complaints about dubious statements Limbaugh made over the years on tobacco, taxes and the environment. But he spent two paragraphs particularly addressing Limbaugh's comments he considered racist, such as the observation, "Have you ever noticed how all newspaper composite pictures of wanted criminals resemble Jesse Jackson?"

Of course, Franken should have known that having no experience in pro football hardly disqualifies a person from being a sportscaster — remember Howard Cosell? But his prediction about Limbaugh's views on race coming back to haunt him proved accurate when Limbaugh became a commentator on ESPN in 2003 and had to resign after just a few weeks on the job when he implied that Philadelphia starting quarterback Donovan McNabb got his position basically because he was black. Since that gaffe, no one has used Limbaugh to do sports commentary.

The ESPN job came about after Limbaugh lost the *Monday Night Football* job when NFL Commissioner Paul Tagliabue heard reports of Ohlmeyer wanting the conservative firebrand. At first Tagliabue considered the news to be a joke or marketing ploy. When he learned Ohlmeyer was serious, Tagliabue voiced his strong objections and lobbied for Ohlmeyer to consider ESPN announcers Tom Jackson or Robin Roberts instead (Roberts became the regular newscaster and later co-host on ABC's *Good Morning America* in 2004).

Neither Jackson nor Roberts impressed Ohlmeyer, but he did concede not to use Limbaugh under Tagliabue's pressure. Ohlmeyer gave considerable thought to Tony Kornheiser, a 52-year-old *Washington Post* columnist with a hit show on ESPN Radio. (Kornheiser later began doing work for ESPN on TV after being passed over for *Monday Night Football*.)

Then on June 12, 2000, came a scruffy-haired comedian and actor who entranced Ohlmeyer and made him his new top pick for the show. The decision prompted possibly even more outrage and disgust than Limbaugh would have, but it did get people talking about *Monday Night Football* again. Which is exactly what Ohlmeyer wanted.

"Way Beyond What We Expected"

The audition by Dennis Miller in a Los Angeles studio doing commentary on a mock broadcast of a 1999 Tennessee Titans–Buffalo Bills playoff game stunned his future booth mate Al Michaels.

"It was way beyond what we expected," Michaels told S.L. Price in *Sports Illustrated*. "I had no idea that he knew as much about football as he did. He made points that other analysts we brought in never made, and his points were more salient, more interesting and better stated. He was giving his riff, analyzing the plays and providing the humor. 'Amazing' would not be an overstatement."

Miller himself said he was not dazzled at all by what he did. It was just the same way he talked back to the TV set over the years while watching football. In fact, he had done the same thing for years as part of his basic delivery as a comedian.

An observational humorist with a caustic edge, Miller came to prominence on NBC's comedy series *Saturday Night Live* when he became a regular there in 1985. For the next five years there, Miller nailed the job of being the "anchor" of the "Weekend Update" sketch satirizing TV news. Especially compared to the so-so results of his predecessors such as Charles Rocket (1980–81) and Brad Hall (1982–84), Miller gave his spot a distinctive presence with a solid delivery of biting jokes. That stint propelled him into hosting his own late night syndicated talk show, *The Dennis Miller Show*, in 1992, but the competition was tough and the show folded after eight months.

Miller recovered quickly and nicely by doing some well-received comedy specials for HBO in 1993, leading to a live series there the next year called, appropriately, *Dennis Miller Live*. It won several Emmys, including Outstanding Variety, Music or Comedy Series in 1996, and kept his name in the public eye.

But Miller's popularity resided on him being a comedian, not a sportscaster, an area of show business where he had no personal experience. Even so, the possibility of failing in this new job did not faze him in the least. "I don't know if I'm the guy to do this, but I'm a decent roll of the dice," Miller told Julian Rubinstein of *The New York Times Magazine*.

Ohlmeyer announced his decision to the press to go with Miller on June 22. He figured Miller would be a bigger draw for young males than the relatively unknown other top contender, Tony Kornheiser. What he may not have expected was how loudly some reacted to Miller as thoroughly inappropriate for the job.

"It's a triumph of latter-day liberalism over conservative righteousness. Of the snide over the pompous ... of the self-important over the self-important," griped Ciro Scotti of Miller's selection over Limbaugh in his column on the *Business Week* Online website. "I thought the game was the entertainment," sniffed John Madden to Julian Rubinstein in *The New York Times Magazine*.

Despite the chorus of naysayers, Ohlmeyer remained behind keeping Miller as part of his revamped announcing lineup for *Monday Night Football*. As it turned out, at least one other new element proved to be questionable with critics as well.

Stark Contrast

During his meeting with Tagliabue, Ohlmeyer convinced the NFL commissioner to let ABC mount miniature cameras onto the caps worn by referees (called the "ump cam") and allow more reporters to roam the sidelines for interviews with players throughout the game. That also meant he now had the resources to use two sideline reporters with the increased access. He decided to do so, only with two new ones rather than keeping his current one.

On the morning of June 22, 2000, ABC senior vice president John Filippelli stunned Lesley Visser by telling her she was fired from *Monday Night Football* after two seasons with the show because Ohlmeyer wanted to go another direction. When it was found out that one of Visser's replacements was 26-year-old Melissa Stark, it was obvious what "direction" Ohlmeyer wanted, given Visser was 20 years older.

"It was Don Ohlmeyer's party, and I wasn't invited," Visser commented to John Walters of *Sports Illustrated* about her dismissal. She did not put down Stark, but she did note that "People are excited about Dennis Miller being young and hip, but the truth is that he and I are the same age." Visser rebounded quickly; her old network CBS rehired her a month later, where she got to cover the Super Bowl in 2004.

The changeover in personnel given the age difference overshadowed the press conference revealing the new *Monday Night Football* team. When one reporter raised the issue with Stark, Miller shot back to him, "Do you have something against 26-year-olds?"

Those who were familiar with Stark's work knew that while she was young, she was not an inexperienced sportscaster. Growing up in Baltimore, her father was an eye doctor whose patients included Colts players that he would treat in the locker room with her by his side. She graduated magna cum laude from the University of Virginia with majors in Spanish and foreign affairs, but she also covered the university's athletic programs for a local station while in school. Hooked by that job, she joined Home Team Sports in Maryland before joining ESPN as a correspondent in 1996.

Recounting what she thought when she received the offer to join *Monday Night Football*, Stark told *People* magazine she was a little edgy about doing it. "Everyone just said to remember that it's the same thing I was doing at ESPN. You can't think about how many more people are watching. But of course it crossed my mind: 'Am I ready for this?'"

The Rest of the New Crew — Fouts and Dickerson

Along with Miller and Stark, ABC was adding two ex-pro footballers to the mix — Dan Fouts in the booth and Eric Dickerson on the sidelines with Stark. Dan was the son of Bob Fouts, a longtime sportscaster for the San Francisco 49ers. He even recorded statistics for his dad prior to his playing career.

Born June 10, 1951, in San Francisco, Dan Fouts attended the University of Oregon before becoming a quarterback for the San Diego Chargers from 1973 to 1987. He led the team to the playoffs from 1979 to 1982, but they never made the Super Bowl under his leadership. Nevertheless, Fouts piled up more than 40,000 yards passing for the Chargers, only the third pro quarterback ever to reach that mark, and he went to six Pro Bowls from 1979 to 1985. The Chargers retired his number when he hung up his cleats, and in 1993 Fouts was elected to the Pro Football Hall of Fame.

Even though his dad had been a sportscaster, Fouts did not follow his footsteps immediately. He finally worked his way to doing color beside Keith Jackson's always steady play-by-play announcing on ABC's NCAA football games starting in 1997. He did the task two more years before being plucked to join *Monday Night Football.*

Adding a person with such limited experience to the unproven Miller did not sound like a winning formula to some reporters, but Ohlmeyer told S.L. Price of *Sports Illustrated* Dan Fouts had "an engaging and impish quality" that he felt would mesh well with Michaels and Miller. Perhaps the most striking and unexpected feature of Fouts' voice was that it was a higher timbre than that of Miller and Michaels.

Like Fouts, Eric Dickerson was also a member of the Pro Football Hall of Fame, earning induction in 1999. Born on September 2, 1960, in Sealy, Texas, Dickerson was a two-time All American running back at Southern Methodist University. His abilities were so well known that he was a second pick in the 1983 draft and played for the Los Angeles Rams through 1987. Following that run, he went to the Indianapolis Colts through 1991, the Los Angeles Raiders in 1992 and the Atlanta Falcons in 1993. He was the NFL's second all-time leading rusher when he retired.

He was not, however, an accomplished sideline reporter. That was a big miscalculation by Ohlmeyer. Dickerson proved to be woefully inadequate, often being inarticulate and ill-prepared during his spots. If the idea was that the team needed to have a black member to reflect the NFL's racial makeup, Dickerson was a poor, inappropriate choice. Someone like Sterling Sharpe, whose name previously appeared under consideration for the booth replacements, would have been much better. Instead, the show would be left with what many thought to be its weakest on-air personality ever, and for two years at that.

Ohlmeyer's Final Makeover Touches

As part of his push to make a mark with his return, Ohlmeyer convinced ABC to let an outside ad agency promote *Monday Night Football* in order to reach new and different audiences. However, the result, "*Monday Night Football*— It's Powerful Stuff," was hardly one of the earth-shattering phrases to emerge in the history of national promotion.

Ohlmeyer also demanded that Miller, Michaels and Fouts ride in limousines, stay in top hotels and leave with police escorts to get to chartered planes, perks that *Monday Night Football* announcers had been denied in the 1990s. Ohlmeyer felt that effort for austerity detracted from the glamour the series had and needed in its future if it wanted success.

Also, Ohlmeyer's work with director Drew Esocoff on the show was more hands on than what Roone Arledge gave to Chet Forte in the 1970s and 1980s. "In simplistic terms, Ohlmeyer is the person who sets policy," noted Dan Caesar of *The St. Louis Post-Dispatch*. "Esocoff, in concert with Ohlmeyer, is the one who decides which pictures go out over the air. They sit in a dark trailer, looking at a wall that contains a bank of more than 78 monitors that can display live pictures, taped features and graphics that can be put on the air with the push of a button. While all the attention is focused on the booth, this is where *Monday Night Football* comes together."

"Our goal is to provide a more enjoyable program for the viewers, and this combination of talent is the start," Ohlmeyer said at the June 22, 2000, press conference announcing his new crew. "What we want to accomplish is to have a team with distinctive voices, distinctive personalities and distinctive points of view."

Did that mean it would it add up to a distinctive show? Well....

Miller Time

After a few preseason games starting on July 31, Dennis Miller's official *Monday Night Football* debut came on September 4, 2000, as the defending Super Bowl champs the St. Louis Rams, led by quarterback Kurt Warner, faced off against the Denver Broncos. After a couple of opening montages and reminders for viewers to check out the NFL and *Monday Night Football* websites and listen to the game in Spanish courtesy of Toyota, Al Michaels threw the conversation to Dan Fouts to discuss defensive strategies and then Melissa Stark on the field to mention the injured leg of Terrell Davis.

Then Michaels told viewers, "One guy we will not ease into our 31st season of *Monday Night Football*, Mr. Dennis Miller. You know, I'm looking at your wardrobe, this is a blast from the past." The camera showed Miller wearing the classic yellow sports coat with the show's emblem from the 1971–83 era. Miller picked up Michaels' cue and ran with it — boy, did he ever. These were his first words, or spiel, if you prefer:

"First game, Al. You know, ladies and gentlemen, you knew I had to break out the colors. I want to talk for a second about Kurt Warner, a man who seemingly is implacable in the pocket as most of us are in a hammock. Now, I attribute this to two reasons. First, his experience in the Arena Football League. I think the compacted nature of that venue must make Warner feel like he's gone from a bumper pool table to a snooker table. Second, and more importantly, is I believe he has a deep and fervent belief in a higher power. No, I don't mean Paul Tagliabue. Indeed, his debut was so preternatural last year, one can assume that Warner is a latter-day Joe Hardy. And the simple fact is, since this guy found Christ, he finds the open man with uncanny frequency. TGIM, Al!"

If your first reaction upon reading that is "Whew!" you're not alone. In about a minute Miller made sometimes obscure joking references to the NFL commissioner (Tagliabue), a fictional crimesolver (Joe Hardy) and ABC's promotional slogan in the 1990s for its Friday night sitcom lineup (TGIF, or Thank Goodness It's Friday). For good measure, he added the Cosell-style big word "preternatural" in there as well.

Things settled down after that, with the casually dressed Eric Dickerson (dark blue shirt with no collar nor tie) reporting on Denver's running game being centered around Marshall Faulk before game activity began. In the early going Michaels remained firmly in control, while Fouts offered well-researched insights on several players and Miller spoke not too often, albeit typically with a good line (e.g., while noting the quickly mounting touchdowns before halftime, he quipped, "Got the feeling the guy working the scoreboard might get carpal tunnel syndrome tonight."). He loosened up more as the game progressed, and even had a nice bit of repartee when he noted, "Everybody's worried about me using profanity, and the only 'F' word I might say a lot this year is Faulk!" "I ain't worried," Michaels deftly underplayed in response.

Meanwhile, Stark gave updates on Terrell Davis and interviewed NFL Commissioner Paul Tagliabue briefly while Dickerson virtually disappeared from view before halftime. During that period, there was shallow assessment by the booth about the game's progress and Chris Berman narrating all-time sports bloopers with lame comic effects before a return to the action on the field for the second half, with little change in what had been happening with the announcers in the previous part of the contest.

The game ended with St. Louis triumphing over Denver 41–36. However, there was less certainty over how America viewed this biggest revamp of *Monday Night Football* in more than a decade.

Mixed Reviews for the New Crew

There were strong pro and con feelings regarding this take on *Monday Night Football*, and most centered on Miller. On the positive side, the *New York Daily News* found him "very likable," while *The Los Angeles Times* termed him "irreverent."

"Dennis Miller was such a hoot Monday night that I can't wait for the next Monday night," wrote Jay Mariotti in *The Chicago Sun-Times*. "There are those who call his addition to the most sacred booth in TV a form of blasphemy, a desecration of the holy testosterone temple. They should be banished to an attic with a lifetime supply of Frank Gifford tapes."

On the other hand, just as many found the production lacking. "Dan Fouts and Dennis Miller ... found new ways to fumble, jumble and mumble their way through the first game of the 31st season," wrote *The Hollywood Reporter*. More harsh was Phil Mushnick of *The New York Post*, who quipped that Miller's "first two games in the booth have found him to be more forced and rehearsed than the lead pilgrim in the fourth-grade Thanksgiving pageant."

For his part, Miller confided to former ESPN sportscaster Keith Olbermann his take on the job after his debut. "Miller was completely exhausted," Olbermann told Howard Manly of *The Boston Globe*. "It was as if he were run over by a succession of steamrollers. The preparation and execution had drained him. But he was really dedicated to making this work."

Manly himself thought Miller needed better execution indeed after seeing the debut. "Miller's performance was underwhelming," he wrote. "His material seemed scripted, his erudite references often missing the mark. Rival networks, who are quick to duplicate anything remotely resembling a hit with viewers, were not calling other comedians to see about their availability."

Indeed, Miller's off-tangent on-air references soon became so arcane that ABC's website posted explanations of them after each show. For those who couldn't wait that long, a wireless technology company called Shadowpack offered for its clients a service called "Dennis Miller Demystified." Via pagers or other wireless devices, Shadowpack members could get instant translations of the announcer's sayings, such as telling them that when Miller said "He looked like George Chakiris in summer stock" during the Jaguars-Colts duel, he meant the actor who won the Oscar for his supporting dancing role in the 1961 film version of *West Side Story*. Or that when Miller quipped during the Buccaneers-Vikings match, "And somewhere on Long Island 'Le Grand Ahi' churgles in his Barcalounger," he was making a French translation of former football coach Bill Parcells nickname "The Big Tuna" and how Parcells was now retired and presumably lying in a comfortable folding chair.

For those who were taught that it wasn't professional or funny for a comedian to have to explain his jokes, Miller's routines were exasperating to follow. Even well-educated viewers probably were perplexed at least once during every show with a hard-to-grasp allusion, such as in the Seahawks-Chiefs meeting when he said one player was "air-dropped in like Red Adair." Fireman Paul "Red" Adair put out the oil fires in Kuwait after the Gulf War in the early 1990s, a fact little reported even then. So why make the comparison if only to show how trivial you can get?

There was less division over one of the new sideline reporters. Eric Dickerson often came across mumbling with little insight in his segments, and he impressed no one. "Eric Dickerson was the human incarnation of Mushmouth from the Cosby Gang," sniped Mark Madden of *The Pittsburgh Post-Gazette*.

While Dickerson struggled, Stark did perfunctory if not outstanding work. She found out that for the best interaction with players, she had to stand as close as possible to the action. This led to distress for her during the New York Jets–New England Patriots contest the week after the opener on September 11, 2000, when her sweater caught fire from the nearby pyrotechnics fired during the player introductions, but she managed to put it out without getting burned.

Assessing her own performance to *People* in November, Stark said: "I get more comfortable with each game. But there's pressure. I feel stress all week." So did the rest of the main staff at *Monday Night Football*, according to most accounts.

Even the starting time for the show now fell under a critical gaze. On October 23, 2000, *Monday Night Football* hosted its longest game ever, when an overtime 40–37 win by the New York Jets over the Miami Dolphins did not get finished until 1:18 A.M. Eastern Time. For the poor East Coast late night anchors who had to deliver a news report after that event, that meant that they could have been leaving their stations the same time the 5 A.M. news crews were coming to work. For the show's personnel, it brought them grief in the media as critics wondered that now given the increase in commercials on the show since the 1970s made it longer, maybe an earlier starting time of an hour or so would be better to make sure a game could finish around midnight even if it went into overtime. Between that complaint and the divided criticisms over how they were doing, the *Monday Night Football* crew felt like they were damned if they did and damned if they didn't.

Mocking the Mondayers

Perhaps the most devastating critique of Miller et al. came from Miller's own TV alma mater, *Saturday Night Live*. The series spoofed them on its October 7, 2000, show with Jimmy Fallon as Miller, Darrell Hammond as Michaels, Will Ferrell as Fouts, Tracy Morgan as Dickerson and Maya Rudolph as Stark. The sketch was laser-sharp funny, one of the series' best that season. Unless you were Miller, Michaels, Fouts, Dickerson or Stark, of course.

The segment mocked every mind-numbing convention the football broadcast critics had noted. Michaels introduced the other talent and set the tone while shilling for ABC's disastrous new 2000 fall series ("Warren Sapp, perhaps the most feared man in the NFC, and this Friday on ABC, it's *Madigan Men!*"). Fouts made the most obvious statements as his insights ("Al, my prediction is that whoever puts the most points on the scoreboard will probably win tonight's football game."). Stark awkwardly tried to fit in and convince viewers she was a worthy sportscaster ("You know, Al, you may not take me seriously because I'm a woman wearing a lavender sweater set from Club Monaco, but I know one thing, Al. I know my football!"). And Dickerson... Well, actually they let him off the easiest, though they did have him recounting a nonsensical interview he had with Minnesota quarterback Dante Culpepper about how the latter should handle Tampa Bay's defense ("I told him you gotta get your freak on, kid.").

The one really roasted by it was Miller and his stylized delivery, which had been great on *Saturday Night Live* but so out of place on *Monday Night Football*. One of the eight strained metaphors used in the sketch went "Hey, Al, I saw the *Madigan Men* pilot. It's got fewer laughs than Molly Blum's internal monologue at the end of James Joyce's *Ulysses*." The whole effort fared so well that *Saturday Night Live* did another takeoff on the series with most of the same cast three months later (January 13, 2001), this time insulting chiefly the title talent in "Eric Dickerson's NFL Pre-Game Special."

But lost amid all the attacks by comedians and columnists were two encouraging signs. *Monday Night Football* increased its audience in its primary demographic, men 18–34, during the 2000 season. That was the first reversal in that category in six years. And while average ratings were down nearly a million viewers from 13.5 in 1999 to 12.6 in 2000, the show still remained a top 10 hit. It actually finished slightly higher in the top 10 than in 1999, once again due to an overall drop in audiences watching network TV.

Given those numbers, with the warped logic existing among ABC programmers at the time, that was all that mattered to them. *Monday Night Football* was back as a qualified success to them, if no one else. They overlooked the fact that 11 of the 17 games were decided by no more than a touchdown, which should have indicated to them that the play on the field was really the main attraction now and not whatever the show's broadcasters did. The executives' failure to see that and stay the course would prove to be injurious for *Monday Night Football* in the fall of 2001.

Exit Ohlmeyer, Enter Gaudelli, Enter (and Exit) the XFL

On March 6, 2001, three days before his first anniversary as producer of *Monday Night Football*, Don Ohlmeyer surprised everyone by announcing that he was resigning from his job there after less than a year.

"I had a terrific time this year producing *MNF*, but I just could not continue to put myself through the stressful traveling that goes with the job," he told reporters.

ABC Sports President Howard Katz commended him. "The sweeping changes he made in the telecast the past year all made *Monday Night Football* a much more enjoyable, entertaining and watchable telecast," Katz said. "Without question, he brought the buzz back to Monday night and made it special again."

In honor of Ohlmeyer's achievement, Katz vowed the on-camera lineup would not change in the fall of 2001, the first time it would remain unchanged since 1997. Ohlmeyer insisted the most controversial new element, Dennis Miller doing color, would continue to get better, and Katz concurred.

"We clearly intend to continue in the direction that Don took the telecasts last season. He has given us a blueprint and built a team of announcers and production people that will execute his vision," Katz said.

To ensure no drastic alterations would occur, he appointed company man Fred Gaudelli as the new producer a week after Ohlmeyer departed. Gaudelli, 40, had worked for ESPN since 1983 in production of such sports as college football and basketball before becoming producer of ESPN's *Sunday Night Football* for 11 years starting in 1990. Gaudelli vowed he would make at first only minor alterations, if needed, for the series.

"The template Don put in place is the direction ABC wants to go," he told Leonard Shapiro of *The Washington Post.* "Over the next few months, I'll study what he did, what worked and what didn't work. The goal is to make it better. That was Don's charge."

While Katz made a smooth transfer of power on *Monday Night Football,* one competitor was having a massive flameout with another version of nighttime pro football. NBC had witnessed a continuing decline in its audiences on Saturday night since 1992, when *The Golden Girls* was its last top 30 hit there. It also chafed under not having any pro football to show since the 1998 NFL contract negotiations awarded rights to other outlets.

Given those factors, and weighing into account the growing popularity of wrestling on TV, NBC split ownership 50–50 with the World Wrestling Federation, or WWF (retitled World Wrestling Entertainment or WWE in 2002 to end a trademark disagreement with the previously established World Wildlife Fund) to establish the Extreme Football League. Going under the title XFL, the league sought to emphasize grittier play while delivering a game with wrestling-style flashiness, including pre-publicity claims of going into the dressing rooms of cheerleaders.

Such a tacky approach appalled sports traditionalists, and most NBC Sports talent such as Bob Costas avoided anything associated with the program. So when the XFL finally made it to air in February 2001, NBC had to employ the lesser-known Matt Vasgersian and Mike Adamle (who already hosted the dubious syndicated sports competition *American Gladiators* in the 1990s) as announcers. Joining them was ex-wrestler Jesse "the Body" Ventura, who in his weekday world just had the minor duty of being governor of Minnesota. Many of his constituents voiced resentment about him spending time on the XFL. One other reporter, Fred Roggin from KNBC Los Angeles, left before the end of the season.

As disappointing as the reformatted *Monday Night Football* could be at times, it looked flawless next to the overdone theatrical antics of the XFL. Critics mocked it, while audiences quickly tuned out. The show hit rock bottom with the March 10, 2001, contest, as it earned a 1.6 rating, the lowest rating ever for a sponsored nighttime broadcast network series up to that time (NBC managed to go lower a year later with a 1.3 for a snowboarding event, which holds the record for smallest nighttime network TV rating for a program as of this writing).

By then, the XFL was an obvious lost cause for having another season. Its final telecast ended a few weeks later on April 21, 2001, then in May NBC officially announced the deal had ended. The WWE announced plans to continue it, but could not find sufficient financial backing to do so. When the XFL finally dissolved, several published reports claimed that NBC and the WWE each lost around $70 million on the venture.

With this potential audience threat out of the way, and no shift in major personnel other than in production, *Monday Night Football* looked poised finally to have a regular team in place. But as in the past, appearances could be deceiving.

The Miller Regime Crumbles

The official start for season two of Miller and company on *Monday Night Football* took place on September 10, 2001. The Denver Broncos prevailed over the New York Giants 31–20. Millions of Americans went to work the next day, with some no doubt eager to discuss the game. What happened that morning made them quickly forget ruminating about it, however.

The attacks by terrorists on the World Trade Center in New York and the Pentagon in Washington, D.C. on September 11, 2001, altered the American landscape in many ways. *Monday Night Football* was one of the areas affected by it. The most immediate impact was that NFL Commissioner Paul Tagliabue cancelled the following week's games out of respect for the thousands of Americans impacted by the lives lost and the damage done.

When the games returned to action, there was a sense of uneasiness in terms of potential threats posed by large stadiums acting as targets for terrorists, and a concern that professional sports should not be as important in Americans' daily lives. Over time, however, most people believed that escapism provided by sports and entertainment helped people cope with the circumstances. But this did not apply squarely to *Monday Night Football* for a couple of reasons.

After the attacks, nervous Americans were not in the mood to embrace a sportscaster such as Miller to crack obscure jokes while watching their favorite sport. His basic wise guy approach, plus the continuing lack of chemistry between him and the other announcers on the show, did not translate well to viewers. While large audiences flocked back to old favorites like the sitcom *Friends* as electronic "comfort food," fewer were willing to sample what *Monday Night Football* had to offer.

As for the sideline reports, Stark showed improvement, but Dickerson's opinions were as worthless if not more so than the ones he contributed in 2000. In the words of Dusty Saunders of *The Rocky Mountain News*, Dickerson "at times acted as if he wasn't sure the NFL existed."

Not helping matters was the new lead-in/lead-out show. ABC ended two unproductive seasons of the Monday edition of *20/20* with a Monday edition of an even more exposed series — *Who Wants to Be a Millionaire?* That ailing game show sunk from 8 to 9 P.M. opposite the top 20 sitcoms *The King of Queens* and *Yes, Dear* on CBS, and their strong performance helped the audience flow into *Everybody Loves Raymond* at 9 P.M. on the network, thus allowing it to beat *Monday Night Football* definitively. As a result, water cooler talk on Tuesdays began to focus more on "Did you see what happened on *Everybody Loves Raymond* last night?" rather than the football games.

At the end of the season, *Monday Night Football* set another series low rating average, losing more than a million viewers in 2000–01 to finish with an 11.5 rating in 2001–02. Due to another decline in audiences watching the networks overall, that still meant a top 10 finish, but the ratings were not strong enough to generate advertising to cover its costs.

And if all that wasn't enough, there was a show airing a week after the season-ending game that prodded people's memories of how good *Monday Night Football* used to be.

Monday Night Mayhem: *The TV-Movie*

Adapting his screenplay based on the 1988 book he co-wrote with the same name, reporter Bill Carter decided that *Monday Night Mayhem* would have a different focus as a TV-movie. The book's history began focused on Roone Arledge and his goals for the game. The film portrayed the series' rise through an emphasis on Howard Cosell, imbuing the sportscaster with a rather benevolent portrayal in the process.

The two-hour TV-movie made its debut on the TNT cable network appropriately on a Monday night at 9 P.M., specifically January 14, 2002. It received generally positive reviews and decent ratings for a cable program.

The characterizations were questionable, however. Kevin Anderson's Gifford came across as a little too humble, John Turturro's Cosell smiled a lot more than I recalled ever seeing him on or off the air, and his voice was not as nasally as the sportscaster's, and Brad Beyer's Meredith, sporting a cowboy hat, gave the impression in early scenes that he was imitating Jon Voight's Joe Buck character from *Midnight Cowboy* when he arrived in Manhattan.

In an effort to condense events and move the plot along, the movie sometimes betrayed history. Two obvious examples were having *Saturday Night Live with Howard Cosell* occurring at the same time Fred Williamson was hired and implying that O.J. Simpson came on as the first occasional replacement for Meredith, with no mention being made of Fran Tarkenton. Other times, events were not clearly explained, and if you did not know the show's story, it might have left you wondering what happened. There was an oblique reference to Arledge not returning Meredith's phone calls; Vin Scully was just referred to as "Scully" from the Dodgers among candidates for the booth; and the hiring of Keith Jackson was not portrayed at all.

Some scenes rang false too, such as Jackson discussing his removal from the show with Arledge at an editing session rather than in his office and Forte joking about the way he covered the games.

However, the TV-movie did succeed in reminding viewers how appealing *Monday Night Football* was in the 1970s and early 1980s on air, and how it never had the same glow about it since then. Coming as it did following one of the program's most lackluster seasons, the comparison was depressing. Even when played by actors, Cosell, Gifford and Meredith, despite their off-air discomfort, had a palpable chemistry evident to viewers that Dickerson, Fouts, Miller, Michaels, and Stark sorely lacked.

It may not have been a determining factor as much as the ratings, but it is curious how just a month after *Monday Night Mayhem* aired, *Monday Night Football* went through another shift that this time knocked off three of its on-air personalities, its biggest transition of on-camera talent ever. Somewhere in the great beyond, Howard Cosell no doubt was smiling.

Glad to Have Madden

On February 28, 2002, after 17 years of off-and-on failed negotiations, John Madden announced he was joining ABC. He signed a four-year contract with them worth $20 million.

"This is where I want to finish," Madden said at a press conference announcing his new affiliation. "I want to be a part of *Monday Night Football* and be a part of *Monday Night* as long as I broadcast."

Madden emphasized that Fox allowed him to pursue the ABC job given the retirement of his longtime broadcasting buddy Pat Summerall, who had been with him for 21 years, including when they moved to Fox from CBS to cover the NFL in 1994. He had one more year left on his Fox contract, but they were planning to offer him significantly less than the $7.5 million annually he got for the next few years there.

The general reaction to the appointment of Madden was favorable, although there were some qualms about his advancing age (he was 65 when he joined ABC) and that his fear of flying meant he would be joining the crew separately via train or bus for each show.

With ABC adding Madden at a relatively high price, that meant it could afford only one analyst for *Monday Night Football* in the upcoming season. The network offered reduced roles to Miller and Fouts covering other sports. Fouts accepted his terms, which included him returning to cover NCAA football for the network with Keith Jackson through the latter's retirement in 2006.

Miller nixed any changes and went back to focusing on his HBO comedy series *Dennis Miller Live*. He voluntarily ended his series on August 30, 2002, then returned a year and a half later on CNBC with a nightly talk show titled simply *Dennis Miller*. There he startled some fans by fully endorsing President George W. Bush's war on terror and giving more conservative opinions. It was low-rated and lasted little more than a year. Miller then concentrated on guest shots and commercials and rarely talked about his time on *Monday Night Football* other than to say he enjoyed the opportunity of doing it.

ABC retained Al Michaels and Melissa Stark on its roster, but it made no offer of any kind for Eric Dickerson, canning him once the contract with Madden was signed. Dickerson's salary and horrendous reviews as sideline reporter combined to assure his departure on the series. Whatever meager credibility Dickerson had as a sportscaster with *Monday Night Football* vanished a year later when he was the captain of the Team Dream in the 2002 Lingerie Bowl pay cable event during the Super Bowl halftime (Lawrence Taylor coached the opposition Team Euphoria in the "contest"). Dickerson must have had some appeal with somebody at the CBS Los Angeles TV station KCBS by the 2005 football season, though, as the affiliate had him as an analyst in its local NFL pregame coverage.

Ending Four Years of Frustration

When the dust settled, after four years with three announcing combinations (Michaels-Esiason-Dierdorf in 1998, Michaels-Esiason in 1999, and Michaels-Miller-Fouts in 2000 and 2001), three different sideline reporters (Visser 1998–99, Dickerson 2000–01, and Stark 2000–02), and three different producers and directors, *Monday Night Football* finally looked to be getting where it wanted to be in 2002. It had two of the best, if not the best, football sportscasters at the helm now that Madden joined Michaels, and a technical team that had remained steady and respected throughout all the personnel turmoil happening around them in the period.

With these elements in place, it was a given that audiences would flock to the show once more to see the best pro football series on the air, and thus ABC could raise ad rates for the increased audience and cover the cost of *Monday Night Football* to network.

Just one question remained: If the ratings did not rise, and thus ABC kept losing $150 million annually on the show, what would the network do next?

11

Leader of a Loser (2002–2005)

The arrival of John Madden to *Monday Night Football* quelled most reviewers' complaints about how the series had been heading and gave most people connected to the series an optimistic view of the show's future. Madden's appeal was far and wide — his NFL electronic game was one of the biggest sellers in its field — and with the series shorn of its more controversial announcers (Dennis Miller and Eric Dickerson), the belief was that it had nowhere to go but up.

Media observers felt the same way, albeit with some caution. "If Madden, the ultimate football guy, can't save *Monday Night Football*, perhaps nothing can," wrote Michael Silver in *Sports Illustrated* prior to the start of the 2002 season. He may not have realized how prophetic that statement was.

Madden Arrives; Not All Viewers Come with Him

In the first show during the preseason in August 2002, Madden called the Houston Texans "the best expansion team we've ever seen" and noted how the Texans' Domingo Graham gave a block to the New York Giants so solid that Madden said "Boom!"

"Let it be duly noted: The first Monday night 'boom,'" Michaels said in response.

It was marvelous repartee, and critics lapped it up. Writing for the Salon website, King Kaufman praised Madden and Michaels, saying their byplay was so casual, it appeared they had been working together for 30 years. "The two are about as good as it gets in their respective jobs," he wrote.

Yet Kaufman fretted that their expertise would be superfluous in terms of attracting new viewers, because by now, he felt, the show's appeal simply was in whatever teams played. "The simple fact is that as much as we all love to play program director, it doesn't really matter who's in the booth for *Monday Night Football*. Football fans aren't going to tune out a good game because they don't like the

154

announcers.... And, as we learned in the unfortunate Dennis Miller era, non-fans aren't going to watch because of some non-football element that's been thrown in."

That judgment proved correct, to the chagrin of ABC leaders. Even with Madden on board, having few truly competitive games (only three that season were decided by the margin of no more than 7 points), and facing stronger competition than ever from CBS's top 10 hits *Everybody Loves Raymond* and new hour-long crime drama *CSI: Miami* all made ratings for *Monday Night Football* unimpressive. The series ended with a stagnant 11.4 ratings average, slightly less than the previous season. It still was a top 10 hit (thanks to broadcast audience levels declining once again), but its failure to improve its audience with the latest configuration at a considerable cost for Madden's salary depressed executives who realized they could not make major ad rate hikes to help cover the more than half-billion dollars it cost ABC to have *Monday Night Football* on air every season.

There was one saving grace, however. For the fourth time in six years, *Monday Night Football* was ABC's top-rated series, and this time its lead was glaring. ABC had only two other top 30 series that year, *The Bachelor* at number 16 and *N.Y.P.D. Blue* at number 29. It was the network's worst performance in nearly 30 years, and as such, it kept programmers more preoccupied on other failures in the schedule. But the lack of turnout for Madden did not escape their memories either.

Lead-In/Lead-Out Blues

Keeping down ABC's average in 2002–03 was the worst lead-in/lead-out slate *Monday Night Football* ever had — the sitcom *The Drew Carey Show* followed by the improvisational series Drew Carey hosted, *Whose Line Is It Anyway?* They were two aging series that held little appeal kicking off or following football, and their failure was awe-inspiring, even in the face of previous loser lead-in/lead-outs.

Begun in 1995, *The Drew Carey Show* had some amusing elements over the years. But by the fall of 2002, the series was entering its eighth season as a tired property, having already suffered considerable audience erosion in the 2000–01 and 2001–02 seasons against *The West Wing* on NBC Wednesday nights.

But leave it to ABC programmers at the time to think the show still had potential. In the summer of 2001, with the series' ratings down 15 percent from the previous year, ABC went ahead and granted the series a two-year deal paying around $3 million per show to let it run through the 2003–04 season. Why? Because they were worried when the show's contract ran out in 2002, it would cost them more to renegotiate a contract with the talent involved in it. Apparently no one considered the possibility that its ratings would keep going down by that time as well.

Whatever the reason, ABC was stuck with *The Drew Carey Show*, and as it faltered against *The West Wing*, programmers thought it might have a better chance leading into or out of *Monday Night Football*, since much of that show's audience was blue collar guys like the one the star himself portrayed. To fill out the bottom half of the 8–9 P.M. hour, ABC installed *Whose Line Is It Anyway?*, an improvisation show hosted by the by-now-overexposed Carey. The results were pathetic.

Debuting in its new slot September 16, 2002, *The Drew Carey Show* finished an unprecedented low for an ABC series of fifth place in its time slot, down not only against the sitcom *The King of Queens* on CBS, the reality game show *Fear Factor* on NBC and a *National Geographic* special on Fox but also the family comedy-drama *7th Heaven* on the WB network. It was the first time ever a WB series topped an ABC show in direct competition. Thereafter, ratings kept slipping to the point where on October 28 *The Drew Carey Show* and *Whose Line Is It Anyway?* finished in sixth place behind the sitcoms *The Parkers* and *One on One* on the UPN network.

Embarrassed by such low numbers, ABC took the shows out of the time slot, but they struggled the rest of the season on other nights.

While *The Drew Carey Show* disintegrated, ABC slotted a spin-off of its *Primetime* newsmagazine series to run the hour lead-in/lead-out spot in the fall of 2003, apparently forgetting how unimpressive a similar clone of *20/20* there bombed in the fall of 1999 and 2000. *Primetime Monday* predictably flopped, so in September 2004 ABC tried out a reality series called *The Benefactor* starring Mark Cuban, owner of the NBA franchise the Dallas Mavericks. It was so off-putting the network cancelled it by November, meaning that ABC in 2005 would start a 13th time in the last 14 seasons with another series or two airing from 8 to 9 P.M. Eastern or 7 to 8 P.M. Central and after the football games in the West. It proved that Martin Starger's fears about programming that slot back in the 1970s remained even more valid 30 years later.

Casting Away Katz

Before *Primetime Monday* and *The Benefactor* bombed, on March 3, 2003, Howard Katz announced his resignation as president of ABC Sports effective March 14 after four years on the job. ESPN President George Bodenheimer took over the reins from Katz while staying as head of ESPN too, a double duty that Katz's predecessor, Steve Bornstein, handled from 1996–99.

"I haven't been happy," Katz admitted concerning his tenure to Richard Sandomir of *The New York Times*. "It hasn't worked out the way I wanted it to. This wasn't the right fit. I'd come home and complain about this or that. I have to clear my head." He planned to leave in 2002, but he wanted to get through supervising the Super Bowl on ABC in 2003 first before going.

During his years of service, Katz renewed or secured ABC rights to the Indianapolis 500, the British Open, the PGA Tour, the College Football Bowl Championship Series and the Big East Conference college football. He also kept football on Monday nights, of course. After reviewing these achievements, Lisa de Moraes, the resident snarky TV critic for *The Washington Post*, sarcastically commented, "Is it any wonder he had to go?"

Of course, Katz could be blamed for allowing the messy transitions from the Esiason-Michaels days through the final Madden-Michaels lineup to occur under his watch too. He also took part in the 2003 post-game Super Bowl show which ran so long that it did not end until after 11 P.M. on the East Coast. That late finish prevented ABC from getting a big ratings spillover after the game for a special edition of its struggling action adventure drama *Alias*, which could have used the boost in viewership normally found after the Super Bowl ends.

Katz's replacement, Bodenheimer, started serving as president of ESPN in October 1999. He joined that company back in 1981. He made a successful bid to get ABC back into covering the NBA in 2003, but his work on *Monday Night Football* was minimal in comparison to the former recent occupants of his seat.

It would also be derided within a few months thanks to a spectacular boner in picking the latest addition to *Monday Night Football*. Bodenheimer learned from Melissa Stark the same month Katz retired that the sideline reporter was pregnant with her first child and so was not returning to the series in the fall of 2003. She retired from the media for a year after giving birth, reappearing in 2005 as a contributor to *Today* on NBC.

To take her place, the new ABC Sports President chose a woman who was slightly more mature than Stark age-wise, 39-year-old Lisa Guerrero. Unfortunately for Bodenheimer and *Monday Night Football*, Guerrero was nowhere near as experienced a reporter as Stark, and she performed so poorly she became the shortest-lived addition to the series since Fred Williamson did only three games in 1974, and was the network's latest source of embarrassment.

The Guerrero Error, er, Era, Begins

Lisa Guerrero's résumé going onto *Monday Night Football* was almost as fluffy as her predecessor Melissa Stark's was substantial. She was not a novice in sports journalism — Guerrero had been a reporter for Fox Sports Network and two Los Angeles TV stations — but prior to those jobs, she had been a cheerleader for the L.A. Rams football team in the mid–1980s before the franchise moved to St. Louis. In the 1990s she had appeared in more than 200 commercials and guest starred on series as varied as the nighttime sitcom hit *Friends* to the NBC daytime soap opera *Sunset Beach*. This sort of entertainment-oriented background already had journalists warily questioning whether she had the chops to do sports reporting right on *Monday Night Football*.

Her first sports reporting exposure occurred in the early 1990s, when she was entertainment director for the New England Patriots and did well enough to secure a local TV series in Boston called *Sports Gals*, being one of three women discussing the athletic scene. That exposure led her back to Los Angeles for acting and sportscasting. By the turn of the 21st century, Guerrero became a reporter filing taped stories for *The Best Damn Sports Show Period* on Fox Sports Network. She undercut her professional standing there when word got out that she started dating Lou Merloni of the Boston Red Sox after interviewing the baseball player in the summer of 2001. (When she was on *Sports Gals* in Boston, she was engaged to but never married Patriots quarterback Hugh Millen.) By the fall of 2002, her paramour was Baltimore Orioles pitcher Scott Erickson.

Guerrero emphasized in interviews how she possessed a lifetime of interest in sports even though she had not pursued covering them in depth as an adult. When her mother died when she was 8, her father raised her along with two brothers, forcing her to learn about games to keep up with them. (She adopted her mother's maiden name as her surname to honor her afterward — she was born Lisa Coles.) But she offered no apologies for not following the standard approach for being a female sports reporter. "I'm a pretty different blend of a real feminine girly-girl and a true sports fan," Guerrero told Bob Rossi in *The Pittsburgh Post-Gazette*. "You don't see a lot of that on television."

You also didn't see many women sports reporters do a pinup pose either, but that's what Guerrero did in *Maxim* magazine in its "Women of Fox" pictorial in September 2002. Such cheesecake posing along with her love life kept lessening Guerrero's credibility among her peers, but she still kept her job with *The Best Damn Sports Show Period*.

On April 9, 2003, Guerrero celebrated her 39th birthday by doing her last day at work with *The Best Damn Sports Show Period*. She was tired of putting in 11-hour days to do just two updates an hour for the show rather than four as she had done originally, and with a job offer in hand to act in a movie starring Alec Baldwin called *The Play Maker*, Guerrero bid sportscasting adieu — or so it appeared at the time.

With Stark's vacancy now official, Guerrero became a candidate to replace her. While supposedly ABC had some 100 male and female applicants for the post, network sports officials preferred to keep the sidelines helmed by a woman, claiming it would attract the female audience. Guerrero obviously fell into that category, and she won over the network officials so well that they gave her a three-year contract to do the show. "I think it's the best job in sports with the two biggest legends, Al Michaels and John Madden," Guerrero said proudly to Jim Baker of *The Boston Globe* after the announcement came out.

However, most veteran sports reporters greeted the news with shock. Why did ABC pick Guerrero over, say, ESPN reporter Michele Tafoya, who had done plenty of sideline reports for sports on her network? Were they favoring looks above all else by going with a former bathing beauty? ABC sports officials denied that was the case, that Guerrero had merit to be in her job and would work out fine. "I'm very confident that she will have great chemistry with John and Al, and with her knowledge and experience covering the NFL, she will provide great insights about the game and its players," sports president George Bodenheimer told *The Toronto Sun.*

For her part, Guerrero felt her pinup status was not an issue, it was just something that happened because of her appeal. "If some 18-year-old thinks I'm hot, then I embrace that," she told Richard Sandomir in *The New York Times.* "It's awesome." (Sandomir then wryly pointed out that such remarks surely never were uttered by Guerrero's predecessor, Lesley Visser.)

Moving onward, Guerrero told Rudy Martzke in *USA Today* she was eager to handle the task set before her. "Al Michaels told me that every word and the color of my lipstick will be discussed, but I can't be afraid of having the best opportunity in live sports television," she said. "I just have to prepare and do the best job I can."

The latter sentence was the key statement to Guerrero's downfall — the need to prepare. While she had been filing taped pieces and giving updates on scores, Guerrero never had interviewed players and fans on the sidelines during a game. That inexperience would come to haunt her and define her rather quickly, and would give *Monday Night Football* some more on-air low points like it had two seasons earlier. Indeed, more than one observer compared her at the start to Eric Dickerson, and often unfavorably so.

One notable exception was Mike Tierney of *The Atlanta Journal-Constitution.* Sounding more like a playboy than a reporter, Tierney spent most of one article following Guerrero's debut in an August exhibition game salivating over her looks. "Even at age 39, she scores a 9 on the Bo Derek 1-to-10 scale. In modern parlance, she is fly," he wrote. He pooh-poohed those who felt she could not do the job and added that "When your audience is overwhelmingly male, why not get a babe for an insignificant role?"

Ending his sexist take, Tierney concluded, "So, lighten up, critics. As long as Guerrero doesn't botch names or pitch inane questions, what harm is there? She can't be worse than Eric Dickerson."

Oh, how soon Tierney had to eat his words....

When an "Ex-Teammate" Isn't One, Leading to More Mistakes

The first pre-season game covered by Guerrero was on August 4, 2003, between Kansas City and Green Bay. She acquitted herself well with interviews of Chiefs owner Lamar Hunt and Chiefs player Priest Holmes. Guerrero's official debut came in a contest between the Washington Redskins and New York Jets on September 4, 2003 (the season opener took place on a Thursday). After Washington won 16–13, she interviewed Redskins quarterback Patrick Ramsey about a discussion he had before the game.

"I saw you talking to Laveranues Coles, your ex-teammate," Guerrero said to Ramsey. "What did he say to you?"

The problem was that Coles still was with the Redskins and apparently Guerrero forgot that (or did not know it, which would be even more embarrassing, as Ramsey threw five passes to Coles for 106 yards during the game). Coles did play for the Jets a year earlier, which possibly prompted the misstatement from Guerrero.

To his credit, Ramsey did not make a big deal out of Guerrero's gaffe and continued talking with her. On the other hand, those watching Guerrero intently to see how she would fare could not believe how she showed her ignorance of the team lineup in this incident and attacked her strongly.

The next week, during the Tampa Bay Buccaneers–Philadelphia Eagles matchup, Guerrero further damaged her reputation with a ridiculous report on the excessive perspiration of Tampa Bay center John Wade. Guerrero told viewers she did not know whether Wade changed his sweaty pants at halftime as he told her he might do, but she would find out. Why? Well, according to Guerrero, "I know it sounds gross, I know it sounds disgusting. But we want to keep an eye on this situation."

That wasn't all, according to Rick Harmon of *The Tampa Tribune*. "Through her first two regular-season games, Guerrero has done nothing but embarrass herself, and it looks like ABC plans to keep her from asking any questions on her own," he wrote. "During her interview with Bucs LB Derrick Brooks, it was obvious the questions were predetermined and in every report she made during the game, she was spending more time looking at her notebook than the camera."

Shortly thereafter, ESPN anchors Stuart Scott and John Anderson mocked Guerrero's initial mistake on their *SportsCenter* news update on September 14. Recapping highlights of Washington's win, Anderson described Ramsey in a play as "using his new ... that's his teammate, Laveranues Coles!" Scott followed that up with, "I saw Laveranues talking to Ramsey before the game. They are teammates."

ABC sports officials reprimanded them for making fun of one of their fellow broadcasters, and Scott and Anderson apologized to Guerrero. Other reporters, however, did not have ABC restraining them and thus let loose against the newcomer.

"Guerrero is quickly exposing herself to be the biggest ditz to star in an ABC prime time vehicle since Suzanne Somers jiggled across the set of *Three's Company*," snickered *Denver Post* sports columnist Mark Kizla in one typical comment.

Adding to the negativity surrounding Guerrero was word she would appear in another layout for a men's magazine, this time the October 2003 issue of *FHM*. Guerrero posed for the seven pictures in lingerie between leaving *The Best Damn Sports Show Period* and getting the *Monday Night Football* gig, but its ill-timed arrival only added to the aura of Guerrero being a bimbo. The situation put the network on the defensive.

"People are taking cheap shots at her," ABC spokesperson Mark Mandel told Richard Deitsch in *Sports Illustrated*. "She has the total support of ABC." Privately, however, the sports department fretted as Guerrero continued to show ineptitude on air, such as looking down at her notes rather than into the camera frequently while giving updates. After her first three weeks on air, Guerrero had a lone defender in Jim Baker of *The Boston Globe*, who pleaded in his column to his colleagues and readers to "Give her a chance." Fewer did each week.

By early October Dusty Saunders of *The Rocky Mountain News* asked Lesley Visser, who was the *Monday Night Football* sideline reporter in 1998 and 1999, what she thought of Guerrero. Visser diplomatically did not address Guerrero specifically, but she did note that "You can't expect people to do a high-profile job if they don't have experience. I've been fortunate to gain experience through an association with talented writers and broadcasters."

That same month *The Houston Chronicle* reported that America's Line, a betting service, already offered odds on who would replace Guerrero. ESPN's Suzy Kolber and Michele Tafoya led the field at 5–1 each, while even Guerrero's forerunner and new mom Melissa Stark got a respectable 12–1 shot.

Another insult occurred in early November, when comedian Frank Caliendo of Fox's NFL pregame show quipped on air that "ABC should not apologize for hiring Lisa Guerrero but for allowing her to speak." Jillian Barberie, weathercaster on the same show, immediately came to Guerrero's defense, calling her "incredible."

Amid it all, Guerrero claimed to be above the fray and unconcerned about her critics. "I don't pay attention to those articles," she told Jim Baker of *The Boston Globe* in November. "I'm too busy working 12 hours a day preparing [for the broadcasts]."

She even had time to do a guest spot on *The George Lopez Show*, playing the sister of the titular character. The program aired December 19, 2003. It did not win her any favors as being taken seriously for her job. Guerrero may not have realized that, but her ABC bosses did.

When the season ended, Guerrero put the reports out of her mind and wed Scott Erickson in Hawaii on February 3, 2004, a day after he turned 36. More good news came to the couple the next day, when the struggling Erickson learned he had a minor-league deal with the New York Mets for the upcoming spring training.

But Guerrero's bad luck on the air continued a month later. "Lisa Guerrero did not do a good job with her questions to the competitors during the women's final of the World Figure Skating Championships," noted Rudy Martzke in his March 29 wrap-up of weekend TV sports in *USA Today*. His chief beef involved Guerrero saying to third-place finisher Michelle Kwan, "You've got to feel good about earning a medal here," even though Kwan had won the championship before—five times, in fact.

This glaring error was the final straw with ABC Sports executives. With the media against her—even Mike Tierney, *The Atlanta Journal-Constitution* reporter who defended Guerrero as having potential a year earlier, now termed her a "train wreck"—and Guerrero herself unable to make coherent on-the-spot commentary away from football, she was a liability to the organization. Five weeks later, they removed her from being the sideline reporter on *Monday Night Football*.

ABC gave Guerrero a chance to stay with the network under the three-year contract she signed in 2003. She chose to leave quietly instead. She mostly disappeared from headlines until, with little fanfare, she came back onto national TV as a reporter for the syndicated informational series *Inside Edition* in June 2006, shortly before what would have been her last season under her original contract for *Monday Night Football*.

Tafoya Love

On May 3, 2004, Michele Tafoya, by now ABC's sideline reporter for NBA games, became Guerrero's replacement. At age 39, Tafoya was a year younger than Guerrero, but she was much more a mature reporter than her predecessor based on her experience. *Monday Night Football* producer Fred Gaudelli made the decision to go with Tafoya jointly with Mike Pearl, the executive producer of ABC's NBA games who came to the network a year earlier after Guerrero's hiring. Reportedly the rapport Tafoya showed with Michaels in filing sideline reports while he announced NBA games made him endorse the possibility of her joining *Monday Night Football*.

Gaudelli made the announcement while explaining why Guerrero had to go. "I am a believer in Lisa's talent. I just didn't think that her talent [and] the role matched up," he said. "The sideline reporter role is an incredibly hectic environment; nothing is predictable. You can be ready to do one thing, and a second later we're doing something 180 degrees in the other direction. I just don't think that Lisa's talent matches up with what that role called for."

That reasoning did not wash with John Jackson of *The Chicago Sun-Times*, who followed the quote with these comments: "Excuse me, but the attributes Gaudelli described are the essence of being a reporter, sideline or otherwise. You must have the ability to react quickly and adjust based on information. Essentially,

Gaudelli is saying Guerrero lacked the basic skills that reporters in every medium — TV, radio or print — must possess to do their jobs properly. So why was she hired in the first place?"

At any rate, Tafoya certainly had the sports credibility Guerrero lacked. An MBA graduate from the University of Southern California, Tafoya auditioned unsuccessfully for the San Diego sports radio station XTRA-AM in 1993 before getting her first job with a radio station across the country in Charlotte, North Carolina. She then went to Minneapolis to do both TV and radio and started working freelance as a game reporter and studio host for CBS Sports in the mid to late 1990s.

In 2000 Tafoya joined ESPN, covering men and women's college basketball games as both an announcer and a reporter. Her work there was solid enough to make her a regular sideline reporter on NBA games on ABC in 2002.

"What I would like to bring to the role is ... to provide perspective from the sidelines, to bring the viewer a little bit closer to the action," Tafoya said to John Jackson. "No one does a better job of explaining the action on the field than John Madden and Al Michaels, but if there are ways we can enhance the telecast with information and things that I see and things that I learn when preparing for these games that are best told from that vantage point, then that is exactly what we want to provide. Just enhancing the broadcast in ways that can't be done from the booth."

Without mentioning Guerrero, Tafoya acknowledged to Jay Posner of *The San Diego Union-Tribune* that one woman who previously did the job she was inheriting complimented her appointment as an improvement for *Monday Night Football*. "Lesley Visser called me and she said something like, 'A return to authenticity.' People have been great that way. I've been getting e-mails and calls from people saying, 'You've earned this.' It's a little bit overwhelming for me, honestly. But it's really nice to hear people say, 'You've earned this.'" (Visser had even more vindication two years later on June 29, 2006, when she learned she would be the first woman to be inducted into the Pro Football Hall of Fame after three decades of covering the sport.)

At the same time, Tafoya realistically noted to Richard Sandomir of *The New York Times* that "I don't expect to escape unscathed. I'm not immune from criticism" about her reporting skills. She need not have worried. As expected, Tafoya blended well with Michaels and Madden in the fall of 2004, providing gaffe-free insights that complemented the duo's work on air. Finally, it seemed, ABC had the right combination working on *Monday Night Football*.

Just one slight problem to that — rumors crept up around the same time that even with the strong team now in place, ABC was considering dropping *Monday Night Football* as its ratings flagged and the network came back from the depths of its overall performance from the last few years.

The Rumors

On Monday, May 19, 2003, *ABC's 50th Anniversary Celebration* ran from 8 to 11 P.M. It didn't matter; viewers were more interested in seeing the competing hour-long episode of Robert marrying Amy on *Everybody Loves Raymond* on CBS. Or the campy TV-movie *Martha Inc.: The Story of Martha Stewart* starring Cybill Shepherd as the title temperamental domestic expert on NBC. Or a special edition of *American Idol* on Fox.

ABC's 50th Anniversary Celebration finished fourth in its time slot against those offerings, and its performance ensured that ABC would do so as well. The network that spent decades trying to overcome a third-place finish now had ended its 2002–03 season with its worst-ever performance, ironically with a special celebrating its own heritage. If that didn't deflate morale at the network, then nothing could.

The next season, ABC apparently had enough confidence in *Monday Night Football* not to include it as part of its "Primetime Preview Weekend" event at Disney's California Adventure theme park on September 6 and 7, 2003. The festival included screenings of all new ABC shows and appearances for autographs and question-and-answer sessions by cast members of new and returning ABC nighttime series—all except *Monday Night Football*, that is. However, it didn't include anyone either from *Primetime Monday*, the newsmagazine leading into *Monday Night Football* (or following it, in the case of West Coast viewers), so ABC might have just been concentrating on promoting its straight entertainment shows at "Primetime Preview Weekend."

Whatever the case, the kickoff did nothing to attract audiences for the network in 2003–04. Only one of the seven new series scored well enough to be renewed for a second season, the sitcom *Hope & Faith*. The other three comedies (*I'm With Her*, *It's All Relative* and *Married to the Kellys*) and three dramas (*10–8*, *Karen Sisco* and *Threat Matrix*) floundered quickly, and their midseason replacements were none too successful either, with the exception of *Extreme Makeover: Home Edition* on Sunday nights. At the same time, returning properties such as *N.Y.P.D. Blue* and *The Practice* were fading fast.

In contrast, *Monday Night Football* was a reliable performer. Its newest addition was a smart and overdue one for viewers—to broadcast the games permanently in high-definition TV (HDTV), as they had done in the 1999 season but since dropped. Once again, *Monday Night Football* would wind up as ABC's top-rated nighttime series at number 10 for the season while the network scrambled unsuccessfully to get out of fourth place. Its closest fellow ABC series in the list was *The Bachelor* at number 23.

Yet even with that distinction, there were disappointments associated with it. Most notably, NBC managed to outdraw *Monday Night Football* by more than 3 million viewers when its season finale for *Average Joe*, a reality series about plain-looking men attempting to be the one to woo a beautiful girl successfully, ran against Al and John on December 8, 2003.

By that time, insiders murmured that the costs of the show were far too high for the budget-minded men at ABC. It also was known within the industry that the next round of NFL TV rights was coming up in 2005, and given the expected increase the league would ask, could or would the network be able to handle it?

By the summer of 2004, experts figured the NFL wanted at least a 5 percent increase in rights fees from TV networks over the last contract, which had cost ABC $550 million annually. In recent years, ABC affiliates had contributed $34 million to help with the NFL contract costs, yet even with that amount and advertising, the show was hemorrhaging money badly. That virtually negated its continuing top 10 status.

Brad Adgate, research director for the advertising buying firm Horizon Media, addressed the network's situation succinctly in August to Meg James of *The Los Angeles Times*. "ABC is between a rock and a hard place. It's been ABC's highest-rated show, but at some point they have to ask: 'How much is too much?'"

One affiliate's general manager told James in the same article he doubted the cost issue weighed as heavily with network honchos as the show's overall prestige and standing. "If they are serious about fixing the network — and I think they are — then fixing the network doesn't equate to losing *Monday Night Football*," Darrell Brown of Denver's KMGH Channel 7 said.

An ABC spokesman told James in the same article the network would not comment before formal talks. NFL Commissioner Paul Tagliabue was as evasive too.

When *Monday Night Football* began its 2004 season, the new element at halftime was "You've Been Sacked," replacing the 2003 segment where players jammed with musical acts. It was like *Punk'd*, the MTV series that pulled practical jokes on celebrities. The first one had Rams wideout Tony Holt being fooled into doing a fake magazine shoot in a tutu. Though critics derided it as asinine, "You've Been Sacked" did seem an apt statement to describe what ABC officials did to the series after the season ended.

The Announcement— Monday Night Football Is History

On April 18, 2005, the word became official — *Monday Night Football* would have no more regular appearances on ABC after the fall of 2005. It would move instead to ABC's cable partner ESPN. "Retaining *Monday Night Football* simply didn't make smart financial sense for ABC," ABC Sports and ESPN President George Bodenheimer said. "We could not reconcile the fees against the revenues."

ESPN got about $2.70 a month per every home subscribed to a cable system carrying it, and that fee helped finance a deal for them. Also, ESPN officials were worried that Fox Sports would scoop up the rights in case they did not win them. ESPN planned to start the Monday games at 8:40 P.M. instead of 9:07 P.M. It had no announcers listed when its rights for the games became official.

Aiding ABC's decision was the arrival of three new hits on the network in the 2004–05 season, taking less pressure on the network to keep nighttime football. *Desperate Housewives* was at number 4, *Grey's Anatomy* at number 9 and *Lost* at number 16 in the ratings when the cancellation of *Monday Night Football* was made official. With those three shows, ABC now found itself competing seriously with Fox for second place for the season (Fox eked out a win), and NBC's failures led it from first to fourth, the biggest decline ever by a network in one year.

Coincidentally or not, NBC had not had rights for the NFL since 1998. In fact, NBC had no major regular sports series on its network since the NBA in 2002. "I think NBC was starting to experience what CBS went through when it lost the NFL," said Neal Pilson, who was head of CBS Sports when it lost the NFL in 1994, to Richard Sandomir in *The New York Times*. "It took almost eight years, but they looked at CBS's experience, which hit much harder and quicker, and saw what it lost without the NFL."

So, in the NFL rights negotiations in 2005, NBC agreed to add Sunday night football to its schedule starting with the 2006–07 season. A pregame show would air from 7 to 8 P.M. Eastern, followed by the game starting at 8 P.M.

The NFC contract for 2006–2011 totaled $4.275 billion, with Fox paying $712.5 million of that figure and NBC paying $600 million of it. The AFC contract totaled $3.735 billion, with ESPN paying $1.1 billion annually and CBS paying $622.5 million of that amount. As Steve Zipay of *Newsday* noted, the yearly rights fee for pro football was greater than the combined rights fees the networks and cable TV paid for the summer Olympics ($894 million), the National Basketball Association ($766 million), Major League Baseball ($559 million), NCAA basketball ($565 million) and the Professional Golf Association ($212.5 million).

The Reaction

"Last year, I would have said it would be devastating to ABC," Marc Berman, senior TV writer at *Adweek*, told Stuart Elliott of *The New York Times*. "But not anymore, because it suddenly has three hit scripted shows, *Desperate Housewives*, *Lost* and *Grey's Anatomy*, which are building blocks for a successful schedule."

Likewise, some operators of ABC stations just shrugged off the change. "I'm not disappointed about it at all," Ron Hubbard, general manager of ABC's Minnesota affiliate KSTP, said to Judd Zulgad of *The Minneapolis Star Tribune*. "If the Vikings played every week it would be fantastic, but they don't. Other than that, [the games] really interfere with our news and people's regular television habits." Hubbard added that he did not think his station got a return from the investment of the previous eight-year contract with the NFL.

But Greg Wyshynski, a writer for the online magazine *Sports Fan*, was livid about football going to ESPN. He used a few analogies to other TV shows to make his point.

"Imagine if I had told you 10 years ago that *Seinfeld* was moving its first-run episodes to TBS," he wrote. "Or that *ER* was leaving NBC to starting running original episodes on TNT. Or that *The Simpsons* had decided to continue the adventures of America's Greatest Dad on the Cartoon Network. Would you think, for even a second, that the gain in prestige for these cable networks was somehow greater than the drop in prestige for these network television programs? Relocating *Monday Night Football* to cable television diminishes the institution."

Yet another columnist gauged the change quite differently. "It has been nearly a week since the big news broke: *Monday Night Football*, after 36 years, is off ABC following this season," Phil Mushnick of *The New York Post* wrote. "Yet we've yet to hear a single soul express remorse, regret, surprise, joy or any reactive emotion of any kind. And it figures. *Monday Night Football* has been dead for roughly half the country — this half — for years. It faded, then faded some more, nearly suffocating in a wallet." Mushnick said the overexposure with games on Sunday and the late ending of many games at around 12:30 A.M. in the East were prime reasons for the show's decline.

One person took a humorous take on it. Richard Sandomir of *The New York Times* called on the spirit of one of the founders of the show to put things into satirical perspective. "Hello again, everyone, this is Howard Cosell, speaking of *Monday Night Football* and its horrifying transfer from ABC, the network that I verily built with the red-haired yoda, Roone Arledge, to ESPN, that citadel of sports veracity…. Obtuse, inane, lunkheaded, presbyopic, vacuous and misanthropic — there is no question that transporting Monday Night to ESPN is all of these." The article ended with Cosell directing his legal team to bar ESPN from using his image to promote Sunday night football.

It was funny, but the sad truth remained — no matter what anybody said or did, and no matter how many people thought they would never see the day, *Monday Night Football* was fated to go off ABC within a year.

12

2005: Prepping the
Final Curtain

As ABC, ESPN, NBC and even CBS and Fox attempted to sort out in the summer of 2005 what personnel would be working which pro football shows in the reconfigured world starting the next year, there was a moment of levity to remind them all just what sort of power *Monday Night Football* still carried in popular culture.

Back on November 15, 2004, as one of ABC's sometimes corny promotional openers for the game, there ran a segment with Nicollette Sheridan, the resident blonde vixen on the network's new Sunday night hit comic soap opera *Desperate Housewives*. She showed up as her character Edie wearing nothing but a towel in the Philadelphia Eagles locker room to talk to Terrell Owens, the team's star wide receiver (Philadelphia was playing Dallas that night and swamped them 49–21). After some suggestive small talk, she dropped her towel, and an impressed Owens said he would forget about the game while he approached her.

That ended that bit, but it prompted a wave of controversy at the time. Even though Sheridan was not shown naked, the implication was obvious that she and Owens were on their way to having sex. Critics attacked that scenario as offensive both racially (a black player would rather have sex with a white woman than play ball) and sexually (Sheridan was nearly naked all the time while Owens was fully suited up). Owens downplayed the incident, saying people were too sensitive, but ABC apologized for the segment, particularly as parents complained their children should be able to watch the games without seeing soft-core sex skits air before them. It also prompted an investigation for obscenity by the Federal Communications Commission (FCC).

That controversy had been forgotten by most people once the spring came around and news about *Monday Night Football* became public. Then, on the ESPY sports awards show on ESPN July 13, 2005, Owens showed up to present one category with Sheridan. Seeing her dressed up next to him, he quipped: "So this is what you look like with your clothes on."

All right, so it wasn't hilarious, and prompted mostly awkward laughs at best.

But it showed despite how ABC downplayed its situation, *Monday Night Football* remained a top attraction for the network. If any ABC executive hoped saying goodbye could be a quiet process that could be expedited for their sake of moving on and getting a more profitable Monday night, he or she was strongly mistaken.

Madden Goes to NBC, Michaels Uncertain

By June NBC made the first definitive public move regarding its 2006 pro football announcing team by revealing that John Madden would be the analyst for its Sunday night games. This decision meant Madden would become the first football announcer to call games on all four major broadcast networks — first CBS, then Fox and ABC.

By the end of July, ESPN had signed Al Michaels as its play-by-play man for Monday games in 2006, joined by Joe Theismann as analyst. Theismann had covered Sunday games for ESPN since 1988 with Mike Patrick at play-by-play (since 1987) and Paul Maguire as co-analyst (since 1998) — neither Patrick nor Maguire would be involved in the Monday NFL coverage. Michele Tafoya would do sideline duty along with Suzy Kolber of ESPN, making them the first pair of female sideline reporters regularly covering professional football. Kolber first started working with ESPN in the mid–1990s.

Also in the last week of July 2005, NBC announced its veteran sports reporter Bob Costas would anchor the NFL studio show for pregame and halftime action during the Sunday night games starting in the fall of 2006. The network already had announced Cris Collinsworth, an analyst with Fox's NFL pregame show, would join Costas in the NBC studio show in 2006 too.

By the start of the season in September, however, NBC had not confirmed who might do play-by-play with Madden. This suggested to some people the network held out the hope of getting Michaels back via last-minute maneuvering and hurting ESPN in the process. For his part, NBC Sports President Dick Ebersol was tight lipped for the time being, only saying that several candidates were under consideration. When word got out later that fall that he had hired *Monday Night Football* producer Fred Gaudelli and director Drew Esocoff to repeat their duties for NBC in 2006, ABC and ESPN officials realized that their plans for Michaels the next year might not be a done deal after all.

The Last Season Begins

"Lame-duck years aren't fun," Michaels told Michael Hiestand of *USA Today* about the atmosphere surrounding the last season of *Monday Night Football* on

ABC. "We all know that. But you've got to be resolute about going to work and making this look like it's always looked or better."

If there was trepidation about doing the work, it certainly did not rub off on much of the TV audience. The official season opening game on Thursday, September 8, 2005, between the Oakland Raiders and the New England Patriots finished at number 1 for that week. Helping it in the standings was the fact most other shows on that week were repeats. Still, it was an impressive accomplishment for a show everyone knew had its days numbered.

Faring worse was the *NFL Opening Kickoff* hour special airing before the game in the East and Midwest and after it in later time zones that same night. A concert featuring the Rolling Stones, Kanye West and other top recording stars, it wound up at number 34, placing third in its period in the early time periods opposite its CBS and Fox competition. Hosted by Freddie Prinze Jr. (whose sitcom *Freddie* was one of the new ABC series introduced that fall, all of which flopped), the special did have the distinction of being aired on a delay of a few seconds for fear the artists might say or sing something offensive — the networks understood that a vigilant FCC could and probably would fine them for obscenity as it attempted in the wake of Janet Jackson's "wardrobe malfunction" during the halftime show of the 2004 Super Bowl. Likewise, *Monday Night Football* adopted a delay in its telecasts for the same reasons during the 2005–06 season.

The Monday night games now had a little bit of old mixed with a lot of new. After having guest artists sing during the opening of the show last year, it went back to having Hank Williams Jr. do "Are You Ready for Some Football?" For the halftime highlights, another country star, Tim McGraw, adapted and performed his 1995 hit "I Like It, I Love It" with lyrics updated weekly to describe recent football events. A more dubious halftime addition were the so-so minute monologues of Jimmy Kimmel, who had his own late night talk show on ABC.

And there remained tie-ins for just about everything else on the show, including having the Visa sky cam able to do coverage in the air and promoting ABC shows and Disney movies in interviews and taped segments, such as having Baltimore Ravens linebacker Ray Lewis interact with the characters from the cartoon film *Chicken Little* on the October 31 show.

The show remained at number 1 during its first official Monday game of the season, with a 19.6 rating, its most popular individual contest since 2002. Aiding that turnout was that the series ran a rare doubleheader, starting a New York Giants–New Orleans face-off at 7:30 P.M. Eastern, then leaving that contest to cover the Washington Redskins versus the Dallas Cowboys 90 minutes later (the former game continued on ESPN). This schedule arose in the aftermath of Hurricane Katrina, which left New Orleans without a regular stadium to play in and forced the NFL to redo the team's schedule now that it had no home venue. Covering the earlier game was ESPN's usual Sunday night NFL team of Mike Patrick, Joe Theismann and Paul Maguire.

To respond to this situation, ABC wisely held a telethon during the game for viewers to contribute money to hurricane relief. Among those manning the phones for donations during the telecast included two faces familiar to longtime *Monday Night Football* viewers — Frank Gifford and (ahem) Eric Dickerson.

Two other notable events occurred as the season progressed. One was the pregnancy of sideline reporter Michele Tafoya. She went on maternity leave by the time of the September 19 doubleheader. To handle her duties, ABC moved its NCAA football reporter Samantha Ryan to take her place the rest of the season. (In June 2006 Ryan relocated to CBS to do sideline reports for the NFL and college basketball.)

On October 10, 2005, the San Diego Chargers came close but lost to the Pittsburgh Steelers 24–22. That game was of note because San Diego had not been on the series since 1996, one of the longest periods of absence ever.

The ratings slipped considerably after the opener, getting a 16.1 rating for September 19, 13.6 for September 26, 15.6 for October 3, 15.7 for October 10, 14.4 for October 17, 14.2 for October 24 and 16.5 for October 31. However, those showings still placed the series in the top 20, and almost always in first place for its time slot (its nearest challengers were the top 20 CBS hits *Two and a Half Men*, replacing the 9–9:30 P.M. slot previously held by *Everybody Loves Raymond*, and *CSI: Miami* from 10 to 11 P.M.).

Then on November 7, the series topped its season opener with a 21.9 rating, then passed that mark even more with a 22.6 rating on November 28. That number was the series' highest individual game rating since December 18, 2000.

That was the top audience for the series that season, however. The next week, December 5, viewership dropped dramatically to a 15.1 and declined even more on December 12 down to 13.6.

By the December 19, 2005 contest, where the Baltimore Ravens had one of the biggest blowouts ever on the series by downing the Green Bay Packers 48–3, only 12 million viewers watched, the lowest audience for a *Monday Night Football* game since 1991. That must have left an odd feeling among ABC executives — relief that interest flagged on a show soon to be leaving the network, but concern that it might be flaming out worse than they had expected.

The Final Game

The show ended on December 26 with a contest between the New England Patriots and the New York Jets. It was a meaningless game, as the Patriots already were assured of going to the playoffs no matter what the outcome was. For diehard *Monday Night Football* fans, however, it was essential viewing.

The series' 550th show was a monument to the series' classic combination of Howard Cosell, Frank Gifford and Don Meredith from 1971 to 1973 and 1977 to 1984. In a show awash in nostalgia, it was telling that little was mentioned concerning other previous announcers for the series. It included opening with Cosell's introduction from the first show and having at the start of the fourth quarter Meredith serenading, "Turn out the lights, the party's over" in a prerecorded bit.

Meredith also showed up in a special two-minute segment taped at his home in Santa Fe. He mentioned how *Monday Night Football* gave its audience "something to talk about at the watering hole" at work the next day. ABC Sports and ESPN President George Bodenheimer told Michael McCarthy of *USA Today* that Gifford persuaded Meredith to come out of retirement and tape the segment, though he turned down the opportunity to be on the show live.

"From the very first day, it was different," Gifford said of the series in his taped bit at the top. He later described the roles the show's classic crew had in a half-time conversation live in the booth with Michaels. "Howard pontificated. Don Meredith was the country guy who kept the big city slicker straight. I kept law and order."

Madden and Michaels even did some discussion about the Cosell-Gifford-Meredith lineup themselves after Michaels admitted he did not know where to start. Madden asked him if it was true that the atmosphere the trio had on air was the same off screen. Michaels sidestepped defining the exact nature of their relationships, saying instead just that the series let the announcers talk about issues that were "verboten until then" on NFL telecasts.

Michele Tafoya had hoped to rejoin her partners of two years, but she did not get to be on the final game. Having given birth to a son on November 18, she was ready to go on the air but started vomiting five minutes prior to kickoff, which forced her not to show up.

At the end, the show turned sentimental when Michaels thanked former ABC Sports president Dennis Swanson for giving him a "20-year E-ticket ride" on the series. (That was an appropriate nod to the network's owner, as rides at Disney parks at first required different levels of tickets for admission, and those requiring E-tickets were always considered the best ones.) He patted Gifford on the shoulder and said simply: "I can't thank you enough." To Madden, Michaels said: "A virtual champagne toast to you, my friend." To which Madden responded: "They can't take the memories away."

The game itself was an anti-climax, with New England quickly and thoroughly crossing the field to score several times against New York in the early going. "I'm not sure if we watched a perfect drive or surgery," Madden quipped about the ease the Patriots had in facing their opponent. Ironically, New England won 31–21—the same losing score the Jets had in the first *Monday Night Football* against the Cleveland Browns in 1970. Jets backup quarterback Vinny Testaverde had the distinction of scoring the last touchdown on *Monday Night Football*.

The game ended at 12:12 A.M. Eastern Time, after a final clip of Meredith singing, "Turn out the lights," followed by Hank Williams Jr. taking over delivery of the song while other past highlights ran. A notation in the credits read that it was done in memory of the now-deceased Pete Rozelle and Roone Arledge.

In the ratings for the week of December 26, 2005, through January 1, 2006, the last broadcast of *Monday Night Football* finished at number 2 that week with 14.4 million viewers, falling considerably behind the top finisher, a repeat of *CSI* on CBS with 17.5 million viewers. That was a nice high finish for the week, but when one considers the show's average audience had been higher than that just eight years earlier, it definitely was nowhere near the ratings grabber that the finales for other network nighttime series that year such as *Friends* and *Everybody Loves Raymond* were. Still, it was a better performance than the shows that were its immediate successors.

The Replacement Blues

With *Monday Night Football* finished, ABC had to address another perpetual headache — what to put in its place the rest of the season. Having known about this situation for months, and realizing that whatever they installed there had a decent chance of staying there permanently, one would expect they would come up with a strong entry or two to make viewers forget about football. But once again, ABC dropped the ball in programming the slots.

Picked to do battle at the start of the workweek were *Emily's Reasons Why Not*, a *Sex in the City* imitation sitcom starring Heather Graham from 9 to 9:30 P.M., and two returning series, *Jake in Progress*, a former hour-long comedy-drama from the spring of 2005 starring John Stamos as a man looking for love from 9:30 to 10, and *The Bachelor*, a reality show wherein a gaggle of women competed to be the companion of man from 10 to 11. With the audience for *Monday Night Football* being more than two thirds male, it was ridiculous for ABC to program these shows that skewed so obviously to females. But the network did, and it paid for it.

When they debuted on the midseason Monday night lineup on January 9, 2006, *Emily's Reasons Why Not* and the newly trimmed *Jake in Progress* came in fourth in the 9–10 P.M. Eastern time slot, with the former getting 6.3 million viewers to finish at number 72 and the latter getting 5.6 million to finish at number 76. Their performance was so poor that ABC canned them immediately and declined to air any more episodes of each, making *Emily's Reasons Why Not* just one of a handful of TV series ever to air only one episode (the others were *You're in the Picture* on January 20, 1961, *Turn-On* on February 5, 1969, *Co-Ed Fever* on February 4, 1979, *South of Sunset* on October 27, 1993, *Public Morals* on October 30, 1996, *Lawless* on March 22, 1997, *Dot Comedy* on December 8, 2000 and *The Will* on January 8, 2005). It was a shaky leadoff for ABC in approaching programming Monday nights without football.

ABC then went with double airings of *The Bachelor* from 9–11 P.M. Mondays through the spring. Even though the series still usually finished last in its time slot against the major broadcast networks, its average was higher than that of *Emily's Reasons Why Not* and *Jake in Progress*, so ABC decided to renew it for the 2006–2007 fall schedule from 9 to 10 P.M. Mondays even though it no longer was as strong a draw as when it started.

For 10 to 11 P.M. Mondays, the network also renewed another mediocre performer that had run four episodes in that slot starting April 24, 2006, the young adult drama *What About Brian*. Even though it finished in third place during its run, ABC apparently felt that since it came from the same production company that gave it the hit drama *Lost*, it had potential to grow.

So that's what ABC decided to use to replace its longest-running nighttime series ever for the fall of 2006, outside of news and movies — an aging reality show and a faltering soap opera, both with little "buzz" surrounding them. Coupled with the return of usual third-place finisher *Wife Swap* from 8 to 9 P.M., which started in that slot in the fall of 2005, the very weak schedule hardly sent shivers up the spines of other network programmers. Maybe ABC kept it weak to help ESPN build an audience, but for a broadcast network to do so is incredibly shortsighted for its own interests in the long run. Many people felt the same way regarding ABC dropping *Monday Night Football*.

ESPN and NBC Finalize Their Plans

The ending of *Monday Night Football* was not the last pairing of Madden and Michaels on ABC that season. The men also had the honor of covering Super Bowl XL (that's 40 to non–Roman numeral fans) where the Pittsburgh Steelers defeated the Seattle Seahawks 21–10 on February 5, 2006. It naturally was the number 1 rated show of the week, though not the biggest Super Bowl telecast. Its 46.1 rating was the highest score for a Super Bowl since 2000, however.

What arguably was more important in the sports announcing world came later that week. On February 8, ABC and ESPN announced that they would release Michaels from their contracts to let him join Madden in the NBC booth the next fall. In making the change, ESPN replaced Michaels with its veteran play-by-play man Mike Tirico to join Joe Theismann in its Monday football night coverage later in 2006, and it also disclosed that Tony Kornheiser would accompany Theismann as an analyst there.

The appointment was sweet justice for Kornheiser, who just missed out on doing *Monday Night Football* in 2000 when ABC went with Dennis Miller. Instead he went to work for ESPN thereafter on the popular *Pardon This Interruption* daily sports review show while keeping his column in *The Washington Post*. Like Madden, Kornheiser feared planes and so announced he would get to games via bus instead.

To complete the Michaels deal, the media was amused to learn, the conditions of his trade to NBC included the latter giving up rights to Oswald the Lucky Rabbit, a cartoon character created by Walt Disney that wound up being owned by Universal, the movie studio that had merged with NBC by 2006. NBC also gave ESPN a few other minor rights to its sports in exchange for Michaels.

With Michaels, Madden, director Drew Esocoff and producer Fred Gaudelli on board, NBC now was ready to tout that its Sunday night show would have the same personnel as *Monday Night Football* and thus be a natural successor to that storied series. Not so, responded ESPN officials, claiming that its coverage would be much more extensive; it would spend all Mondays promoting that night's game and use more personnel to cover it.

Meanwhile, NBC unveiled its 2006 fall season schedule in April 2006. The opener was to be the Miami Dolphins visiting the Pittsburgh Steelers on September 7 (a Thursday), then the first Sunday game would be on September 10 with the Indianapolis Colts facing the New York Giants.

The next night, ESPN's first edition of football on Monday nights would kick off with a doubleheader — Minnesota at Washington starting at 7 P.M. Eastern, then San Diego at Oakland at 10:15 P.M. The ESPN games thereafter would have a regular starting time of 8:30 P.M. Eastern (the kickoff actually would be at 8:40 P.M.) The preseason games would begin on August 14.

Also in April, NBC said another ESPN veteran, Andrea Kremer, would be its sideline reporter for the Sunday night games. Though she had not done sideline reporting in her 17 years with ESPN, NBC officials assured skeptics that her extensive sports coverage elsewhere would compensate for that fact and not make her another Lisa Guerrero.

The final addition to NBC's Sunday games came in May when the network finalized its studio show lineup. Five regulars, a rather large crowd for the job, would do the pregame and halftime honors. Joining the already mentioned Bob Costas and Cris Collinsworth were Jerome Bettis, freshly retired as a running back for the Pittsburgh Steelers and affectionately known as "The Bus"; Peter King; and Sterling Sharpe, formerly of ESPN and, yes, a candidate for *Monday Night Football* several times earlier.

Many of the names involved with the new NFL nighttime games were connected in some way to *Monday Night Football*, so it was obvious they hoped to emulate that show's success. But with NBC facing a more competitive Sunday night (when football would face two top 30 hits in the 9–10 P.M. Eastern slot alone — *Desperate Housewives* on ABC and a relocated *Cold Case* on CBS), and ESPN being unavailable to some 20 million viewers who watch only broadcast television, the success rate for either enterprise looked iffy going into the season.

Do viewers want a Sunday night game after being able to watch two others earlier in the day on other networks? Do they desire to see Mondays on ESPN focused on that night's contest? Or will the saturation turn off the public, as many have feared over the years? The only way to find out, as any TV expert could tell you, is to keep watching those who are watching TV.

Final Thoughts

The collapse of *Monday Night Football* grew from many factors. Its roots began with its failure to cultivate analysts that could fill the shoes of Cosell and Meredith. Both had their faults, but at their best, Cosell was a keen observer of the plusses and minuses for each team, equally able to praise the coaching skill of Don Shula for a masterful stroke of taking a safety to preserve a win for a game as to condemn a faltering player who needed to retire but whose arrogance prevented him from doing so. In contrast, Meredith was a man with a laid back approach whose humor could prick but never sting, except when he and Cosell were really on the outs, of course. He was a natural ham, whereas many analysts thereafter have come up with forced jokes that seem rehearsed.

Too often thereafter, ABC seemed content to install men in the booth who all agreed with each other and thus sounded bland and obvious, the Gifford-Michaels-Dierdorf combo being the most egregious example. Or they cast their team with little concern about cohesion and competence — think of the Michaels-Miller-Fouts-Stark-Dickerson grouping for that example. It all but drove away people who would have watched the game purely for entertainment alone, because it failed the basic criteria one looked for in an unscripted TV show, of chemistry and variety among the regulars.

Increasing costs also had an impact on the series, but let's keep in mind that ABC's parent company, Disney, was willing to shell out more than $1 billion to get ESPN to host Monday night games, more than it ever spent for football on ABC. Indeed, for a network that mentioned so often how much pro football cost them in the last few years, it's hard to figure out how they think it will be more profitable on an outlet with less exposure, particularly for lower-income viewers who make up a substantial part of the *Monday Night Football* audience. Another explanation may be in order, but it's a sad one.

Since the early 1980s, pundits had been predicting that all sports would leave the networks for cable or pay-per-view, as the old-style school of television (broadcasters) could not or would not be able to pay the growing exorbitant rights for those events. They were wrong then, but it may be coming finally to that era now, thanks in part to Disney's effort, hopefully unintentionally, that has led to the continuing decline in quality and quantity of ABC Sports.

In June 2005, Disney leaders decided to have the department's programming, public relations, legal, marketing and finance units all fall under ESPN management, ostensibly to save costs (there were cutbacks in staff associated with the announcement). ABC Sports production managers would have control of some ESPN personnel working underneath them, but that really is inconsequential in light of the other alterations. Sports on ABC now are nothing more than ESPN presented on a broadcast network, a bad precedent to be sure.

Does NBC have its cable partners MSNBC or CNBC produce its news? No. Likewise, does CBS allow MTV or VH-1 to produce all its music specials? No again. No other broadcast network allows the setup ABC has with ESPN right now, and for a network that stood apart from the others during its earlier days specifically in this field, it is humiliating to watch. Roone Arledge never would have allowed this situation to exist.

That's all speculation now. What's important in the minds of *Monday Night Football* fans and network executives is whether the NBC and ESPN offerings begun in the fall of 2006 will prove to be worthy long-term replacements for what they had been getting. My vote is that they will not, at least in terms of popularity.

The Sunday NFL shows did do better in the ratings in 2006 than the flagging entertainment shows NBC had aired previously (e.g., *American Dreams*). But the combination of Madden and Michaels is getting as old as the men themselves (both are older than 60), and unless it's a compelling match-up, it's hard to see how it will make younger viewers inclined to watch the series all the time, particularly with all the competing media available to them via the internet, DVDs, electronic games, etc. Additionally, the studio show preceding it from 7 to 8 P.M. Eastern has to deal with spillover games from contests on Fox and CBS cutting into its audience, and while many switched channels in 2006 to see NBC's NFL game, far fewer did so for its pregame show.

As for the ESPN games, starting them at the bottom of the hour is a questionable move. That risky decision assumes that potential viewers will have no competing hour-long shows they will have to stop watching to change the channel and check out the start of the series. And let's face it—Mike Tirico and Tony Kornheiser are personalities familiar only to ESPN viewers, while Joe Theismann's fame as the Washington Redskins quarterback occurred back in the mid–1980s. True, ratings in 2006 set records for cable—but they were lower than ABC's in 2005.

In the meantime, ABC has lost a piece of its history that led it from its perpetual upstart reputation to become the leader among the networks in the mid–1970s. The NFL has lost a venue that offered the league its greatest and biggest regular exposure ever in its nearly 80 years of operations. Together, they showed that nighttime sports could be a top TV attraction, able to compete and even beat the best entertainment shows put against it.

It's possible that both parties may find out after the current TV rights deal expires that the moves with NBC and ESPN were not as productive in the long run and therefore will try to revive *Monday Night Football*, but that would be a return in name only, no doubt requiring another crew to take over the property. As anyone familiar with TV revivals know, all that will do is make people regard the original even more fondly while ignoring the reincarnation.

So, *Monday Night Football* now joins the pantheon of *The Ed Sullivan Show*, *Gunsmoke*, *What's My Line?* and a few others as legendary TV series whose long runs and massive popularity made them transcend the medium into becoming modern-day classic pop culture. The reverence and attention shown to Cosell, Meredith and Gifford in the press and on the show during the December 2006 finale attested to that. It's become one of those "They don't make 'em like that anymore" series when people refer to the current state of television. As it well should be.

Turn out the lights — the party is definitely over.

Appendix A: *Monday Night Football* Cast and Crew

Announcers: Howard Cosell (1970–83), Don Meredith (1970–73, 1977–84), Keith Jackson (1970), Frank Gifford (1971–97), Fred Williamson (1974), Alex Karras (1974–76), Fran Tarkenton (1979–82), O.J. Simpson (1983–85), Joe Namath (1985), Al Michaels (1986–2006), Dan Dierdorf (1987–98), Boomer Esiason (1998–99), Dennis Miller (2000–01), Dan Fouts (2000–01), John Madden (2002–06).

Sideline Reporters: Lynn Swann (1994–97), Lesley Visser (1998–99), Melissa Stark (2000–02), Eric Dickerson (2000–01), Lisa Guerrero (2003), Michele Tafoya (2004–05), Sam Ryan (2005–06).

Executive Producers: Roone Arledge (1970–85), Dennis Swanson (1986–96), Steve Bornstein (1996–99), Howard Katz (1999–2003), George Bodenheimer (2003–06).

Producers: Chet Forte and Dennis Lewin (1970–72), Don Ohlmeyer (1973–76, 2000), Dennis Lewin (1977–79), Terry O'Neil (1980), Bob Goodrich (1980–85), Ken Wolfe (1986–99), Fred Gaudelli (2001–2006).

Directors: Chet Forte (1970–86), Larry Kamm (1987), Craig Janoff (1988–99), Drew Esocoff (2000–2006).

Others:

Replay Unit Director (1973): Joe Aceli

Technical Director (1973): Bill Morris, John Broderick

Associate Director (1973): Dick Buffinton

Appendix B: *Monday Night Football* Seasonal Ratings

1970-71*	1982-83: #10	1994-95: #5
1971-72: #25	1983-84: #21	1995-96: #5
1972-73: #18	1984-85: #25	1996-97: #7
1973-74: #19	1985-86: #15	1997-98: #5
1974-75: #32	1986-87: #18	1998-99: #4
1975-76: #30	1987-88: #16	1999-2000: #7
1976-77: #22	1988-89: #15	2000-01: #5
1977-78: #16	1989-90: #10	2001-02: #7
1978-79: #28	1990-91: #9	2002-03: #10
1979-80: #37	1991-92: #12	2003-04: #10
1980-81: #20	1992-93: #7	2004-05: #10
1981-82: #11	1993-94: #8	2005-06: #12

Figure not available, but believed to be between #35 and 40

Sources

Introduction

Wai, Leila. "Don't Close Your Eyes for Football Anymore," *The Honolulu Advertiser* website, April 19, 2005.

Chapter 3

Adams, Val. "Monsters to Be Just Plain Folks on a CBS-TV Comedy Series," *New York Times*, Feb. 15, 1964, p. 50.

Durslag, Melvin. "Pro Football Tackles Doris Day, Carol Burnett and the Movies," *TV Guide*, Sept. 19–25, 1970, pp. 14–16.

Chapter 4

Amory, Cleveland. "Review: *Monday Night Football*," *TV Guide*, Dec. 19–25, 1970, p. 25.

Axthelm, Pete. "Football's Long Weekend," *Newsweek*, Oct. 5, 1970, p. 63.

Boyle, Robert H. "TV Wins on Points," *Sports Illustrated*, Nov. 2, 1970, pp. 14–17.

Deford, Frank. "TV Talk," *Sports Illustrated*, Oct. 5, 1970, p. 9.

_____. "I've Won. I've Beat Them," *Sports Illustrated*, Aug. 8, 1983, pp. 66–82.

Dunham, Wayne. "Football Action from Every Angle," *The Chicago Tribune TV Week*, Sept. 3–9, 1978, pp. 5 and 6.

Leonard, John. "Cosell: Milder, But Does He Satisfy?" *Life*, Nov. 13, 1970, p. 24.

Chapter 5

Birmingham, Frederic A. "Frank Gifford: A Sense of Style," *Saturday Evening Post*, October 1978, pp. 62, 63 and 117–120.

Daley, Robert. "The Man They Love to Hate," *The*

New York Times Magazine, Sept. 1, 1974, pp. 10, 11, 27–31.

Shrake, Edwin. "What Are They Doing with the Sacred Game of Pro Football?" *Sports Illustrated*, Oct. 25, 1971, pp. 96–106.

_____. "The Defection of Dandy Don," *Sports Illustrated*, April 22, 1974, pp. 38–42.

"Welcome to the 1,000-Hour Season," *Sports Illustrated*, Sept. 16, 1974, p. 97.

Chapter 6

Amory, Cleveland. "Review: *Saturday Night Live with Howard Cosell*," *TV Guide*, Nov. 15–21, 1975, p. 44.

"Due Bills," *Time*, Sept. 29, 1975, p. 84.

Leggett, William. "ABC Has the Monday Blahs," *Sports Illustrated*, May 10, 1976, p. 60.

Lorge, Barry. "Drysdale Pleasant, But Not ABC Baseball Coverage," *The Washington Post*, April 14, 1978, p. D-5.

"Mongo at the Mike," *Newsweek*, Oct. 28, 1974, pp. 91 and 92.

New York Times, Nov. 22, 1977, p. 43.

Rhoden, Bill. "Howard Cosell Tells It Like It Is," *Ebony*, December 1976, pp. 76–84.

Sanoff, Alvin P. "Sports Are Not 'The Answers to All of Society's Problems': A Conversation with Howard Cosell," *U.S. News and World Report*, Sept. 16, 1985, pp. 74 and 75.

"TV's Impact on Pro Football: Size-Up by the Commissioner," *U.S. News and World Report*, Aug. 12, 1974, p. 53.

Chapter 7

Brady, Dave. "Meredith Limits TV Talk Role," *The Washington Post*, Oct. 25, 1978, p. C-5.

_____. "Vike QB to Join ABC-TV," *The Washington Post*, May 9, 1979, p. E-1.

Durslag, Melvin. "How Monday Night Carried the Day," *TV Guide*, Aug. 30–Sept. 5, 1980, pp. 24–28.

Kowet, Don. "Backstage at *Monday Night Football*," *TV Guide*, Nov. 29–Dec. 5, 1980, pp. 28–32.

Leggett, William. "Ol' Don May Be a New Danderoo," *Sports Illustrated*, Oct. 3, 1977, p. 42.

MacPherson, Myra. "Dandy Don, Away from the Mike; Dandy Don Meredith's Different Ballgame; When It's Not Monday Night, Meredith Is Taking a Whole Different Ballgame," *The Washington Post*, Oct. 2, 1978, p. B-1.

Schwartz, Tony. "TV Notebook: Shogun's Opener on NBC Attracts Almost Half of All Viewing," *The New York Times*, Sept. 17, 1980, p. C-27.

Taaffe, William. "Fresh Juice But Sour Ratings," *Sports Illustrated*, Oct. 31, 1983, p. 103.

Vecsey, George. "The Dulcet Tones," *The New York Times*, Oct. 30, 1980, p. 23.

Chapter 8

Dodds Frank, Allan. "The USFL Meets the Sophomore Jinx," *Forbes*, Feb. 13, 1984, pp. 41 and 42.

Fierman, Jaclyn. "Advertisers Show Signs of Football Fatigue," *Fortune*, Oct. 15, 1984, p. 141.

Flax, Steven. "As Fans Return to the NFL, TV Ad Sales Bomb," *Fortune*, Nov. 25, 1985, p. 61.

Friedman, Dick. "How Good — or Bad — Is *Monday Night Football?*" *TV Guide*, Dec. 10–16, 1983, pp. 39–42.

Gunther, Marc. "Monday Night Fever," *TV Guide*, Aug. 27–Sept. 2, 1994, pp. 24–27.

Hoffer, Richard. "Fine and Dandy," *Sports Illustrated*, July 31, 2000, pp. 124–127.

Leonard, John. "Pigskin Parade," *New York*, Jan. 9, 1984, pp. 73 and 74.

Merwin, John. "Who's Getting Clipped?" *Forbes*, Nov. 5, 1984, pp. 38 and 39.

Norman, Geoffrey. "After the Fall," *Sports Illustrated*, May 20, 1991, pp. 72–88.

Raissman, Bob. "Sports View: Simpson on Cosell," *TV Guide*, Sept. 15–21, 1984, p. 29.

Rushin, Steve. "All Al, All the Time," *Sports Illustrated*, May 10, 2004, p. 15.

Sandomir, Richard. "Suddenly, Cosell's Back and He's Still Cosell," *The New York Times*, Oct. 29, 1999, p. D-7.

Taaffe, William. "Howard, the Guys Need You," *Sports Illustrated*, Oct. 1, 1984, p. 89.

_____. "Hey Joe, Turn Out the Lights," *Sports Illustrated*, Oct. 7, 1985, p. 55.

_____. "It's Bottom-Line Time," *Sports Illustrated*, Oct. 12, 1987, pp. 51–54 and 73.

Chapter 9

Baker, Jim. "ABC Punts Away Musberger," *The Boston Herald*, Dec. 6, 1996, p. 92.

Candler, Mark. "The Too-Wide World of Television Sports," *Business Week*, Dec. 10, 1990, pp. 220 and 221.

Gifford, Frank. "High-Tech Touchdowns," *Popular Mechanics*, February 1988, pp. 10–13.

Hyman, Mark. "How to Lose Fans and Get Richer," *Business Week*, Jan. 26, 1998, p. 70.

Jares, John. Special advertising section, *Sports Illustrated*, Sept. 4, 1989, p. 5.

Kingwell, Mark. "Men's Night Out," *Saturday Night*, December 1996–January 1997, pp. 111 and 112.

Levitt, Shelley and Mary Huzinee. "But They're Truly a Pair for All Seasons," *People*, Nov. 16, 1992, pp. 133 and 134.

Martzke, Rudy. "Swanson Steps Down from ABC," *USA Today*, April 1, 1996, p. 2C.

McGraw, Dan. "Send Michaels, Gifford and Dierdorf Packing," *U.S. News and World Report*, Dec. 29, 1997–Jan. 5, 1998, p. 66.

"Swanson Named WNBC President," *The New York Times*, June 27, 1996, p. B-18.

Taaffe, William. "The Midterm Grades Are In," *Sports Illustrated*, Nov. 28, 1988, pp. 105–108.

_____. "Monday Man," *Sports Illustrated*, Nov. 28, 1988, pp. 105–108.

Walters, John. "Stalk Softly," *Sports Illustrated*, Aug. 23, 1999, p. 20.

Chapter 10

Armstrong, Mark. "Dennis Miller Takes 'Monday Night' Pigskin," *E! Online* website, June 22, 2000.

Caesar, Dan. "Monday Night Run Was a Grand Tour for Dierdorf," *The St. Louis Post-Dispatch*, Feb. 7, 1999, p. D-4.

_____. "Technically, 'MNF' Isn't That '70s Show," *The St. Louis Post-Dispatch*, Dec. 3, 2000, p. 127.

Carter, David. "How to Fix Monday Night Football," *Business Week*, July 10, 2000, p. 52.

Chad, Norman. "Monday Night Fever Has Evolved into Insipid Virus," *The Boston Globe*, Oct. 16, 1998, p. E15.

Fink, Mitchell, with Emily Gest. "To Air Is Human, Cosby Learns," *The New York Daily News*, Oct. 16, 1998, p. 15.

Franken, Al. "Block That Rush!" *The Nation*, June 19, 2000, pp. 6 and 7.

Grossberg, Josh. "Miller Scores Mixed Reviews," *E! Online* website, Aug. 1, 2000.

_____. "'Monday Night Football' Producer Punts," *E! Online* website, March 6, 2001.

_____. "Madden to 'Monday Night'; Miller Out," *E! Online* website, Feb. 28, 2002.

Hiestand, Michael. "In Ratings Chase, TV's Still Waiting for a Home Run," *USA Today*, Sept. 9, 1998, p. 2C.

Hooper, Ernest. "Dierdorf, Esiason Were Bad Mix," *The St. Petersburg Times*, Feb. 5, 1999, p. 2C.

Manly, Howard. "Miller's Rants Get Few Raves," *The Boston Globe*, Sept. 3, 2000, p. D-8.

Mariotti, Jay. "Miller Might Just Be Getting Warmed Up," *The Chicago Sun-Times*, Aug. 15, 2000, p. 110.

"Monday Night Footnotes," *Harper's*, January 2001, pp. 31 and 32.

Pergament, Alan. "ABC Takes Big Gamble by Using Two-Man Crew," *The Buffalo News* (New York), Sept. 9, 1999, p. 27S.

Peterson, Bill. "Boom, Boom, Out Go the Lights," *CityBeat* (Cincinnati, Ohio) website, March 23–29, 2000.

Price, S.L. "Can Dennis Miller Save Monday Night Football?" *Sports Illustrated*, June 3, 200, pp. 82–96.

Rubinstein, Julian. "Monday Night Football's Hail Mary," *The New York Times Magazine*, Sept. 3, 2000, pp. 46–49.

Sandomir, Richard. "ABC Losing Its Hold on Monday Ratings," *The New York Times*, Sept. 25, 1998, p. D-4.

_____. "ABC Sports President Named," *The New York Times*, March 26, 1999, p. D-7.

_____. "Monday Night Games at 9," *The New York Times*, April 2, 1999, p. D-2.

Saunders, Dusty. "ABC Sports Proves Louder Isn't Better," *The Rocky Mountain News* (Denver, Colorado), Sept. 14, 1998, p. 3C.

_____. "It's Quite Apparent 'MNF' Lacks, Well, Some Gray Matter," *The Rocky Mountain News* (Denver, Colorado), June 30, 2003, p. 2C.

Scotti, Ciro. "A Not-So Neutral Corner," *Business Week Online* website, June 29, 2000.

Shapiro, Leonard. "Three-Part Harmony on 'Monday Night Football,'" *The Washington Post*, Sept. 16, 1998, p. B-7.

_____. "ESPN Veteran to Produce 'Monday Night Football,'" *The Washington Post*, March 13, 2001, p. D-5.

Slusser, Susan. "'MNF' Fine with Boomer, But 'Blast' Is a Bummer," *The San Francisco Chronicle*, Sept. 18, 1998, p. E-2.

Walters, John. "Rethinking MNF," *Sports Illustrated*, March 20, 2000, p. 30.

_____. "Break a Leg," *Sports Illustrated*, Aug. 21, 2000, p. 24.

Wulff, Jennifer, and Marianne V. Stochmal, "Stark Victory," *People*, Nov. 13, 2000, pp. 241 and 242.

Chapter 11

Baker, Jim. "Guerrero Graces 'MNF,'" *The Boston Herald*, June 27, 2003, p. 94.

_____. "Sports on the Air," *The Boston Herald*, Sept. 21, 2003, p. B-30.

_____. "Guerrero Survives," *The Boston Herald*, Nov. 2, 2003, p. B-19.

Barron, David. "Tafoya to Replace MNF's Guerrero," *The Houston Chronicle*, May 4, 2004, p. 7.

De Moraes, Lisa. "ABC Sports Hands the Ball to ESPN's Bodenheimer," *The Washington Post*, March 4, 2003, p. C-7.

Dietsch, Richard. "Under Review," *Sports Illustrated*, Sept. 22, 2003, p. 21.

Elliott, Josh. "Under Review," *Sports Illustrated*, Oct. 11, 2004, p. 28.

Elliott, Stuart. "NBC Decides It Can't Live Without Football," *The New York Times*, April 20, 2005, p. C-1.

Fee, Gayle, and Laura Raposa. "Inside Track: Famous Femmes, Sports Studs Make Dynamic Duos," *The Boston Herald*, Dec. 12, 2001, p. 8.

Harmon, Rick. "Guerrero's Blunders a Monday Embarrassment," *The Tampa Tribune*, Sept. 12, 2003, p. 2.

Harris, Elliott. "Movie Time: Small Parts No Longer Part of Game Plan," *The Chicago Sun-Times,* April 9, 2003, p. 141.

_____. "A New Lisa on Life: Righty Erickson Gets Hitched to Guerrero," *The Chicago Sun-Times*, Feb. 9, 2004, p. 97.

Hiestand, Michael. "Sanders' Talk of Coaching Is Cheap Shot for Publicity," *USA Today*, Nov. 3, 2003, p. 2C.

_____. "NFL Shuffles TV Lineup for 2006," *USA Today*, April 19, 2005, p. 1C.

Jackson, John. "Tafoya Hiring Spotlights What a Mistake Guerrero Was," *The Chicago Sun-Times*, May 7, 2004, p. 144.

James, Meg. "Will ABC Sack 'Monday Night Football'?" *The Los Angeles Times*, Aug. 23, 2004, p. C-1.

Johnson, Peter. "NBC Revels in Reality Ratings," *USA Today*, June 25, 2001, p. 4-D.

Kaufman, King. "Boom! Madden on Monday Night," *Salon* website, Aug. 6, 2002.

Kizla, Mark. "Guerrero Bad News on Football Sideline," *The Pittsburgh Post-Gazette*, Sept. 10, 2003, p. C-2.

Lankhof, Bill. "The Last Word," *The Toronto Sun*, June 26, 2003, p. 119.

Martzke, Rudy. "Versatile Guerrero Gets Sideline Role for *MNF*," *USA Today*, June 26, 2003, p. 3C.

_____. "'MNF' Reporter Guerrero Hits Sidelines Running," *USA Today*, Aug. 5, 2003, p. 6C.

_____. "'SportsCenter' Anchors Unfairly Put Joke

on 'MNF' Reporter Guerrero," *USA Today*, Sept. 17, 2003, p. 2C.

_____. "CBS Announcers Score Big with Timely Observations," *USA Today*, March 29, 2004, p. 2C.

Mushnick, Phil. "Coffin Corner — Once Must-See MNF Kicked Off Long Ago," *The New York Post*, April 24, 2005, p. 63.

Posner, Jay. "Guerrero's Performance Leaves Plenty to Be Desired," *The San Diego Union-Tribune*, Sept. 12, 2003, p. D-6.

_____. "Tafoya a Long Way from XTRA Audition," *The San Diego Union-Tribune*, May 7, 2004, p. D-6.

Rossi, Bob. "Out of Bounds ... with Lovely Lisa Guerrero," *The Pittsburgh Post-Gazette*, May 20, 2002, p. C-2.

Sandomir, Richard. "Katz Leaving ABC Sports," *The New York Times*, March 4, 2003, p. D-7.

_____. "Sideline Reporter Has It Both Ways," *The New York Times*, June 27, 2003, p. D-6.

_____. "Guerrero Wasn't Ready to Be Prime Time Player," *The New York Times*, May 5, 2004, p. D-7.

_____. "Why Is 'Monday Night' Different from Others?" *The New York Times*, April 21, 2005, p. D-4.

_____. "As *Monday Night* Moves, an Old Voice Weighs In," *The New York Times*, April 25, 2005, p. D-9.

Silver, Michael. "Monday Evening Quarterback," *Sports Illustrated*, July 29, 2002, pp. 34–39.

Simers, T.J. "Maybe a Soak in a Hot Tub Will Make Weaver Smile," *The Los Angeles Times*, June 30, 2005, p. D-2.

"Sunday People in Sports," *The Houston Chronicle*, Oct. 5, 2003, p. 20.

Tierney, Mike. "Guerrero Spices Up 'MNF,'" *The Atlanta Journal-Constitution*, Aug. 5, 2003, p. 2C.

_____. "'Monday Night' Goes for Sideline Substance," *The Atlanta Journal-Constitution*, May 4, 2004, p. 2C.

Wyshynski, Greg. "The Jester's Quart: The New Monday Night Football," *Sports Fan* magazine website (www.sportsfanmagazine.com), April 22, 2005.

Zipay, Steve. "ESPN to Take Over in '06," *Newsday*, April 19, 2005, *Newsday* website.

Zulgad, Judd. "No Monday Night Blues," *The Minneapolis Star Tribune*, April 22, 2005, *Minneapolis Star Tribune* website.

Chapter 12

Hiestand, Michael. "Michaels: NBA Finals Will Be Fine Matchup," *USA Today*, June 6, 2005, p. 2C.

General

Arledge, Roone. *Roone*. New York: HarperCollins, 2003.

Brooks, Tim, and Earle Marsh. *The Complete Directory to Prime Time Network and Cable TV Shows 1946–Present* (8th ed.). New York: Ballantine, 2003.

Castleman, Harry and Walter J. Podrazik. *The TV Schedule Book*. New York: McGraw-Hill, 1984.

Cosell, Howard, with Mickey Herskowitz. *Cosell*. New York: Playboy, 1973.

_____, with Peter Bonventre. *I Never Played the Game*. New York: William Morrow, 1985.

Gifford, Frank, and Harry Waters. *The Whole Ten Yards*. New York: Random House, 1993.

Goldenson, Leonard H., with Marvin J. Wolf. *Beating the Odds*. New York: Charles Scribner's, 1991.

Gunther, Marc, and Bill Carter. *Monday Night Mayhem*. New York: William Morrow, 1988.

Harris, David. *The League: The Rise and Decline of the NFL*. New York: Bantam, 1986.

Hyatt, Wesley. *The Encyclopedia of Daytime Television*. New York: Billboard, 1997.

Internet Movie Database. www.imdb.com.

Jenkins, Dan, and Edwin Shrake. *Limo*. New York: Atheneum, 1976.

Karras, Alex, with Dennis Graham. *Tuesday Night Football*. New York: Birch Lane, 1991.

Patterson, Ted. *The Golden Voices of Football*. Sports Publishing L.L.C., 2004.

Patton, Phil. *Razzle-Dazzle*. Garden City, N.Y.: Doubleday, 1984.

Quinlan, Sterling. *Inside ABC: American Broadcasting Company's Rise to Power*. New York: Hastings House, 1979.

Smith, Curt. *Voices of the Game (Updated Edition)*. New York: Fireside, 1992.

Sugar, Bert. *"The Thrill of Victory": The Inside Story of ABC Sports*. New York: Hawthorn, 1978.

TV Guide. Various Issues, 1967–2006.

Variety. Various Issues, 1970–2006.

Wikipedia. www.wikipedia.com.

Index

Index